(YOU DON'T KNOW)
THE HALF OF IT

(YOU DON'T KNOW)
THE HALF OF IT

A Memoir

by

BOBBI WILLIAMS

with

GEORGE WILKERSON

Columbus, Ohio

Published by Gatekeeper Press
3971 Hoover Rd. Suite 77
Columbus, OH 43123-2839
www.GatekeeperPress.com

Library of Congress Control Number: 2017962812

ISBN: 9781619848078

Printed in the United States of America

To Barbara
For loving George
And putting up with me

========================

Special thanks to my son, John, Linda Brunton, and Editor, Allison Loris, for their proofreading, suggestions, and comments and to those friends who provided financial support for this publication: Richard Barron, Emily Bradbury, Green Daniel, Frank Einstein, Terry Galloway, Amy Hall, John Heim, Lewis Kaem, Liz Margolies, Mark Kishego, Melissa Middlebrook, Gretchen Polnac, Steven Rambo, Jim Rice, Mark Russell, Laura Ricci, Todd Richards, and Lydia Winter.

CONTENTS

FOREWORD

ONE AFTERNOON, WHEN THE FOG of my presence has momentarily lifted, I get George to tell Mother our secret. "There's a girl in me," he says, his eyes following the wooden spoon slowly stirring the soup.

She pauses, stares down, sighs, and gathers her thoughts. Then she turns to us. "Don't be silly," she says. "You're a boy." She pauses over the awkwardness of the subject. "You have a penis. Girls do not have penises."

George considers the words a bit, mulls them over, then replies: "I'm a girl."

Mother stops stirring and turns to face us. "No."

The soup spoon is suspended over the steaming cauldron; her other hand is firmly planted on her hip. "You are <u>not</u> a girl."

George is uncomfortable, but I won't let him leave without a logical explanation. "You <u>are</u> a girl." I tell him, "You're a girl with a penis." And he understands, for now, but he also knows he can't tell anyone. Not anyone.

☜ ❏ ☞

There is a theory based on the fact that many more twins are conceived than born. In many cases, early on in their development, one of the twins is absorbed into the other. Occasionally, a child is born with a remnant of that other twin—an extra hand or leg or internal organ. So maybe this is where I was once; George's potential twin sister. The only extra parts, are in our consciousness. Perhaps there are a lot of people like me, living within or alongside of others. Perhaps many of us stay in that

1

area of the other's consciousness without ever fully emerging. Perhaps some of us, like me, are of a different gender, but some are not. Whatever shape it takes, all of us are tasked with caring for the 'other,' the one with the freedom to be. We function at various levels and in various ways. We're not a psychological condition, not part of a multiple personality. We simply <u>are</u>. And perhaps one day, in a future world, science will parse it all out and the secret will be public. But for now, we must float in the space no one thus far has found.

ONE
In Brooklyn

GEORGE WILKERSON AND I WERE born on February 13, 1942, in Lutheran Hospital in Brooklyn, New York. For a long time, I stayed quiet, resting in his heart of hearts, far outside of his consciousness—watching, listening, and waiting.

The Grandparents

My first awareness is of standing at the top of the stairs in the house on Weldon Street looking down through George's eyes at Mrs. Catipano, who is calling up to our Mother, extending a large bowl from her chubby arms and asking if she wants some of the spaghetti she just made. She's an Italian Hattie McDaniels, as neat as a ribbon of fettuccine in her red and white apron, the bib barely managing to fit over her enormous breasts. Her accent is thick. "You gonna like, I know. I know."

Later George and I are sitting on the curb, watching older boys play stickball in the street. When the broomstick-turned-bat smacks softly against the pink rubber ball, the kid who hit it runs

3

towards first base (beyond where we're sitting) and heads toward second—a white piece of cardboard. Some of the kids are shouting after him, while others are yelling at the kid from the opposing team who has missed the ball and is now chasing it down the street.

Later still, we watch as Grandfather Cook struggles to get the tricycle out from under the porch (no room for it in our apartment, which is across the street). George was named for him— father's attempt to make points with the father-in-law. We call him Gramps and he owns a hardware store in Canarsie. It's a solid business which turns a decent profit and sometimes he takes us there and we get to shuffle through the sawdust on the floor, past the long row of nail bins labeled two-penny or four-penny, as the scent of sawed lumber tickles our nose. It's a man's place; I don't find it very appealing, but even at this age the gender message comes through, the distinction is clearly drawn. We watch him, standing behind the cash register, a Grandfather who could not be any more grandfatherly, sporting a hefty paunch, balding, with side swatches of white hair, and a cigar clenched between his teeth.

The grandparents house is two stories tall, with an attic, a basement and a fair size yard in back with lots of shrubs and a white trellis arching over a seat. But the main attraction is in the living room; the television—one of the first in the neighborhood. The gold Philco logo gleams beneath the small round screen, a bubble which we sit in front of every afternoon, watching a test pattern and listening to the single tone screaming hypnotically "eeeeeeeeeeeeee...."

The test pattern is all that was broadcast before actual TV shows came on. The profile of a Native American (similar to the one on Gramps' Red Man tobacco pouch) is all there is to watch until 5:00 in the afternoon when it's replaced with the face of *Howdy Doody*, a marionette whose daily program includes characters like Buffalo Bob, Clarabell the Clown (the actor later became Captain Kangaroo), Mr. Bluster, the Flub-a-dub, and Princess Summerfallwinterspring.

Howdy is a little boy who wears lipstick. Of course, that's never mentioned, but I notice it. I always notice things like that, but since they make George uncomfortable, I remain silent.

☜ ❑ ☞

Santa Claus lives in the grandparents attic. Grandfather calls upstairs to him and he responds in a deep voice with an ominous sounding '*Ho Ho Ho*'. George is very afraid of him. Maybe he knows it's his grandfather's voice and that's who he's really afraid of because of the cruel "trick" Gramps plays.

"Do you want to see a match burn twice?" he asks, and before George can answer he strikes a match (as if to light his pipe), blows it out, then touches it to George's arm. When George cries out, Gramps laughs. That trick and having trapped Santa Claus in the attic are the roots of a cynicism that stays with both of us for the rest of our life.

Fortunately, most of the time, Gramps is harmless. While we watch *Howdy Doody*, he sits at the kitchen table and plays Solitaire. Grandmother sits across from him, snapping string beans or mashing potatoes—preparing the evening meal. At supper she chides Grandfather for speaking German.(Later we find that the strange words are obscenities.)

So we're sitting on the curb on Weldon Street watching the big kids play stickball. Or we're standing at the top of the stairs, behind Mother talking to Mrs. Catipano. Or we're riding the tricycle up and down the sidewalk in front of the grandparents house. They're memories George shares with me now. But then, he had no choice. In fact, in those early years, he doesn't even know I'm there. I have no name. That comes much later. I'm nothing more than a spirit now.

☜ ❑ ☞

During those days in Brooklyn, Father worked a variety of jobs. For a while he was an ice cream truck driver, a *Good Humor* man. (This bit of information is just hearsay, just remarks from Mother and Sister, but over time are confirmed enough to believe.) To kids of that time, *Good Humor* means standing at the curb clutching ten cents and watching the man dressed in white open the little door to the refrigerator at the back of the truck and as a cloud of dry ice smoke billows out the door, watching him reach inside to find the ice cream we want. (George's favorite is the *Dreamsicle*.)

There are bells that announce his approach, but no music, just a row of bells that hang across the front window, where the visor is usually located, and the Good Humor man rings them by pulling on a string. But all of that was during the first five years. There are no memories of *Father the Good Humor Man*, but maybe it's better that way.

☞ ❏ ☞

Over the years George has embellished his stories of the early days. In some versions, he grows up in Brooklyn, plays stickball himself, and rather than moving to Long Island and then commuting to high school in Brooklyn, he simply stays there, hanging out with the children of Mafia dons or joining a street gang or running numbers out of Tony the Gimp's barber shop. He tells people whatever he knows will impress them. People love a good story. That's something he learned early on. I honestly think that he got that skill from me. Sometimes I think that I may be his muse.

An unembellished fact of the early years is that we were born with a cleft palate. The evidence is there in his mouth. The uvula bends sharply toward the left. The crack in the ceiling of his mouth was repaired when he was 18 months old and it required two surgeries. He had already begun to talk before they operated and after the surgery he had to learn to speak all over again.

Then, at two years he had a hernia. That was repaired too. So he was something of a burden, both physically and financially. Later in life, as George struggled to figure out where I came from and what made us the way we are, he couldn't come up with the sort of trauma therapists love—an early significant event that might have shaped us. We tried to blame the surgeries. We tried to say that Mother was overprotective as a result of the time we spent in hospital. We theorized that George was abducted by aliens who merged me into his being, and that we were dropped off back at the apartment on Weldon Street.

But what does it really matter? Why do we need to know? Those are the questions the therapists always asked.

GEORGE WILKERSON

TWO
On Long Island

WHAT HAPPENED? ONE SECOND WE'RE sitting on the curb in Brooklyn and the next we're at the dinner table in the house in the suburbs. Did I doze off? What did I miss? Sometimes I fade so far into the background that I lose track of what's going on and when I come to, I frantically search George's memories for what went on in my absence. But there's nothing there. It's like driving on a smooth highway and suddenly you find yourself on a muddy dirt road.

The dinner table is in the house in Rockville Centre, one of a long stretch of villages from the Queens border to the end of Long Island. It's the last house at the end of a dead-end street. There's an unfinished basement with a pool table on one side and Father's workbench on the other. On the ground floor there are five rooms: the living room at the front of the house, the dining room on one side of the center and the kitchen on the other side, where the back door is located, and if you come into the house by way of that back door, there's a bathroom to your left.

The second floor has three bedrooms in the front half of the house and an efficiency apartment in the rear. Above that there's an attic and on the back of the house there's a screened-in porch Father added or maybe just screened in. No matter. He laid claim to so many things. As for the furnishings, when they needed a set for the TV show *Leave it to Beaver* they made duplicates of our furniture, including the tin top, red and yellow kitchen table with the built-in silverware drawer.

Out there, beyond the back yard, just past the shrubs that define the property line, there's a large vacant lot that goes all the way to the next street. It's overgrown with weeds so we don't play in it much, but it's a good place to get away.

The house is from the thirties. Father fancies himself a handyman and spends a lot of time making improvements. These almost always involve large quantities of gray or white high-gloss paint. He has a workbench in the basement and a table saw and other assorted tools that are essential to his need to define his manliness.

That efficiency apartment on the second floor was one of his projects. There's an entrance from the front porch of the house to a stairway leading to the second floor, making access somewhat private. You can also get to those stairs through a door in the living room, but in either case you have to walk up the stairs to a landing, then turn right and go up five more stairs to arrive at a small hallway. From there, to the right, there are three doors: one to our sister's bedroom, one to the parents' bedroom, and a third to the attic which later becomes George's bedroom. A fourth door, to the left, goes into the apartment. Step through <u>that</u> door and there's a kitchen to the left, a bathroom straight ahead, and a living room to the right. There is no bedroom; the sofa in the living room folds out to become a bed.

Our house is the last one at the end of a dead-end street—Scott Place. An old childless couple live next door, a family with two older girls is next to them, and the Shultse family is at the corner. The best feature of our location is that in the winter, when the snow plow pushes all the snow to the end of the street, leaving a giant mountain of snow directly in front of our house. I'm not a snow bunny, but George is, so long as a fort can be built and the snow is dense enough to make solid balls.

In addition to our sister, who is something of a mystery at this time, there's an extended family which includes Aunt Katty (Father's sister), Aunt Betty (Grandmother Cook's sister) and her husband, Uncle John (the Jack Spratt to Aunt Betty's Butterball figure), Aunt Sally (Aunt Betty's sister, a great aunt as well) and Uncle Jimmy (Grandmother's brother), who is the subject of many of the gossipy whispers that fill our house. Our parents said he was a 'rummy,' but he was our mother's uncle, and so our great uncle, and despite the remarks, she seemed to sincerely care about him. The rest of the family are in Kentucky, although Aunt Georgie, another sister, has, herself, spent some time in Brooklyn.

Aunt Katty

Aunt Katty is our favorite. She lives back in Brooklyn and on many Saturday mornings Father takes us to her apartment on Liberty Avenue to spend the night with her. The apartment is on the third floor, level with the 'El' and from her living room window we can watch the trains go rattling by, a scary yet exciting experience.

Katty sold tokens in the subway for a while. And there is an occasional mention of an 'Uncle Peck' but we never knew him. Katty was married to a man named Peck Doppman and though I never met him we somehow knew that they never divorced. But since he's not around now we have her all to ourselves.

By the time we started visiting her, Aunt Katty no longer worked for the subway. She had been caring for an old man, keeping house for him, preparing his meals, and seeing to his medications. This is before 'health care aid' and 'home care' were in the American vocabulary. Our parents say that it's done not out of kindness, but out of selfishness, that she's exploiting these men. For some time after leaving the token-selling job, she would move in with this or that old man and care for him and get left something in his will. Our parents (especially Mother) were masters of gossip. The house was always full of whispers, knowing glances and nods, asides spoken with raised eyebrows. "I'll <u>bet</u> *she* takes care of him," mother would say. Those whispers swirled around us like pieces from a jig saw puzzle caught in a whirlwind, unable to be assembled. And we didn't connect the pieces until years later.

Aunt Katty has two distinguishing features. She always wears rouge. It's the only make-up she wears. It looks like she's covering up something. In the right light you might think her cheeks were bruised.

The other feature is her stockings. Women didn't wear socks in those days and there weren't knee highs. So, being a very practical person; she simply rolled and tucked—rolled down her stockings, twisted the top, and tucked the knot into the rolled area, so that the stockings stopped around mid-calf.

On the Saturday mornings when we are driven to Aunt Katty's, toting our paper sack containing pajamas and clean underwear for the next day, Father parks the car and we enter through the front door to the vestibule of the apartment building. There's a row of mailboxes against the wall on the right. Father presses a button under the appropriate mailbox and we are 'buzzed in.' Once upstairs, Father visits for a while, making small talk, before leaving us in her care. That's none too soon for us because we're already looking forward to whatever treat is coming.

In the summer that treat is watermelon. Aunt Katty picks one from a bin outside a nearby grocery store and we take it back to the apartment where she cuts it up and we eat big, wet slices of it. The juice runs down our arms and onto the floor and Aunt Katty laughs and spits out the seeds. So George joins in, giggling and slurping on the juice, and doing his best to spit out the pits too and soon it evolves into a distance pit-spitting contest which Aunt Katty always wins.

In the winter the treat is chocolate éclairs, which Katty buys by the dozen at a bakery just down the street—not as messy as the watermelon, but just as much fun. Licking off the chocolate icing, sucking out the lemon filling, Aunt Katty and George can barely finish off two of them apiece. And they're always accompanied by coffee. (George's is half coffee and half cream and lots of sugar.) After the éclairs and coffee we are wired for action, which usually comes in the form of a board game. And that evening George sleeps contentedly and I drift off as well.

Uncle Jimmy is equally a favorite. He was once a mechanic and had his own auto repair shop for a while. He fought in World War I and when he left the Army he 'bummed' around the country. He 'rode the rails,' worked on oil rigs in Texas, and was in El Paso when Pancho Villa was crossing the border to make raids into the U.S. He was always with us for dinner on Thanksgiving and Christmas.

Father drives to Jamaica to pick him up for the holiday and we go with him. Uncle Jimmy lives in a single room in the back of an old three-story house in a run-down part of Brooklyn where, in our memories, everything is sepia. His rented room has only a single bed and a dresser with a wash basin. It's a very sad place, so we're glad we don't stay. Uncle Jimmy is ready when we arrive and back in the car he sits in front, next to the driver, so we don't hear whatever conversation he and Father have, but we're pretty sure it's trivial.

On those holidays, Uncle Jimmy plays with George. He puts a sheet over a card table that is set up in the living room and it becomes a fort. Or they play 'Go Fish' or Gin Rummy. And at dinner, at the end of the meal, Uncle Jimmy says how hungry he is and then proceeds to eat his plate. Practical matters, like where the plate really went, intrude on the adult memory, but at six or seven, George is thoroughly convinced that Uncle Jimmy has eaten the plate. He then proclaims that he's so full he couldn't eat another thing 'til at least five o'clock. The clock in the kitchen shows that it's five 'til five.

Later, Father drives him home, but we don't go.

Aunt Betty and Nana (Grandmother Cook) are built the same; each is a sack of bubbles. Aunt Betty chain smokes; there's a dirty yellow nicotine stain on her upper lip that even her bright red lipstick can't hide. Whenever she and Uncle John come to visit, she insists on kissing George. He dreads that. At times like that I'm happy to slip farther back into the fog and not participate.

Uncle John is a skinny man with a bright smile. Uncle John plays with us. He takes a piece of cardboard and draws the front of a house, then cuts out windows, takes a pen and draws little faces on his fingers—dots for eyes and a nose and a curved line for a mouth—and they become little people who live in the house, poking their heads through the windows and talking to us. Uncle John's kindness is in those fingers; the little people are his surrogates.

Occasionally we go to visit Uncle John and Aunt Betty in their apartment in Brooklyn. It's very dark there; everything is swathed in thick carpets and draperies. The furniture is expensive, made of dark, heavy wood decorated with fancy carvings; it looks antique, with gargoyle-looking carvings for legs and Mother and Father have made the instructions clear: *Do not touch anything*.

Uncle John and Aunt Betty do not have any children. Both work and by our family's standards, they are wealthy. Mother often makes that point by insisting that George return Aunt Betty's kisses with heavy doses of feigned pleasure and that he be on his best behavior because she believes that one day Aunt Betty will pay for his college education.

But when she dies she doesn't leave anything for us in her will, which leaves our mother cursing her mother, her mother's family, and anyone associated with them…under her breath so that only George and I can hear.

☜ ❑ ☞

Aunt Sally and Uncle Joe are also wealthy. Father says that Uncle Joe stays home and 'clips coupons.' This is some sort of reference to the stock market, but we don't really know what it means. All we know is that they live in the better part of town in a better house and have a better class of friends. And we rarely see them.

For a time, our sister cleaned house for Aunt Sally. It may have been our aunt's way of giving her some money, but in the classic American tradition, making her work for it. Sister reported that she would find money under the carpet or tucked beneath a seat cushion and that Aunt Sally told her she could keep any money she found.

Reflecting on all of that, George and I now suspect that Aunt Sally might have intentionally placed the money there. Uncle Joe, on the other hand, expressed his generosity by telling Father that if he would give him a thousand dollars to invest for George, by the time George was college age there would be enough money to pay for it. Father politely refused, believing for some reason that Joe was trying to "put one over on him."

GEORGE WILKERSON

THREE
Cowboys and Indians and Teeth

JIMMY JINGLES. THAT REALLY IS the name of the little boy who lives across the street (and down a few houses) on Scott Place. Jimmy Jingles has a dog named Sniffy. *Jimmy Jingles and Sniffy.* It could be the title of a TV show for pre-schoolers. But it's not. It's the real name of a real little boy. And Father says he is "effeminate." Father calls him a sissy and so George becomes more concerned about <u>me</u>. Is George 'effeminate?' Does he walk like a girl? Act like a girl?

Father mocks Jimmy's parents because they're very tolerant and 'modern.' They don't spank Jimmy; instead, they speak to him in a very adult manner. His mother calls to him and says very slowly, enunciating every syllable, 'Now Jimmy, you know that just because Sniffy eats his poo does not mean it's all right for you to eat yours.'

Young Cowpoke George

OK…she probably never said <u>that</u>, but that's the way she speaks to him. And as a result, that's how Jimmy speaks to <u>us</u>. And to his parents. And even to Sniffy.

One of the games Jimmy and George play is the classic 'Cowboys and Indians,' patterned after the B-Westerns that run on TV on Sunday afternoons; the ones in black and white, where the lines between the good guys and bad guys are clearly drawn. Ken Maynard and Hopalong (*Hoppy*)Cassidy (William Boyd) are two of George's favorites (not mine, but I kept my opinions private back then.)

When they play, Jimmy feels the need to provide background music, the kind that indicates suspense. There's a stock tune that seems to be used in all of the westerns. It goes

DAA, DAH-DAH, DAH-DAH, DAH-DAH, DAAAAAA

over and over and whenever Jimmy is the bad guy, hiding in the tree waiting to ambush George, George knows exactly where he is because he's humming the music. But George never mentions this to him; Jimmy just thinks that George is very clever. No matter where he hides, George finds him:

DAA-DAH-DAH, DAH-DAH, DAH-DAH, DAA
Behind the fence
DAA-DAH-DAH, DAH-DAH, DAH-DAH, DAAAAAA
Or in Sniffy's house.
DAA-DAH-DAH, DAH-DAH, DAH-DAH, DAAAAA
We know where you are Jimmy Jingles.

☜ ❑ ☞

Mother and Father both have false teeth. They got them when they were very young—Mother when she was in her late teens; Father when in his twenties. That's how dental problems were dealt with back then. Pull them all out and put in false ones. (Mother's father was not one to waste money on dental work.)

Their teeth are part of the bathroom décor. Every night, there they are, sitting in a glass of water on the back of the toilet, grinning up at us. (Later, the glass is replaced with plastic containers with lids. If you weren't educated in such matters you'd never know what was in them.)

One day, when Mother's teeth are firmly planted in her mouth and she's standing at the sink, preparing to wash the dishes, George is outside and has discovered a fairly large worm. It's fat and juicy and would have made a substantial meal for some hungry bird, but for George, it's a prize. And like a cat proudly bringing a mouse to its owner, he brings the worm inside, still alive and squirming, and stands next to Mother, and says: "Look!"

She turns, and seeing the worm, she jumps back, terrified, and screams, and that scares us a bit, but not nearly as much as what comes next because, as she cringes and steps away from us, shaking, gasping for air, her false teeth come bouncing out of her mouth—not all the way, but just enough to reach beyond her lips. And they are clacking together, like those wind-up teeth at the gag shop. She looks like something from a monster movie—*The Thing* or *Creature from the Black Lagoon*.

Somehow, within moments, she manages to suck the teeth back into her mouth and scream "Get it out! Out!Out!" And as we run back outside, the vision of those teeth and her bright red face and her shaking and gasping are forever burned into our brain. I beg George, please, don't <u>ever</u> have false teeth. And I know he hears me.

↜ □ ☞

Mother says George's teeth are bad because of all the anesthesia given to him (for the cleft palate and hernia repairs when we were younger). It's one of those things she believes and since science, research, and logic are not part of her operating system, she's convinced of it.

At age ten the family dentist tells us that George's mouth is too small and that four teeth need to be pulled to make room for those coming in. The plan is that two will be pulled that coming Saturday and two more two weeks after that. So Father takes us to the dentist's office where we're strapped into a chair with wide, thick leather straps around our wrists (not unlike the electric chair straps from the gangster movies of the day.)

It wasn't me! I was framed, I tell ya! It was Louie what done it!
You ain't got nothin' on me! I'm innocent! Innocent I tell ya!

The rubber cone is placed over our nose, the gas seeps in, and George drifts off, but within minutes I'm awake and I can feel it, the instruments in the mouth, like a fish with a hook lodged in the back of its throat, being tugged and yanked, and it hurts, but I can't do anything. George won't wake up and no one knows I'm there. His mouth is propped open with a fat chunk of rubber, so I can't scream and I can't make George move. I want to tell them to stop, because they think George is unconscious, but I'm not. I'm awake, unable to move, unable to struggle. I'm pinned to the chair and trying to scream: "Stop! Please! You're hurting me!"

But to no avail. When George is finally awake enough to struggle against the restraints, they're too tight. And the assistant is holding us down. The dentist's hand is on George's shoulder and the assistant has her hand on his forehead. The pain and the fear are rolled into one massive hurt and all we can do is cry.

And then it's over and we're home. George's mouth is stuffed with bloody gauze. The first part of the ordeal is done…for now. But we know the plan. Two weeks and then the other two teeth must be pulled. And we're terrified. So when that day comes, I make George sick—upset stomach, diarrhea, whatever can't be confirmed. (I'm good at this sort of thing; fear is a powerful tutor.) Every week thereafter, a new appointment is made and every week George is sick.

Father knows we're faking it to avoid the dentist, but George can sell it to Mother and she, in turn, keeps Father at bay while George feigns 'sleeping in' every Saturday until we are tricked into thinking we're going to some church function and instead we go to the dentist. But for this round he's determined to avoid the angst of the previous visit and pumps enough nitrous oxide gas into us to thoroughly knock us out.

☜ ❑ ☞

We are 11 years old now and the bedtime routine is set: go upstairs and brush your teeth, get into your pajamas, come back downstairs, and kiss everyone goodnight. But on this night, Father holds out his hand against George's stomach and stops us short.

"Men don't kiss," he says. Then he takes George's hand and shakes it. At that I creep out of the fog; not so much that George can completely feel me, but enough that he knows someone (or something) is there, feeling his sadness and telling him it's OK, telling him it's wrong, it's wrong. And so sad.

Thereafter, George never kisses or even hugs his father until just before Father dies, years later. As George is leaving Sister's house, where Father lived out his final days, at the end of a visit, he reaches out to shake hands and Father pulls him close and puts his arm around him and whispers "Take care of your family."

But for now, at age eleven, I am clearing away some of the fog so I can let him know he has me inside and I will take care of hm. Father, sensing something, hangs onto the tiny hand and asks: "What will you be...when you grow up?"

When he grows up? Why, he wants to be famous. He wants people to know him, or at least to know _of_ him.

Father tsk-tsks at him. "No..." he tells him, "that's not a good thing to say...or to want. Where is your humility?" Father can't stand anything that would make him look arrogant. So we are warned—we must always be humble. Always.

☜ ❑ ☞

When in public, Father introduces George as _the boy_. "This is 'the boy,'" he says; not his boy, or our boy. Just the boy, for by default, then, Father is "the man."

With Mother, though, he is George, her son. So one afternoon when I the fog of my presence has momentarily lifted, George tells Mother about me. "There's a girl in me," he says, as she stirs the soup.

She pauses, stares down at the soup, sighs, and gathers her thoughts. Then she turns to us. "Don't be silly," she says. "You're a boy." She pauses over the awkwardness of the subject. "You have a penis. Girls do not have penises."

George considers the words a bit, mulls them over, and replies: "I'm a girl."

Mother stops stirring and turns to face him. "No."

The soup spoon in her hand is suspended over the cauldron and the other hand is on her hip. "You are <u>not</u> a girl."

George is uncomfortable, but I won't leave until a logical conclusion has set in. "You're a girl," I tell him, "a girl with a penis." And he understands now, but he also knows he can't tell anyone.

And I'm oddly happy.

FOUR
Abusers and Minstrels

I WATCHED IT HAPPEN, BUT ALL I could do was cringe. Father didn't beat him with a belt or his fists, but he abused him with things like slaps on the back of the head during dinner. And mentally, through constant criticism, comments about how he wasn't manly or how he was uncoordinated, clumsy, and generally not good at anything. Never any praise and nothing was good enough. If he brought home an 'A' paper Father would find errors in the punctuation or the spelling. If George was the boy, Father was the man in charge, the Father-man, and his approval was paramount.

In sharp contrast, Sister was Father's pride and joy. She was perfect. She could do no wrong. And if George received slaps on the head, Sister's worst punishment was admonishment, or simply not having anything said to her, because you didn't hit girls. *If I was in the forefront, if I was the girl, and George was hiding in my place, things would be different. Daddy would love me. He would be proud of me. And the expectations would be of things that I could attain.*

It was around that time that George began to pray at night after he was in bed. He prayed that he would wake up and find that God had turned him into a girl, or that he had been a girl all along. But of course that never happened. So the object of the prayers changed. George gave up on God and instead, he prayed to Satan, saying he would do whatever Old Scratch wanted from him; he would deliver any sin, render him any evil, if he would just turn George into a girl. All he really wanted was to give me my freedom.

But neither God nor Satan responded. So we began to sneak into Mother's lingerie drawer and George would wear her things in private and look at himself in the mirror and see me, the little girl that Daddy would love.

☜ ❑ ☞

Mother's abuse comes in bottles of Clorox and Air Wick. Those are the smells of our house, though regardless of how much she uses, Mother cannot wash out the musty odor of damp walls and cigarettes. She loves her Clorox—uses it straight out of the bottle to mop the floor, wash down the sink, clean the toilet bowl, bleach father's T-shirts, and the sheets. Maybe she gets high from it. At the very least, she probably has suffered some brain damage. The portion of her cortex that otherwise would have made her capable of enjoying things was most likely destroyed in the early days of her marriage, burned away by the antiseptic fumes until all that was left was a little hole in her brain which gradually filled up with bitterness. And that's probably what killed her; the cigarettes just sped up the process.

George and I spend a lot of time in the bathroom where it smells of Air-Wick. Every bathroom in the house has an Air Wick sitting on the back of the toilet. (Today's models have floral designs and are disguised as nick-knacks. They look more like pieces of sculpture. But check out the old ad that shows what it looked like, with the wire handle you pull up to expose the wick.) There's also a can of Lysol spray in the cabinet under the sink.

The primary purpose of the Air Wick, according to Mother, is to cover the odor of Father's shit. Father objects, though, because he is proud of his poo. He touts his foul-smelling bowel movements as a symbol of his masculinity. A real man produces massive, odious turds whose scent rivals those emanating from the fires of hell and whose girth often plugs up the bowl. (And just to ensure his turds live up to his reputation, he favors limburger cheese as a snack and makes a point of eating Bermuda onions and cucumbers doused with sour cream.)

In contrast to his poo, Father never mentions the size of his penis. In fact he never even acknowledges that he has one. But at least once a week he emerges from the bathroom with an expression of success and lets out a deep-throated whoop, shakes his head and say "I'm sure glad <u>that's</u> over". Mother responds by holding her nose and grabbing the Lysol spray off the back of the sink, she begins a thorough sweep of the area, blending the Air Wick and Lysol to a level that would make an elephant swoon. Then she returns with an admonishment to Father about how many times she has told him to spray when he's done, to which Father has no reply. If anything, he sees her comment as recognition of his achievement.

There's a special element of the bathroom that has a secret attraction for me. The dirty clothes hamper is situated so as to be unobtrusive between the bathtub and the toilet. Because I am desperately looking for more ways to show myself, I've got George rummaging through it. To George, the rummaging is an unexplainable impulse, an urge without a name or rational explanation. But I need to be and he needs to let me be and this is the only way it can happen…for now.

So, often, that's where you will find us, locked in the bathroom, digging through the dirty clothes to find something of Mother's or Sister's to try on. George is like a desperado, a criminal alternately frightened and excited, embarrassed and pleased, ashamed and yet driven. It's our dirty little secret and will remain so long into George's adulthood, kept hidden until he gets up the courage to confront me.

☜ ❏ ☞

We're six or seven years old and Father is in charge of a funding-raising event for the local chapter of the Knights of Columbus (a Catholic "fraternal" organization). Being born and raised in Kentucky, he drew on his childhood memories and came up with this idea—a Minstrel Show, with men in blackface telling racist jokes and innocent kids like me performing in skits and Catholic high school girls trying to sing like the Andrews Sisters.

The Knights of Columbus' Minstrel Show

One of the awful jokes in the show went like this:

INTERLOCUTOR: Say, Mister Bones, you seem like a mighty strong fellow. How did you get such fine, large muscles?

MISTER BONES: Well, Mister Interlok-a-toor, that's cuz evr'a day ah eats mah Wheaties.

INTERLOCUTOR: You don't say. Well, tell me then, how come you have such fine square shoulders.

MISTER BONES: Why sho' nuff, suh...that's cuz ah eats the boxes too.

Father included a bit at the opening of the second act where a rope was laid out across the stage and one of the End Men walked over and picked it up, whereupon the rest of the rope (which disappeared off the other side of the stage), became taut and the man, who now was trying to pull in whatever was on the other end, was having difficulty, so another of the End Men got up and grabbed the rope too. But that proved to be too difficult. So one by one the remaining End Men got up and grabbed the rope and finally they were able to pull it toward them and slowly they reeled it in to reveal little six year old George, in his little cowboy outfit, holding on to the other end.

There are few indignities in life that measure up to those Father is capable of.

One dreary, fall Thanksgiving day, Father takes us to see the Macy's parade, lifting us onto his shoulders so we can watch as it all streams by somewhere along Seventh Avenue. It may have been on the same day or maybe another that he took us to see Santa Claus at Macy's too. Santa sits inside a castle at the end of a dimly lit tunnel strung with tree lights leading to his chambers. Christmas music plays softly and kids and parents stand in line for what seems like hours. George is sure that this is the real Santa Claus, the one who is in the sleigh at the end of the Macy's parade, and George is going to tell him what he wants. He's rehearsing the speech and nearly trembling with anticipation. I'm sure he's going to shit in his pants.

But he doesn't. On a cue from an elf, he goes up to Santa and sits in his lap and tells him…a doll, a Donna Reed paper doll. It's not much, really. Not a doll at all. Just a cardboard cutout of Donna and a few sheets of outfits (skirts, dresses, bathing suit, etc.) you can cut out and stick on the doll. (We're talking about early Donna, from "It's A Wonderful Life" not the one later on her own TV show, although that would have been OK too.)

"Donna Reed?" Santa asks.

We nod enthusiastically. "Please?"

Santa sighs. It's clear he has no idea who we're talking about. "Wouldn't you rather have a truck?"

FLASH! The elf's camera goes off and we're escorted away. A truck indeed.

☜ ❑ ☞

And all the while, we are attending St. Agnes Catholic Diocese Elementary School because Mother was born and raised Lutheran and Father, being Catholic, was required by the church to sign a legal document declaring that any children from the marriage would be raised Catholic and sent to Catholic schools. Her parents, being of German Lutheran descent, were not at all pleased when she married Father. And that was not helped by the fact that she was ten years younger than him. There are many layers to the situation that the analysts we see later in life can't begin to comprehend.

There's George, wearing his little white shirt and corduroy blue tie with the St. Agnes insignia, marching with the third graders from the parking lot/playground into the classroom to the strident sound of John Phillip Sousa blaring through the school's loudspeakers.

In Third Grade at St. Agnes Elementary School
(George is second from the left of the boys
standing in the back)

Inside the classroom, Sister Marian calls for order. There are about sixty children, seated at old wooden desks and chairs. (See the photo) They are so old that the desk portion has a hole in the upper right corner drilled out for an inkwell. And the entire desktop is hinged so it can be lifted to reveal a storage area. Add to this rigid classroom, seats that fold up against the back with the fold so perfectly located that George's ass is pinched whenever he leans back.

We are seated very near the rear, the result of an alphabetical arrangement, and behind us there's an innocent little girl, a Shirley Temple wannabee who doesn't realize she is about to have her face bashed in. This is because Sister Marian has a practice of throwing things (chalk, erasers, textbooks, etc.) at students who *act up*.

On this particular day, George is engaged in a surreptitious conversation with the student next to him when out of the corner of his eye he spies Sister Marian, the dictionary from her desk in hand and winding up for the throw. But as she lets fly, natural instinct kicks in and we duck to the right, clearing a path for a perfect strike, right between the eyes of the innocent little girl.

Of course, George is to blame for the result, but is disregarded as quickly and quietly, Sister Marian dashes down the aisle, consoles the sobbing little girl, ushers her off to the nurse's office, and then turns toward us. Without a word, she snaps "a corner-of-the-ear-grab," marches us to the front of the room, guides us to the trash can in the corner, and forces us to sit in it.

And just then, and none-too-soon, Sister Agnes Clare, the Principal, arrives to follow up on the incident and brands George as a troublemaker and reports the incident to the parents. Thus, the reputation and our future life at St. Agnes are cast in concrete. And George is well on his way to becoming an atheist. (I already am.)

☙ ❏ ☞

We've been told that Sister Marian, Sister Agnes Clare, and all of the other sisters at St. Agnes are married to Jesus. They are the wives of our lord and savior, but will never know the pleasure of a wedding night, the joys of pregnancy, or the thrill of a Saturday night in the back seat of a Chevy coup. And not one of them has signed a pre-nup.

Each Sunday we go to the 'children's mass.' But there's not much different about it than any other mass, except that each class sits together in the front pews and the priests try to 'spin' their sermon toward us, but they rarely hit their target. We are the itchiest, most uncomfortable collection of children ever made to sit through a mass, made more itchy by the nuns who patrol the aisles, making sure we are being reverent and choreographing our behavior via a toy, commonly called a 'cricket, 'hidden under their robes. It's a piece of metal inside a metal shell that when released makes a loud, clicking noise. Squeeze it once and it's our cue to stand, twice kneel, once again, sit. Click, stand. Click, click kneel. Click, sit. Pavolv would be proud.

The communion ceremony is also choreographed. Sister Mary Whomever comes to the end of the aisle and clicks once. We stand, then she steps back and, single file, we parade to the altar rail where we kneel and, when the priest arrives, his chalice full of wafers, we stick out our tongues, lap it up, and close our mouths, remembering how Sister Thomasina sternly warned us. "You must never let the host touch your teeth. The host is the body of Jesus and you would be biting Jesus."

The responsibility is awesome. But it gets even better.

"There once was a little boy," Sister says, "who spit out the host into the palm of his hand and when he looked down he saw a pool of blood."

We all gasp.

Except for George. And me. (There are some things we totally share.) We can't wait for the next Sunday when we march reverently to the altar rail, take the wafer onto our tongue, and parade back to the pew where, after checking to make sure none of the sisters are watching, we spit the host into our hand and wait for the miracle.

No such luck. Just soggy bread. The least it could have done was assume the shape of Christ's face. But no…just soggy old bread.

George considers showing the evidence to Sister Thomasina, but I advise against it. We simply file the experiment away with the unanswered bedtime prayers about our gender. It's not likely any of the sisters would have appreciated our scientific curiosity.

Feelings about these women of god are a mixture of anger and love. Here's why.

George is small for his age; all through elementary school he is the shortest in his class and not strong or aggressive, so on the playground he is the favorite target of the school's bullies. One form their assault takes is of a circle within which the main bully throws us to the ground and traps our head in a scissor lock, legs wrapped around our neck as the encircling group chants "Squeeze! Squeeze!" until George cries "Uncle" and assumes the shameful role of the defeated.

As the crowd walks off, at least leaving us alone, we lie motionless on the ground until one or the other of the nuns comes to console us. She drapes her woolen habit over us and escorts us to the nurse's office. ("Sister," I want to scream, but George won't let me. "Where were you when we were being assaulted? Did you watch and wait for the crowd to disburse? Did you secretly enjoy the melee?" Is this how the brides of Jesus get their jollies?)

But the fresh, warm woolen smell of the habit makes us feel safe and secure. These are the times when we love the sisters and wish we could stay with them forever, keeping George away from the bullies and out of the reach of Father, whose only response when we get home with a disheveled shirt and bruises is to berate George for 'not fighting back.')

31

By fifth grade such sisterly love is short-lived, thanks in part to Sister Mary Thomasina. We are marching to the classroom, and again, George is talking to another student. This time it's the boy behind us. Already the class clown, George is doing an imitation of one of the sisters or one of the priests and as we step into the classroom and George turns to climb the last stair, Sister Thomasina grabs us by our hair and drags us to the front of the room. Our pleas and complaints for mercy are of little use. She's angry and George is her favorite target.

"BAM!" She slams his head against the blackboard—Slam! Bam! Slam! —shouting, though we can't tell what she's saying, what with the ringing in our head and the bam, bam, bam as it strikes the blackboard over and over. The slamming serves as punctuation for whatever she's saying—something about Jesus, about sinners, about how important discipline is, and about how rude it is to talk when we should be filing quietly into class. The warm woolen smell of the habit becomes overwhelming. The memory of the innocent little girl years ago being consoled clashes with the pain of the blackboard against our head. The sisters are married to Jesus, so they cannot sin. They can do no wrong. Therefore, whatever the reason, whatever the felony, it <u>must</u> be <u>our</u> fault. <u>We</u> must be the one who is bad. We are the sinner. Or more to the point, George is the sinner, and because I am within him, I am the sin.

FIVE
Sick Days and Commies

A TUMMY ACHE IS LIKE A life-vest for someone falling overboard at school. George moans; he has a headache. He aches all over. "I'm gonna throw up." And I help, for I am a master of feigned illnesses and George is my all-too-talented puppet. This is long before *Dr. Oz* and *The Doctors*. There's no access to TV shows where one can learn the symptoms of a multitude of afflictions on a daily basis. We have to be creative in those days. At these times we work as a team. I come up with whatever I know will work to keep us out of school and George plays the part. He is at least good enough to convince Mother that he should stay home, despite Father insisting there's nothing wrong.

Mother opens the couch (which folds out to a bed) and makes it up for us and we slowly make our way under the blankets. Then she pulls them up around us and feels George's forehead, debating whether or not to call the doctor, but he's good, managing to feign the symptoms to a level just below that of the call-the-doctor level. So Mother turns on the TV and we watch the soap operas while she irons the sheets.

Yes. She irons the sheets. She's a stay-at-home mom and she irons everything—sheets, handkerchiefs, underwear, pants, shirts—nothing in our home goes un-ironed. She would iron our shoes if it were possible.

Sometimes, on these days, George and I get to read comic books—*Archie, Casper the Friendly Ghost, Tom & Jerry* (later replaced by *Tales from the Crypt* and *Mad*, which are banned in our house.) And we have lunch! Lunch at home, even when "sick," is so much better than school. Tomato soup and a grilled cheese sandwich and not the standard baloney on white bread. (If the complaint includes a sore throat, chicken noodle is substituted for the tomato.) And amazingly, by evening George declares he is feeling much better.

∾ ❏ ☞

You can blame me for some of the strange things George does on these sick days when Mother leaves him home alone for a while and goes shopping or on a weekend when the parents are out visiting friends and the Sister has gone on a date. It's my only chance to try myself out. I'm well aware of George's body; it's not that much different from the one I would have if our roles were reversed. So I have him put on Mother's stockings and slips and Sister's skirts and blouses. And when there is a tenant in the upstairs apartment who has stored clothing in the attic we can try those as well.

George is terrified and confused by this, but on some level he knows I can't remain in the fog, quietly watching and listening. I need to come out to myself. And more important, I need come out to him, to make him realize who this secret sharer is.

How old am I on these days? It's hard to say. George's age is easy. He lives each day and the clock rings up the years, but I have no such clock. Sometimes I sleep for days and though the events that occur then are registered in the mind we share, I can only retrieve as George's memories and when I do that, only rarely can I make sense of them. But here's the bottom line. I am always there and late at night, I listen as George prays to the god he already doubts: "*Make me a girl. Please God, when I wake up tomorrow, make me a girl.*"

I try to tell him that someday <u>he</u> can make that happen, not god. <u>He</u> will create that "girl with a penis." He will set me free and when I emerge and we will at last be as one. But for now, we must accept the status quo.

👈 ❑ ☞

Unlike much of life there, Christmas in the house on Scott Place is magic. The few good childhood memories are from those days when the tree gets put up the day before Christmas eve and Father strings the lights. Then Mother, Sister, and I add the ornaments and silver garland strands.(George unconsciously turned chores like that over to me.) Lastly, Father tosses tinsel at the tree, but Mother stops him and carefully places one or two strands on the very end of each tree branch. He chuckles and she shakes her head.

All of these things—the tree stand, the ornaments, even the garland strands, are saved from year to year, stored in cardboard boxes in the attic. Each ornament is carefully wrapped in tissue paper and gently placed in the same box it came in. And the strings of lights are placed in their original boxes as well, each wrapped around the notched cardboard designed to hold them so they are evenly distributed and will slide neatly inside their original packaging. (The bubble lights get careful treatment, as they are expensive and hard to replace.)

The Christmas tree occupies a full one-quarter of the living room. Furniture has to be moved to make room for it. It brings a warmth and comfort to the space that is missing the rest of the year. It sits in a stand which is not in the center, but toward the back of a square piece of plywood, which Father cut and painted white. A miniature white picket fence which Grandfather made from popsicle sticks, marks off the perimeter of the board. There's a front, latching gate and at evenly spaced intervals there are sockets into which tree lights can be screwed. An HO gauge oval track and a tiny trolley circle the tree just inside the fence.

The tree stand is draped by a white sheet and there is a *crèche*, a Manger with the traditional characters, Mary, Joseph, Jesus in his crib, the wise men, and a sleeping sheep with an ear broken off. All but one are ceramic; a plastic cow has somehow snuck in. He doesn't fit with the other pieces; he's too big. But he's there and no one comments.

Perhaps the most unique piece is a dirty ceramic angel, a cherub, actually, which is Mother's and which she insists must be placed at the top of the tree. Father loathes it and every year he complains about it until one year when it goes missing. All of the storage boxes are checked and the wrapping paper is dug through in our efforts to locate it, but to no avail. It's gone.

Mother is crying and it becomes clear to us that Father probably disposed of it, because now he produces a plastic star, which he says is more appropriate anyway, and from then on the angel is never mentioned again.

Christmas eve we have to go to bed and try to sleep—all but impossible, since George's adrenalin level is soaring. There is no fireplace, so George hangs a stocking on our bedpost. During the night, he wakes up at least three or four times and reaches in the darkness to feel the stocking. Still empty. He's aching to go downstairs and watch for Santa, but the orders are strict. We must be invited down.

When at last the stocking is filled, as quietly as possible, George creeps to the dresser and retrieves a flashlight, then lifts the stocking from the bedpost, and crawls back into bed, pulling the covers over his head and turning on the flashlight to assess the booty which always includes two or three comic books. There might be a small toy or two—a slinky or some sort of plastic musical instrument. And some kind of candy. It's all good. We settle in with it all, sucking on the candy and reading the comic books until it's daylight and Father invites us to come downstairs.

There, the glow from the tree lights twinkle through the windowed door to the living room. Slowly stepping inside, we stand for a moment and let the scene wash over us: the colors, the reflected sheen of the tree lights covering the ceiling and walls, and the presents; oh god, the presents, all wrapped and ribboned and piled around the base of the tree. If only….

And then the day officially starts (when the parents and sister are awake as well), and we open presents, taking turns tearing away the wrapping paper and squealing at each other, adding each new gift to our own pile. And I'm thinking *It doesn't get any better than this. If only…* I think, knowing it will be over too soon, *if only it could always be like this*—not the presents or the decorations or the lights, but the warmth, the feeling that being loved is possible, the feeling that all of us, George and me, Father and Mother, and Sister, are the happy family.

To be fair about it, Mother can't cook anything exotic, interesting, nothing different or "fancy" because Father won't eat it. He is a "meat and potatoes" guy. With the exception of Thanksgiving and Christmas, the menu rarely varies from meatloaf, mashed potatoes, and kale or spaghetti and meatballs. But no matter. It's a nightly drudge. Whatever the meal, it must be eaten; everything on the plate must be consumed. If not? Well, we were never beaten, not in the sense of being whipped with a belt or punched around, but there were slaps on the back of the head during dinner. Father had a firm set of rules, insisting that George hold his head over the plate, eat with a piece of bread in one hand to shovel stray food onto his fork, and "eat around the plate." (a bit of this, then a bite of that—never consuming all of one thing). Criticism is constant—comments about how George isn't manly enough or how he is uncoordinated, clumsy, and generally not good at anything. Never any praise. Nothing ever good enough. (I don't want to hear this, but I have no choice. I am here. I am part of George, part of the unmanly, uncoordinated, clumsy George.

So it is that often, when everyone else has finished their meal and left, we are forced to sit by ourselves at the dinner table, staring at an untouched mound of cold mashed potatoes, chinks of cold meat, a dish of half-eaten spaghetti. We must stay at this table until everything on our plate has been eaten.

The food and the mealtime rules did nothing to add any flavor. But at some point Father would leave, usually to go downstairs to his workshop, and Mother would quickly scrape the potatoes into the garbage and shoo us away, telling us quietly as if it had to be kept secret, "Your father really loves you."

And I think *Father doesn't even know **me***.

☜ ❑ ☞

That's Lucille Ball. He says she's a Communist (a "Commie" he calls her). At least that's what Father thinks. You see, he's an American. He's not a Commie. No siree. He made sure we knew that. He's 100% behind Senator Joe McCarthy's 1950's witch hunt, exposing 'commies' in show business. So in 1953 when Lucy testified before the House Committee on Un-American Activities, that cinched it. (Her testimony was that in 1938 she had registered as a Communist party member in order to appease her grandfather who was a Socialist, but she had never voted for a communist and any indication that she had Communist sympathies were false.)

But no matter. Lucy was a Commie and we were not about to watch a Commie no matter how funny she was. (And it didn't help that she married a Cuban.)

SIX
To Brooklyn and Back

Mother & Father

A T A.A. MEETINGS, ADULTS WHOSE parents were alcoholics talk about the terrible things they did when they were drunk. That wasn't true for our drunken parents. Father might have a beer with dinner (especially if we had spaghetti) and Mother might have an occasional drink of 'rock and rye,' but there are those occasions when they have friends over and Father makes High Balls (usually whiskey mixed with ginger ale).

They must have been fairly strong drinks because after just one of them their personalities change. And after a couple of drinks they become warm and fun-loving. Father gets a silly grin on his face, makes jokes, and Mother turns warm, softer, and almost playful. "Bottoms up," Father says to the guests, and raises his glass and everyone toasts him. All of the anger and bitterness they usually carry around is gone and George and I wish they drank more often, even daily. These are the parents we both want—relaxed, caring, loving.

At A.A. meetings a speaker might say "Whenever he got drunk my father beat me." And we think of the times we laid in bed and prayed to god for Father and Mother to become drunks.

☜ ❑ ☞

Father is unaware of what he is doing to us. Certainly, he wasn't aware of me, not as anyone in my own right. You can be sure of that. But it can't be neatly sorted out. Our relationship is like the weather, cold fronts and warm fronts, always moving from west to east or edging down from the north. Growing up in the middle of the storm center, we don't worry about getting wet. We look for some indication of what to do or how to respond to things, but for all we try to do, we are just who we are. All we want is to get through it. So, for much of the time, I let George be George and I stand back and hold on, waiting for it to blow over.

As time passes, I watch George learning how to act and, more important, how to feel. It's all largely a reflection of what Father and Mother say and do, but he doesn't know what I'm supposed to do, or more properly, what he's supposed to do with me. For most of my life, I say and do things along with George as because that's all I have to go by. I see and hear what George is doing and I know much of it came from them, but there's nothing I can do about it. So I tuck my impulses away, am trapped in him and, for the time being, George can't even consult with me. I'm just the leaf on the tree that's blowing in the wind. And it will take a long time for that to change.

There are two high schools in the Catholic Diocese of Brooklyn—one for boys (Bishop Laughlin) and one for girls (Bishop McDonnell). In the eighth grade, a test is given at all of the elementary schools in the diocese. The top scoring boy and girl from each school is given a scholarship to the respective high school. At St. Agnes Elementary School, George is the boy with the highest grade. So we get to go to Bishop Laughlin High School. We get to go back to Brooklyn.

To get there we have to ride the Long Island Railroad (LIRR) to the Flatbush Avenue station which is located underground, below the *Williamsburg Savings Bank*. About ten blocks away is Bishop Laughlin High School.

We ride to and from school on the morning and afternoon LIRR trains along with other students from Long Island. In the morning, about halfway along the walk from Flatbush Avenue to the school, there's a soda fountain where we stop in the afternoon for an Egg Crème (A drink indigenous to Brooklyn, it's just syrup—usually chocolate or strawberry—milk, and seltzer.

Egg cremes are the only good part of our time at Bishop Laughlin. Local kids that live along the walk from the subway intimidate us and in the winter the cold is bitter and the wind is cruel and once we're at school it only gets worse. Our teachers are Christian Brothers. Some still have their Irish accents and they delight in beating up on us. Of course, George is an easy target, being the class clown, imitating Brother Alphonse losing his place in the Latin textbook or pretending to write notes when what he's actually doing is drawing stick figures on the corner of the pages in our notebook so that when you flip them the figures appear to move.

We're not happy at Bishop Laughlin. The school work is boring. We flunk Latin and Algebra and when we try out for the school paper our writing is rejected. We get slapped around by the teachers and picked on by the older kids. The school building is cold and decaying—windows stick, floors creak, and the tall fence around the schoolyard makes it feel like a prison.

By Sophomore year we are miserable. Our life is like an arcade game. George is bouncing around like a pinball and I'm the lever, swinging as he flies by, disrupting his game, while all he can do is try to keep his balls in play. But more to the point, he plays with his balls. Puberty has struck like a rampant cancer; it attacks at every turn. And the need for me to get out is stronger than ever. George tries to sort things out, but confusion and craziness reign. Nothing makes sense. We both envy the other boys for whom everything seems to be neatly wrapped in a wooden shipping crate being unloaded from a freighter onto the dock, designed perfectly to adolescent specifications. But not us. We're square and our crate is round. We don't...we can't...sit solidly on the ground; we toil without destination or design. We just don't fit in it.

And as it was in elementary school, George is often the target of those who need to affirm their masculinity. He's smaller than everyone else in his grade and the ease with which he reacts to their taunts make him the butt of their jokes. We can call only two or three classmates friends, but not so much that they will stand up for him, and who can blame them? It would simply make them targets as well.

The best part of the situation is the daily train ride home. Each day, on the LIRR ride from Brooklyn to Rockville Centre, the boys from Bishop Laughlin occupy one of the cars on the train. The conductor knows us by now and sometimes reminds us when it's our turn to get off. After Jamaica, we split off, depending on where we live. Those from the north shore ride that line; those from the south shore stay on: *Rockville Centre, Baldwin, Freeport, Merrick, Bellmore, Wantaugh, Seaford, Massepequa, Massepequa Park, Copaige, Amityville, Lindenhurst, and Babylon.*

❧ ❑ ☞

Uncle Joe belongs to the Rockville Country Club. Though not involved in the discussions, we learn that the Aunt and Uncle have used their influence to get George a summer job at the club: washing dishes in the club restaurant kitchen. Father believes that it's important for a boy to learn the value of work at an early age. (There are things a girl like me should learn too, but that opportunity doesn't exist. All I can learn is what George learns.)

Because he is underage, George must get a work permit. Then, permit in hand, he reports to work. His hours are weekend evenings and his first job is washing glasses. Glasses are washed in a soap-and-water filled sink with brushes and a motor. The glasses are shoved up and down on the brushes, then rinsed in a second, adjacent sink filled with cold water.

Perhaps the worst part of the job (apart from having to deal with the dirty glasses of all sizes and shapes) is the clock on the back wall that's visible through the open area above the sink. The secondhand moves at a snail's pace and he constantly struggles with the impulse to look at it.

The job is boring and unpleasant. Many of the kitchen staff are immigrants who have escaped from Hungary during the recent revolution. They speak little or no English, with the exception of vulgarities and swear words. The head chef is a man named Matson and the crew delights in mocking and insulting him, but he gives as good as he gets.

DISHWASHER: *Fucking Matson, you fucking you mother's dog.*
MATSON: *Shut up. Mother's dog is fucking your mother. That's what.*

SOUS CHEF: *Yes. You shut fucking hole. Is easy to get dishwasher, you fucker.*

DISHWASHER: *What! You sucking Matson's cock, you cock sucker!*

This probably is not what Father had in mind when he got George the job, but for us it's definitely new and interesting and after a while we move up to washing dishes. (The sous chef is right. The turnover in dishwashers is frequent.) The dishwasher stands at the short side of an L-shaped stainless-steel counter which has a hole in the middle and a large trash bucket under it. To the left there's a large square stainless steel 'box' (the washer itself), open at both ends. The openings are covered with a plastic drape and the racks filled with dishes are placed on a conveyor belt. The busboys and waiters stack the dirty dishes on the counter and the dishwasher scrapes off whatever is left on them into the hole. The dishes are then placed in the racks and pushed onto the conveyor belt and into the washer unit.

Do you know what people do to their discarded food? They leave piles of uneaten vegetables, chewing gum stuck to spoons, and cigarettes doused in their leftover mashed potatoes. At first George gags at the sight and smell of it and I slip back as far from it as I can, but after a while we both become accustomed to it all and learn to focus on the task at hand: clear the counter, get the dishes in the rack, get the racks in the washer. Time passes a lot more quickly here.

The pleasant part of the entire kitchen scene is mealtime. Kitchen staff (as opposed to wait-staff and chefs) eat from a common pot, usually a stew of some sort. It's an opportunity to sit and hear the others talk. More often than not they speak Hungarian, but they may lapse into English vulgarities and curses, most of which are totally new to us.

Matson, one of them says, is a 'shit-fuck.' We're perplexed. "What's a shit-fuck?" George asks, knowing that the question can't be asked at home, and they chuckle and finally one of them, whose English is reasonable, explains. "A shit fuck is a guy who is so excited when he's fucking that he shits himself." And they all laugh and nod and one of them says. "Yes. Matson. He is a shit-fuck."

After a while we learn that many of these men are professionals—doctors, lawyers, and the like—but because they can't speak English they have had to take jobs like these until they learn enough English to take qualifying exams or do whatever they must do to transfer their professional skills. Many of them live in a kind of bunkhouse behind the clubhouse. The rooms are equipped with little more than army bunks and night stands. They often work double shifts, sixteen hour days.

During a break, one of them takes us to his room, which he shares with three other men. From beneath his bunk he produces a large, black carrying case and opens it to reveal a brand new accordion, obviously a very expensive model, trimmed in gold and mother-of-pearl. We're cautioned not to touch it and when George asks him to play it he explains that he cannot. He doesn't know how to play it. But why spend his hard-earned money on something like this? He explains that in his country, owning such an instrument is the equivalent of owning a Mercedes...even if you can't drive it; it shows the world you have arrived.

It's in this strange world of cursing immigrants and discarded food that George meets Charles, who is on the maintenance crew—he changes light bulbs, sweeps and mops the floors, and empties the trash, including that big trash can under the dishwasher's counter.

Charles befriends us and one evening we go to the bunkhouse and sit on the steps and talk to him and he patiently listens to our complaints until finally George gets up the courage to tell him our secret—that when he is alone he puts on Mother's or Sister's clothes and he is not a boy—he is a girl, a girl with a penis. I emerge from the shadows and, I explain how I am part of him, and then pause, out of breath and frightened because this is the first time I have had a voice and it terrifies George.

But Charles treats this confession casually, remarking that everyone is different and that we all need to take care of whatever special need we have. And so it is that one evening when we're invited, we go inside Charles' room in the bunkhouse and after some time Charles asks George to help him. He explains that he needs a favor, this small help, and explains what it entails and while we're seated on the bed he slides George's pants down and we lay down, and he lays beside and behind us, and we can feel his penis against our bottom and we are both suddenly filled with fear. We pull away, trembling, trying to sit up as he tries to calm us down, but we can't stop the trembling as we pull up our pants and run back to the kitchen, ashamed, and afraid, wondering who knows, wondering what if. And...

...we never talk to him again. Soon after that, providence resolves the situation. George, a good worker, is moved to a job in the clubhouse, shining shoes. Compared to the kitchen, it's a luxurious position. The boss is a good man, an 'old hand' who not only shows George 'the ropes' but tells him ways to get some perks. That includes ordering from the menu and one day he asks if George has ever had lobster.

'No,' George says, not even on Fridays. So the boss orders the lobster tail for him and we are enchanted. Never have we ever tasted anything so good.

Never has life been as good as it is, shining shoes and eating lobster.

⤙ ❑ ☞

To some degree Father's foray into the upper middle class has come by way of the Knights of Columbus (the K of C), a Catholic organization of men, described as "a fraternal benefit society." He is an active member of the local chapter and gets to wear a funky hat and sash, carry a sword, and eventually get the title of *Grand Knight*. Many nights when he gets home from work he hurries to change into "the outfit" and go to one of their meetings.

There are rare occasions when we get a tiny glimpse inside the club. He brings us to a K of C communion breakfast and makes George dress in a tie and white shirt and listen to a priest make a couple of jokes and introduce a missionary from Africa who talks about the poor heathens and how the K of C is helping them with food and clothing.

The only connection we can make to all of this is through TV shows like *The Honeymooners*, wherein Ralph Kramden and Ed Norton are members of the *International Order of Friendly Sons of the Raccoons* or the *Amos n' Andy* show where the men are members of the *Mystic Knights of the Sea*.

It's all pretty foolish, but Father takes it very seriously. It's clear he relishes the secretive nature of it even though he mocks Grandfather's membership in the Masons. He sees being part of the K of C as being of a certain class of people, much like playing golf, which he plays poorly, but feels is necessary if he is to be a part of that social status he wants so badly to join.

GEORGE WILKERSON

SEVEN
Work Ethics

EVERY WEEKDAY MORNING FATHER IS up by six a.m. He dresses in trousers from Barney's (the discount clothing outlet), a shirt and tie (sometimes the shirt is a print of some sort and the tie is striped; it's his idea of a fashion statement) and a sport jacket (in the winter he wears a topcoat). He has coffee and a Danish and by 6:50 he is at the LIRR station, waiting with the other Ward Cleavers for the 6:57 to "the city."

Father at Work

When the train arrives at Penn Station he takes the subway downtown to the old, Gotham City steel and concrete building where he works. He takes the freight elevator up to the fifth floor and goes to the Men's Room, hangs up the topcoat and changes out of the shirt, tie, trousers and sport jacket, and dons a blue work shirt and coveralls. He then moves into the workshop and takes his place at the monotype machine.

(Later, when Offset Printing, Word Processors, and Laser printers take away his job and, at the age of 62, with the help of a heart attack, he will be forced to retire.)

One Saturday Father takes us with him. We share his space on the train platform, clinging to his topcoat, frightened by the crowd, and when the train pulls in, clinging even tighter, we follow him onto the train.

Many of the seats face each other, like a series of V's. Most of the passengers are quietly looking out a window or reading a newspaper. As the train begins to pull away, the conductor calls out the upcoming stops. Then, travelling slowly down the aisle, he stops and punches the tickets stowed under the little clamps on the seat backs.

When he reaches us, the conductor smiles and looks over at Father. "Yours?" he asks.

Father nods and the conductor moves on. The rules are clear: nothing that might embarrass, nothing that might cause a scene. Father's glance at us says it all. *Behave.* So George and I content ourselves with looking out the window as Father takes the newspaper he has been carrying, opens it to its full width, then folds it, folds it again, and refolds it, until it resembles a neat runway for his eyes.

As the train approaches Jamaica, the scenery changes rapidly. The little bungalows and tiny plots of land give way to brick buildings, factories, graffiti, narrow streets and old stone and mortar apartments piled high one after the other. Whenever the train stops many of the riders leave, but we don't move until the train pulls into Penn Station where we quickly exit and walk further below the street to the subway. The trains there rattle loudly, their approach echoing inside the tunnels. When the right one pulls up we board and, like most of the riders, stand, but after a moment Father steers us into a seat beside a man who is sleeping. The man smells like grapes and snores loudly, occasionally mumbling to himself.

Thankfully, the trip is short. We exit the train, climb a long flight of stairs, and emerge onto the street where it seems as if we have been released from prison, seeing the sun for the first time. Everything is suddenly wondrous, but there's no time to take it all in. In a few moments we're inside a luncheonette and as soon as we enter a man behind the counter steps up, smiles, and puts out a cup of coffee for Father.

"Whattaya got there?" he asks, gesturing toward us.

"This is the boy," my father says.

"How about some pancakes?" the man says to us.

Father turns to us and gestures. "Answer the man. Do you want some pancakes?"

"Yes, please."

"You got it," the man says, snapping his fingers and pointing to Father.

We watch as Father stirs his coffee, then lifts the cup to his lips. There's a soft sipping sound, then a gasp. "Hot," he says, puts down the cup, and reaches for his water glass. He spoons out an ice cube and places it in the coffee, stirs it, then raises it to his lips again, sipping it carefully, then puts it down. "That's better".

When the pancakes come there's only one.

Father shakes his head. "He won't eat it all, you know."

The man smiles. "Eat as much as you want," he says to us.

Father takes his newspaper from his pocket and lays it on the counter. The man returns with a plate of two eggs and two slices of toast. Father eats quickly, then turns to us.

"Ready?" he asks.

George shoves the last piece of pancake into his mouth and jumps down from the counter stool. Father puts the newspaper under his arm, turns, and waves to the man. "See you, Joe!"

"Put that kid to work!" Joe calls back as we leave, but Father doesn't answer.

We walk a block, turn a corner, then another block, and in the middle of the block, we turn into an alley. At the end of the alley is a large metal door. Father pushes a button on the wall and a loud bell sounds, followed almost immediately by a clunking sound somewhere behind the door. A few moments later, the door slides open. Father steps inside the elevator and motions for us to follow.

We ride the elevator to the fourth floor. When the door opens, a wall of heat smacks us in the face. The noise of machinery blends with noises coming through open windows from the streets below. We follow Father through the machinery maze, past men dressed in aprons and caps leaning over clanking steel and metal behemoths, to a short hallway and through another door. There, a row of bent and rusting lockers lines one wall. Father steps up to one of them, takes off his trench coat, removes his tie, dress shirt and pants and hangs them inside. He then takes a stained and torn denim shirt, a pair of coveralls, and an apron from the locker and puts them on, then reaches out to us. "Here," he says.

George quickly removes his coat and cap and hands them to Father who hangs them inside the locker. Father removes a heavy, black pair of shoes from the floor of the locker, leans down and takes off his shoes and replaces them with the work shoes, and closes the door.

We return down the hall and through the machine room, past the elevator and into a separate room. At the threshold, Father steps inside, stops, and turns to us. "This is where I work," he says. "Don't touch anything."

Most of the floor space in the room is taken up by two large machines. Their armatures and fittings are exposed, like the skeleton of some prehistoric, cold-blooded beast. At the front of each machine is a keyboard. It looks like the typewriter we have at home, but there's no platen, no place to put the paper, and the keys sit higher on their levers.

Father reaches under one of the keyboards, pulls on a handle and swings out a large pot. He motions for us to come closer. "That's 600 degrees," Father says, pointing to the thick, silver fluid bubbling inside the pot. Then he turns and reaches into a wooden box along the wall, pulling out an ingot. "This is lead," he says, slowly letting the ingot slip into the pot and dissolve, melting like a bar of butter, and then swinging it back into its place under the keyboard.

He sits down and motions for us to stand behind him. "When I type a letter," he says, pointing, "the lead in that pot is forced through a die back there. It gets cooled over there and then it's placed in the galley."

He begins to type and as he does the machine groans to life. The armatures rise and fall and the hiss of air being forced through the narrow spaces of the die creates a damp stream. After a few minutes, Father gets up and leads us to a table behind the machine where there is a narrow, flat wooden box. Inside the box, "slugs" sit in neat rows. "This is the cold type," he says. "It goes to that other room, where the presses are."

He looks down at us staring at the galley of type, reading the upside down and backward letters. "Do you know why I do this?" he asks.

George shakes his head.

"I do this so that you won't have to . . . so that you can go to college."

But his point is wasted on George. *What kind of a statement is that? Why would anyone not want to do this? Why go to college when you can do this?*

"O.K.?" the father asks.

George nods. "O.K." he says. And clearly, I am not a part of this. I'm not charmed by the heat or the machinery or the noise.

Satisfied, Father rises and leads us out to the larger room where the presses are located. Standing in the doorway, he points to one of them. It's churning like a jump rope; a large cylinder rolls forward, stops, then rolls back, then rolls forward, stops, then rolls back in a continuing, heavy rhythm. As it begins the next cycle, a long sheet of paper rises from somewhere beneath its skeleton and the roller flattens it, pressing hard against the paper and leaving a mute impression.

"The galleys come in here," Father says, "and the presses make the newspaper's pages.

The sound and motion, the *mise en scene,* have George totally transfixed, but then a man steps from behind the beast and waves at us. Father nods and the man yells something.

"The boy!" Father yells back.

The man smiles.

"C'mon," Father says, returning to his own space, to his own machinery.

We follow him and he places a chair against the wall and motions for George to sit. And for the rest of the morning, except for the times when we go to the bathroom or follow Father into the front room to deliver the galleys, we stay in this space, reading the proof sheets, staring out the window at the brick wall across the air shaft, or watching in rapt fascination as the machinery responds to Father's commands. *Why would someone not want to do this?* George thinks.

When it's time to leave, we reverse the process that brought us here. Father changes back to his shirt and tie and we walk to the subway and then take the train to Rockville Centre where Mother is parked at the station, waiting for us. We walk to the car, climb in, and say nothing as Mother slides across the seat so that Father can drive us home.

There is such irony in all this, in George being wound up, in an odd way, over what Father does. That he sat at a keyboard and triggered the production of 'cold type' to create words and sentences that were fed to a printer, and now, as you read this, we sat at a keyboard, triggering the production of words and sentences that were fed to a printer. But there's no longer a behemoth spitting molten lead and casting shiny letters into wooden galleys—just zeros and ones casting tiny letters on a screen.

George thinks: *Why would someone not want to do that?*

And I answer: *Because it's dirty and hot and sweaty.*

But the machinery has touched the testosterone and that suit trumps my queen-high flush.

☜ ❑ ☞

When George and I are fifteen years old, the train ride to Brooklyn, the cold walk to Bishop Laughlin, the raps on the knuckles and slaps on the head by the Christian Brothers, and the harassment by the older kids and the teasing by classmates are wearing us down. George is now terrified of my being discovered. We don't fit in anywhere and nothing I do to find a way to help him to get by is working. He's confused by my desire to escape and he's anxious and to make matters worse, his male hormones are surging. Finally, I decide to do something.

I have a plan, but I'm not ready to share it. I see to it that George saves some money; not a whole lot, but it's what I think will be enough and one fall day, instead of changing trains at the Jamaica station (to go to Brooklyn) we stay on the local and go to Penn Station in Manhattan and find our way to the Port Authority Bus Terminal where George buys a bus ticket to Columbus, Ohio. (My plan required a ticket to Louisville, Kentucky, but we don't have enough money, so George asks how far we can go on what we have and Columbus is it.)

We are in the far back of the bus and slowly, as I'm coming to further into George's consciousness, I realize I have no plan for what we'll do when we get to Ohio. We're running away from something, not toward anything. So for now, I make him aware that we're doing <u>something</u>, that we had no choice; it was either ride this bus or jump in front of one.

GEORGE WILKERSON

EIGHT
Oceanside High (By Way of Kentucky)

COLUMBUS, OHIO IS THE HOME of Ohio State University and this bus is one of many the University students living in New York take back to campus after Thanksgiving vacation. We are surrounded by a dozen or so of them and one of the co-eds finally asks where we're going and why. So, through George, I tell them the truth, the story of the cruelty of the Sisters and the Brothers and how we feel lost and confused and they are sympathetic. And George tells them of this something he has no words for (me). They ask us questions about religion and god and for the first time George is able to talk to people who understand our doubts and fears. They offer us food and soda and seem to be impressed by our curiosity and honesty. The conversation becomes heated. One of them is an atheist; another has 'communist leanings.' One of the girls is studying to become Hindu and explains the role of Krishna, a way of thinking that we've never heard of. We're challenged and excited to be able to express ourselves and to let out the thoughts and fears we've hidden from family, from the priests and nuns, and even from friends. They regard George's efforts to explain me as something positive and encourage him to confront me. They have given us a glimpse into a world we never realized existed, a world where people can question, explore, and learn without fear.

When we reach Columbus and must leave the company of the students, some give us money and encourage us to hitchhike to Kentucky, so we head to the highway and begin, but we're unsuccessful and after a short while a man comes up to us and starts a conversation, asking George if he wants to get laid. For just $20, he says, he can hook him up with a prostitute. So George gives him the $20 (nearly everything the students donated to us) and is directed to a hotel down the street and given a room number.

I can feel George's testosterone at work, but what about me? This is a whole new problem. I have watched George masturbate and play out his fantasies and the object of these is always female, but when I'm 'alive' what is my role? If I share his fantasies am I a lesbian? If I don't, am I gay? I am thoroughly confused…so I retreat. I leave him to summon up the courage to go to the hotel and knock on the door, but of course, no one answers. He's been had. Stupid George.

We head back to the street and George sticks out his thumb at passing cars and very shortly a car pulls over and an overweight, balding man in need of a shave, wearing a dirty white shirt, and smoking a cigarette invites us to get in.

"Where are you going?"

"Louisville."

"Me too," he says. "I'll take you there."

We climb in and pull away and before long we're on the open highway and he's telling us he's a Korean War veteran and pulls up his pant leg to show us his artificial limb. It's metal and has holes through it; for ventilation, probably. And he continues to talk and before long he has his hand on George's leg and he's talking about sex and women and how he knows we're dying to get laid, but explains that sex between two men is a whole lot better.

George asks to get out.

"Relax," he says. "I know a nice place in Louisville."

George asks him to please let us out.

Sensing our anxiety, he pulls over and as we climb out we can see in the back seat an array of children's toys and somehow it makes us feel a little sick because he probably has kids, though looking back on it now, maybe the toys were enticements for kids younger than us.

So there we are, on the side of the road. It's now early morning and, fortunately, rides (better and safer) come along and before nightfall we arrive in Louisville at the home of Uncle Thornton and Aunt Elsie May.

The arrival is not entirely welcome. It doesn't take long before they call our parents. Uncle Thornton hands George the phone. "Talk to your father."

George takes the phone, but before he can say anything, Father says. "You come home…right now. Is that clear?"

Maybe the long distance gives George the courage to stand up to him. Or maybe he feels my anger. "I'm not coming home if I have to go back to Bishop Laughlin."

"Forget about that. You come home…now."

George hands the phone to our Uncle. "He's OK here," Thornton says.

There's a long pause followed by a few uh-huhs and yeses, then he hands the phone back to George. "It's your mother."

"George?"

"I'm not coming home if I have to go back to that school."

She sighs. "I know. Don't worry about that."

"I don't want to go back." (I'm on the verge of tears and whenever that happens, George cries as well.)

"Don't worry. You won't have to."

And at that we know it's true, because it doesn't matter what Father says, if Mother says we won't, we won't.

The next morning we're on a bus back to the city. The parents pick us up at the Port Authority terminal and very little is said on the way home. But we don't go back to Bishop Laughlin.

There's more of me in George than there is of George in me. George doesn't fit into the standard male persona. He'll never be a John Wayne or a Humphrey Bogart. He's smaller, weaker, and not at all aggressive. And no matter how hard he tries, he can't adopt the trappings of masculinity. He has managed to assume some of the elements of the gender, but they are just that—assumptions. They don't come naturally. Although they require less effort as time goes on, George is now fully aware of my presence and at times I leak out. My femininity oozes through his pores and keeping me at bay can be a struggle, but it's a struggle of which no one is aware. George has become a fine actor.

Within a week of getting back from Kentucky, George is attending Oceanside High School and we are saved.

It's the "Blackboard Jungle;" era, but even if Oceanside isn't New York City, the influence is there. Gender roles are sharper. There are about half a dozen sororities and four "Social Clubs" (a euphemism for 'gang' though these groups are more like fraternities). They are the *Counts*, the *Dukes*, the *Gents*, and the *Emeralds*. And there are periodic rumors of an upcoming 'rumble' on this or that Saturday at *Nathan's Roadside Rest*, the local hotdog and milk shake hangout, but when driving by on such a Saturday, the place is quite calm.

George wants to fit in with the guys. So he adopts the persona of a 'hoodlum,' telling anyone who will listen that he has come from Brooklyn, land of the "tough guys." And the he shoves me down as deep as I can go.

But it doesn't work. Despite the Elvis Presley hairstyle and turned up collar, he can't pull it off. He's still the 'delicate kid' from St. Agnes Elementary School and by summer he has dropped the swagger and the attitude and settled into the role of class clown and as he relaxes I slowly work my way back up to a comfortable level of his consciousness.

❧ ☐ ☞

Come Fall, George tries a variety of ways to be popular. First, there's *Dee Jay Georgie J*, the guy who joined the A-V club so he can check out the record player during lunch and play 45's in the cafeteria so the girls can dance. He uses his allowance to buy the latest hits and brings them to school every day. Everyone seems to like it, but it doesn't win him any fans.

So next there's *Choral Comedy George*, the Chorus class student whose job is to make the gang laugh. This is primarily accomplished by writing little poems and song parodies. One of them, to the tune of Johnny Cash's *Don't Take Your Gun to Town*, is about the withered right arm of the chorus teacher. His name is John Race and the song goes like this:

> *Johnny Race was twenty-one when he first noticed it*
> *He tried to tear or chop it off and throw it in a pit*
> *But his Mom said "Don't do that. Just let it dangle there.*
> *No one will notice it, my son, and that way you'll have a spare"*
> > *Don't take the arm to school son,*
> > *Leave the arm at home, John*
> > *Don't take the arm to school.*

It's disgusting, but George is so hungry for attention, he willingly perverts his writing talent for attention of any sort—even revulsion..

And finally, there's *Intellectual George*, who somehow is befriended by two other boys, Maris and Mitch, avid readers and truth-seekers who accept him into their cabal. It's the reading that makes the common ground.

The addiction to reading began at pre-school age when Mother read the Little Golden books to us. Books were precious and we always had them in our room; everything from the Hardy Boys to science fiction novels by Bradbury and Asimov. With Maris and Mitch we read Heinlin, Bradbury, and whatever else we can get, including, of course, *Catcher in the Rye* and stuff by and about Freud (passed to us by Maris as fuel for late night discussions.) Freud is especially interesting because he talks about sex and gender and George knows that buried somewhere in those pages there's bound to be something about me.

George's SAT score on the English portion is in the low 700's (top score is 800), most likely because of the reading, though what's assigned in school (e.g. *The Red Pony*, *The Old Man and the Sea*) are easy, so grades don't reflect his language skill. That's one of the reasons we're called to the counselor's office where we are chastised because of the contrast between the low grades and high test scores. "You're not performing up to your potential," the counselor says

"Potential for what?"

"Your potential," he repeats. "Your academic potential."

George shrugs and I'm thinking *What is this guy saying?*

"Can I go now?" George asks.

The counselor nods.

Ironically, Girls scare the bejesus out of George. They intimidate him while at the same time they intrigue <u>me</u>. Maybe that's why he's intimidated. Over the course of just one year our sensibilities are so interconnected that we often share the same feeling, although we give them different names: *intimidated…intrigued.* It's both really.

At fifteen years old, the notion of asking a girl on a date does awful things to George's innards—stomach cramps, diarrhea, nausea. But he knows it's a necessary part of appearing 'normal,' So he finally asks a girl on a date. She isn't very attractive and when he asks she seems to be grateful. Her name is Vickie and she's about five inches taller than us. She has a Romanesque face, her skin chiseled into sharp corners—the kind of girl people called 'gawky. And it's possible that George is the first date she's ever had, if it's a date at all.

This date, such as it is, has a roundabout arrangement. George is afraid to tell his parents, so he invents a story about meeting friends at the movie theatre and tells Vickie he'll meet her there.

George's mother drives us to the theatre early, so we can be out front when Vickie's mother drops her off. When her mother drops her off, George buys the tickets and we go inside. Because Vickie is taller, George sits on our legs, in the lotus position, so it's not so obvious, and puts his arm on the back of her seat, intending to slide it over her shoulder, but he never gets there because he is petrified of what could happen if he touches her.

"Yaaaaa....help!" she might scream. "I'm being raped!!! He touched me!!!"

As an observer, I'm finding it humorous—much better than the Dean Martin and Jerry Lewis movie we're watching.

George has a wonderfully vivid imagination and which is neither inspired nor endorsed by me. So, sadly, by the end of the movie our right arm and both legs are numb.

For a time, that's the way subsequent dating experiences go. And to add to the confusion, if George's thoughts are elsewhere and a girl sees me staring at her, she probably thinks George is flirting, but in fact, I'm the one looking and I'm looking at her outfit, her shoes, how she did her hair, and envying all of it.

Then Pat O'Reilly comes along.

GEORGE WILKERSON

NINE
Of Girls and Boys

GEORGE'S GRADES AREN'T VERY GOOD, so we have to go to summer school. The daily walk is about a mile and usually uneventful. Pat O'Reilly, a girl we've seen and know of from school, but never actually met, lives halfway between our house and the school.

It all begins one day when we walk home with her. It's nothing more than a coincidence. We're simply both walking and we start to talk and that's how it goes until eventually George is invited to come in and meet the parents.

The O'Reillys are Irish immigrants with classic brogues. The father is a laborer, probably much like ours, but without the middle-class affectations. The mother is kind, but nervous and though we don't fully grasp the situation, George and I get the sense that all is not right in the O'Reilly household.

So we start hanging out at Pat's house, in the basement, where we watch *American Bandstand* and (ostensibly) do our homework. The advantage of the location is that we can immediately tell if either parent is coming downstairs. The footsteps and creaking stairs signal their imminent arrival. And so, gradually, over time, George is reaching under Pat's sweater and fondling her breasts and after a while she is fondling his penis and after a while longer, he opens his zipper so she can slip her hand inside. The fire this ignites is something George has only imagined and not anything I ever considered possible. I don't feel like part of it and yet I can feel it. After all, it's my penis too.

The movies and books of the day that attempt to deal with adolescent sex are rarely on target. The fear of being caught coupled with the thrill of entering forbidden territory sets off sensations that will never be equaled because the experience can't be recreated. That first time happens only once.

George was in love and I had enough sense to just stand back and watch, though there was always a sliver of my being that was fascinated by Pat's girlishness—the bra, the skirt, the hairstyle. But I was content to take notes and share the romantic feelings.

Years later we realized that there was something uncomfortable about Pat's relationship to her father. She had tried to tell us what it was, but it was always in such an oblique fashion that we couldn't process it accurately. She was such a sweet, but sad and lonely person, trying hard to escape from it and looking to George to be the rescuer. And what could I do?

☜ ❑ ☞

The word hasn't hit the common vocabulary yet, but if it had, George would be called a nerd. He's in the A-V Club; he gets to truck the Audio-Visual equipment from the storage area to the various classrooms. That's how he meets Maris. And Maris introduces him to Mitch.

Maris Cakars, the son of Latvian immigrants, has the face of an Eastern European child, punctuated by a devilish smile that slyly creeps out of the corners of his mouth. And Mitch is the Garfunkel to Maris's Simon. He's a tall, curly blonde-headed poet. Both are children of radical 1930's bohemian parents.

George and Maris and Mitch are ahead of the curve when it comes to mind-altering experiences. Some weekend nights they stay awake for as long as they can (meeting at a diner and drinking coffee, mostly) because they heard that sleeplessness causes hallucinations (though they never had any). The three of them are simpatico brothers and George makes sure I stay in the background, letting me out only occasionally, in private, to try on Mother's or Sister's clothes when left home alone. Bohemian children though Mitch and Maris may be, there is no confusion about gender identity in their world.

On their weekend adventures they travel into the city and play at being Beatniks, going to coffee houses and listening to poetry and snapping their fingers instead of applauding. They talk about radical ideas, revolutions, and protests. I listen and find it amusing, but more often than not, I doze off and don't wake up until George awakes the next morning.

One of the trio's more unusual exploits involves bathroom passes. There are two for each classroom in the high school: one for the boys bathroom and one for the girls—each a slab of wood painted orange with black letters for the classroom number. The trio decides to steal them, somehow managing to accumulate a couple dozen or more and they are never caught. And then they put them in a box and mail them to the principal and revel in the success of the *Great Oceanside Bathroom Pass Robbery*. It's the beginning of an odd collusion.

Unaware of the robbery, the school administration, in an effort to co-opt a couple pains in the ass, give Maris and George a role in the production of the daily morning announcements. I have a part in this, but George has a creative bent that sometimes rides roughshod over my efforts to temper it. I'm the Ginger Rogers to his Fred Astaire, the Harriet to his Ozzie, but in no way am I the Lucy to his Desi.

George and Maris write little skits and fun "announcements" and things go well for a while, but their need to rock the boat gets the better of them and one day they end the announcements by dedicating a popular song to the Principal (Charles Mossback— could you ask for a more descriptive name?) The song is called *Lotsa Luck Charlie* and it's an innocent joke, but "Charlie" isn't impressed. Immediately after it "airs" they're called to his office and as I sit in the background watching George desperately trying to squelch his laughter, the Principal solemnly recites phrases heavy with 'meaning' (Abraham Lincoln and Dwight D. Eisenhower evoked in the same quote). He talks about the responsibilities of citizenship and of American values and how they are on the path to humiliation and degradation and concludes his remarks by announcing that they are henceforth suspended until their parents are called in, ending the pronouncement with the classic threat that "*This is going to go on your permanent record.*"

At that point. Mossback steps out of the office to get the records and Maris looks at George and declares that the whole thing is "a crock" and "we just ought to leave." And without hesitation, Maris rises and walks out of the Principal's office (via the hall door rather than the one Mossback just used) and George follows.

Maris has his parents' car that day. He has just gotten his license and they're letting him take the car to school. So George and I go to his car (as usual, what choice do I have?) and Maris gets behind the wheel and George gets in and turns to him and asks "What now?" And Maris flashes that devilish grin and says dramatically "Greeby Street."

Greeby Street is in Philadelphia and was the subject of a number of conversations Maris and Mitch and George had because Mitch had lived there before his parents moved to Oceanside. Maris, it turns out, has an address on Greeby Street which Mitch had given him and he had been saving it for just such an occasion.

So off we go.

The drive is uneventful and, after a little scouting around Philly, Maris finds Greeby Street. It's near dark, but enough light is left to find the front door of the brownstone row house and knock. In a few moments, we are greeted by a girl our age who, it turns out, has already heard from Mitch and seems thrilled we're here and invites us inside, asking if we're hungry (we are) and makes us sandwiches. And when we tell her what happened and what we've done she's clearly impressed. Of course, George is delighted. But I have an ugly sense of foreboding which George totally disregards.

In a short while we follow the girl to another house where, in the basement, we find at least a dozen kids who already know the story of how we got there and what we did and they celebrate us like heroes. So now I'm thinking this isn't so bad and I sit back and bask in the shared glory of it all, forcing thoughts of repercussions and consequences out of our minds. We listen to music, talk about our respective schools, and "play it cool," but later, when we return to Mitch's friend's house, we are greeted by the girl's mother and grilled until we confess everything and agree to call our parents. And that changes the complexion of everything. Dreading the aftermath, we silently drive home to face our parents collective wrath.

The aftermath is this: we're suspended from school for three days and we have to return to the Principals' office, along with our parents, and listen to a repeat of the Principal's platitudes and must repeatedly apologize for our behavior. And afterward our parents declare that Maris and George are not to hang out with each other anymore. They have little control over that because by now we are excellent liars, but things just aren't the same.

That adventure with Maris still sits warmly in George's consciousness and though it was not strictly my doing, it served me as well, as a model of behavior for the rest of the life I shared with George. It seems a shame that we never went into politics.

In the years since, George has searched off and on for Maris. There were occasional news reports of his activities with the War Resisters League, but then he went "off the radar" until we uncovered a news article indicating he had become a fireman and died, though the cause of death was never clear.

We were all atheists, Maris and George and I. Nonetheless, we think what great fun it would be, if there was an afterlife, to see Maris again, to see him smile and hear his laugh and drive off to Greeby Street with him.

GEORGE WILKERSON

TEN
Track and Feelings

WHEN WE MOVE FROM CATHOLIC to Public school George discovers running. The Oceanside High School Phys Ed teacher, whose stature is somewhere between Mickey Rooney and Joel Gray, makes his class run the perimeter of the schoolgrounds and George discovers he can hold his own fairly well if the distance is over a half-mile or more. So the teacher encourages George to go out for the track team. (And of course, I must go along for the ride.) George joins the track team primarily because competing in track is an acceptable excuse to be away from home.

Track is a sport, but it doesn't rely on a team. It requires no hand/eye coordination, dexterity, or accuracy. With the exception of the relay races, it's an individual competition. And the coach, as it turns out, knows his stuff. He's a runner himself, the Metropolitan and UAA champion in events like hurdles, long jump, and relay races.

So we're into running, all year round. In the fall we run cross-country where the races are two-and-a-half miles long (usually on a golf course, with a few in city parks) and we often run early in the morning, before the dew has a chance to clear, so the humidity carries the sweet green scent of fall and the steady rhythm of feet hitting the damp ground is hypnotic. The quiet cadence sends us into a dream state where there's just the two of us, floating together, wending our way between the trees and the gray sky and all around, the smell of life and the feel of our oneness carried along by our feet.

George loves running because it gives him something masculine he can feel good about. The gender conflict makes him want to be more masculine, to fit in, to be one of "the guys." *Try hard enough and she'll go away*, I hear him think. And George actually likes the competition (although it's not something I'm really into. I'm like the little monkey on the dog's back—strapped in and bouncing along.)

He trains his eyes on the runner ahead of him, sets his pace just a little faster so that he can catch up to him, then sets his eyes on the next runner. And so on, passing one runner at a time, gradually moving ahead,

He's a running comedian, too. When he's close to another runner he tells jokes and cracks wise. They're panting, struggling to catch their breath, and George makes them laugh, upsetting their pace and their breathing and it pisses them off. Some of them disregard him as best they can while others yell at him: "Fuck off, ass hole!"

"I sure hope your shoelaces are tied well," George says. "You wouldn't want them to come open and have to stop and tie them." Invariably, they look down and that's when he speeds up and leaves them behind.

Or sometimes he's more subtle. "Man…" he says, sighing, "I really hate it when one of my balls slips out of my jock strap…you know…or maybe just a bit of scrotum rubs up against your inner thigh. Ooooh that's tough."

It's a wonder he didn't get the crap beat out of him.

☜ ❏ ☞

Senior year requires a decision. George's race times are good enough to qualify for the Varsity team. He can earn a letter, be a big man on campus, an athlete, wearing a school sweater with a big blue 'O' sewed over the left side pocket. But if he chooses Varsity status, he will be the eighth member of a team of eight, which means that he will never finish among the top three in any race. The other seven will be ahead of him. And that includes Grover Dodd.

Grover Dodd (yes...that's his real name) isn't a great runner, but he always looks good--perfect form, uniform neat as a pin, and the most up-to-date equipment money can buy (stylish shoes, warm-up sweats, etc.). Grover is a metrosexual before there is a word for it. His running style is impeccable. If you take a picture of Grover at any time before a race (warming up), during a race (running), or after a race (cooling down) you can put it on the front of *Sports Illustrated* with the headline *Dodd Shows Them How It's Done!*

(It's the Grover Dodds in life, the models of perfection, that make George and me cringe. We know they aren't really perfect, but that doesn't matter. It's the appearances that count. We are both the victim of expectations of perfection.)

If not the eighth member of the Varsity, George has the option of being first on the Junior Varsity team. No letter. No BMOC. But a good chance of coming in first in some of the races.

"What'll it be?" the coach asks.

George doesn't have to think about it. "J.V." he says.

The coach shakes his head. "You disappoint me."

George doesn't have a reply.

"Go ahead," the coach says, pointing to the gym. "Shower up."

The coach is truly disappointed and for a moment George feels like he has let him down. *But hey,* he thinks, *who wants to be last when you can be first?* And I whisper: *Not Grover Dodd.*

❧ ❑ ☞

Oceanside doesn't have an indoor track like the city schools, so the team trains outdoors, even on snow days. The maintenance crew plows the track and we run a cinder oval surrounded by white. Sometimes we run sprints down one of the school's hallways. Then, usually on a Saturday, the team rides into the city and runs against schools like Boys High or Brooklyn Poly at the 168th Street Armory in Manhattan or the Armory in Brooklyn.

We arrive at a big box of a gym or basketball arena, hollow venues where voices echo, and we sign in and get our numbers which we pin to our running shirts, tearing off all of the excess paper around the number because we believe this will improve the run by cutting the wind resistance, though George probably does it because it's 'cool'(and I watch and wonder if maybe this is a fashion statement.) Then we spend an hour or two seated on the floor, under the bleachers, alongside the outermost racing lane, waiting for our race to be called. We're wearing sweat suits over our shorts and T shirts and we each have a small duffel bag where we store the sweats when our race is called. There's not much of an opportunity to stay warm and loose. It's not like being outdoors where we can jog around and get limber right up until the race. It's cramped and the line moves slowly, so all we do is stretch—except for Fudgie Morgan.

Fudgie is a nickname derived from his habit of saying "Oh fudge," as opposed to another 'F' word. Fudgie always has a bottle of *Thunderbird* wine in his duffel bag and whenever he sees an opportunity he reaches into the bag, takes a quick swig from the bottle (which is wrapped in a brown paper bag), and shoves it back in the duffel bag. Then he turns to one or more of us, flashes a goofy grin and says "What's the word?" and we all smile and answer "Thunderbird!"

I like Fudgie a lot more than Grover.

And so does George

⌐☞   ☐   ☞

Audrey, our sister and scholar, graduates at the top of her high school class and is accepted at Hofstra College and during the summer before he first year of college she begins dating a man, Ed Thornlow who has just got out of the Navy, having served on an aircraft carrier during the Korean War, though he never saw combat.

Father does not like Ed and the feeling is mutual. Neither of them score very high on the sociability index. Father has banned Ed from our house and from seeing Sister. This culminates in a confrontation which we witness from behind a tree across the street. We watch as Ed drives up in his new 1957 black and white Chevy, steps out, and walks to the porch, whereupon Father steps out wielding a baseball bat and threatening to bash his head in if he takes a step closer. All the while Sister is standing just inside the front door, sobbing. (What a fine irony, since the bat belongs to George and Father never plays ball with him or ever wielded that bat for any other purpose than today's threat.)

Of course, all of this makes their relationship that much more attractive. It is forbidden and therefore exciting. And a short while later, they elope, to New Jersey, but they can't get married due to her age or the residency requirements or some other restriction, so they come back and Father relents and a wedding is quickly planned. George was an usher or maybe he carried the ring. But I am fascinated by the wedding gown, the idea of a garter (having never seen one), and the entire notion of being able to get 'all dolled up' and parade down an aisle in front of everyone.

Given the hurried nature of it all, there are rumors that Sister is pregnant. Whether she is or not doesn't matter. There is a kind of 'black cloud of evil' hanging over it all, as summed up in words overheard from Mother, muttering in a hushed tone, trying to explain Sister's attraction to Ed: "What power does he have over her?" Given the taboos of our clan, those words carry a connotation of sexuality. They conjure up visions of Ed performing oral sex on her, driving her into wild paroxysms of ecstasy and thus making her his love slave, the daughter of Satan, mesmerized by Ed's Svengali-like control.

But more likely she is just in love with him.

☞ ❏ ☞

Grandfather is well-off and retired, having sold the hardware store and moved to Rockville Center not far from where we live, into a large house with a rentable apartment on the second floor. After Grandmother dies, Grandfather starts taking bus trips designed for *Senior Citizens*. And that's where he meets the soon-to-be second Mrs. Cook.

The new Mrs. is about his age, so it's not some May/December affair, but Grandpa insists on bringing her to the annual holiday family dinners where they behave in ways that are embarrassing, repeatedly hugging and kissing (we're talking flailing tongues here)—not considered acceptable old folk behavior back then. (Is it now?)

Mother decides that the new Mrs. Cook is a gold-digger and in no way could she ever replace the original. Then Grandfather dies and leaves his "fortune" to her and Mother goes ballistic, alternately crying and yelling about it.

From where I sit (or float or whatever it is I do) I see this as just another part of the strange family dynamic of which I'm an abstract spirit. I realize that it's the stew that bred George and me. And to be clear on the breeding, I know I'm a separate thread in the family fabric, but I am also intrinsically woven into it. Events affecting George affect me as well; sometimes even more so.

ELEVEN
Ol' Shep n' Gay Skip

WHO WANTS A GENUINE RED Ryder carbine action two hundred shot lightning loader range model air rifle?

Not George. And certainly not me. Guns don't do anything for either of us. Even during the Cowboys and Indians games with Jimmy Jingles, the guns never felt comfortable. And while George did that thing with his index finger and thumb, I forced him to stop as soon as I could, making him aware that our hero (or make that heroine) ought to be that shady girl at the saloon who wore a red bustier and fishnet hose and made eyes at the cowboys.

Jean Shepherd, our radio hero, wanted that BB gun when he was a kid. We heard about it every Sunday night when we would crawl off to bed early to listen to his show, which was on from nine until one in the morning. Shepherd talked about his childhood, about his 'old man', about his life as a kid, and especially his desire for a BB gun. And he read poems to us—like *The Shooting of Dan McGrew*.

> *A bunch of the boys were whooping it up in the Malamute saloon;*
> *The kid that handles the music-box was hitting a jag-time tune;*
> *Back of the bar, in a solo game, sat Dangerous Dan McGrew,*

And watching his luck was his light-o'-love, the lady that's known as Lou.

And as I lay with George in the dark attic bedroom listening to Jean Shepherd read that poem I pictured myself as that lady, in my red bustier with a black bustle and fishnet hose. "Oh yes," I whispered to George, "call me "the lady that's known as Lou."

Then I ducked my head, and the lights went out, and two guns blazed in the dark,
And a woman screamed, and the lights went up, and two men lay stiff and stark.
Pitched on his head, and pumped full of lead, was Dangerous Dan McGrew,
While the man from the creeks lay clutched to the breast of the lady that's known as Lou.
These are the simple facts of the case, and I guess I ought to know.
They say that the stranger was crazed with "hooch," and I'm not denying it's so.
I'm not so wise as the lawyer guys, but strictly between us two —
The woman that kissed him and — pinched his poke — was the lady that's known as Lou.

Every Monday at school, Maris and Mitch and George review the previous night's Jean Shepherd show, revisiting everything Shepherd talked about and conclude with Maris nodding his head and saying "He says it for all of us" to which Mitch and George nod and smile knowingly as all three race to the school library to find a copy of the poem.

Whoever succeeds in finding it shares it with the others who savor it like starving artists, which is how they picture themselves. I know this because one of the more curious aspects of my existence is that I can "see" whatever George imagines. These imaginings get George in the habit of thinking about things he doesn't understand. Or maybe it's better to say things <u>we</u> don't understand, like our "selves." Neither of us can sort it out. Could Dangerous Dan also be the lady that's known as Lou?

☜ ❑ ☞

When not hanging out with Maris and Mitch, George has developed a friendship with Skip Cortelyou, one of the more popular guys at school. He's very down-to-earth and genuinely seems like a *Skip*. Not *Skippy*. Not *Skipper*. Just *Skip*, a fun guy with freckles and curly hair. He talks to George sometimes and genuinely seems to like him and one of those times turns out to be something more.

Tradition has it that seniors will go somewhere in "the city" after the senior prom, to a night club or late night restaurant and stay out all night. But sadly, prom night is not a fun event for George. It's a ritual. The girl he takes is someone he has dated and they go through the standard prom routine—rented tuxedo, corsage, dancing in the high school gym. And afterward, they spend some time at a prom party in the basement of the girl's friend's house, hosted by parents who want to make sure the kids don't drink.

But the post-prom ritual had a different effect on Skip. He double-dated for the prom with a friend named Mike, who made arrangements to go to a night club in Queens (one of the boroughs that comprise New York City). It's not Manhattan, which is across the East River; it's on Long Island and the club they go to is the *Town and Country*, an upscale place, where there's a show playing called the *Jewel Box Revue*.

On the Monday after the prom, Skip takes us aside in a quiet corner of the lunch room to talk. He's clearly agitated.

"I think I'm queer," he says in hushed tones.

"How's that?" George asks.

"You know that show Mike and I went to after the prom?"

He describes the place and describes the show. "There were these…er…guys…they were dressed up as women." He takes a deep breath. "And they were like…you know…really gorgeous. I mean…if you didn't know they were guys…"

Skip didn't know about me. Of course, no one did, but I had to wonder why he picked George to confide in. And George is now worrying that he may have tipped his hand, that his dark secret was out.

"So?"

"So…" Skip takes another deep breath. "I got a hard-on." Skip is looking everywhere now, worried that someone might have heard him.

George considers the statement, then asks: "When this happened, did you know they were guys?"

He shakes his head. "<u>Everyone</u> knew," he says, urgently. "They all knew…but nobody told <u>me</u>. I didn't know until the end."

"So you thought they were women and they turned you on."

He nods and looks us in the eye and blinks.

"Hey…" George says, "Relax; you're not queer."

"But…"

"If you <u>knew</u> they were guys and you got a hard-on you'd be queer."

"Are you sure?"

"I'm positive."

Skip breathes a sigh of relief. "Just don't…you know…don't mention…"

George nods. "Not to worry."

Skip stands up, shakes George's hand with a firm, especially manly grip, says "Thanks, man" and walks away.

Without knowing it, Skip has opened another door to George from my world. It wasn't a comfortable place for George, but it becomes very clear that sexuality is part of the problem and as time goes on it only causes more confusion. That little talk was the first time we ever had any kind of discussion with anyone where cross-dressing was part of the topic. And it would be a long time before we ever did again.

TWELVE
A Court Date and College

I N 1959 GEORGE GRADUATES FROM Oceanside High, but since he doesn't go to college right away he hangs out with some of the class of '60 folks. Maris and Mitch and Skip go away to school, but not us. We stay home and get arrested.

George wanted to go to college, but when he asked the High School counselor about it he just laughed and told him to forget it. George's grades averaged out to 68. With grades that low, colleges won't even look at him. So he gets a job working for the *Red L Food Corporation* as an Office Boy.

Red L makes frozen seafood dinners and George is the errand boy. The office is in Great Neck, about 15 miles from Rockville Centre, and once a week George drives to the Fulton Fish Market and picks up cases of frozen dinners and brings them back to the office where they're stored as samples for sales reps to give away.

Some days he spends hours opening envelopes from customers who send in newspaper coupons entitling them to a refund or a free sample. When not doing that he makes copies of documents or does filing. He and I are both incredibly bored, though I guess I'm lucky since I can easily slip back into the fog of his unconscious and doze off.

That Thanksgiving, Skip comes home from college and we go for a beer and George asks him what it's like.

He breaks into an odd grin, puts down his glass, leans forward, and in a nearly inaudible whisper says *"Fuck God."*

George and I both gasp and blink.

"That's what college is like," Skip says, grinning. "It's all the stuff they were afraid to teach us about in High School."

"Like Freud?" we ask, remembering how along with Maris and Mitch we had read *The Interpretation of Dreams* and all about the ego and id. We weren't supposed to read those. Not only were they banned at school, they were on the Catholic church's list of condemned books. Which was all the more reason to read them.

"You need to go," Skip said. "Take the state exam. You're not stupid. Ace that and you can pick any of the state schools. Free tuition."

"Really?"

He nods.

So we go back to the high school counselor and he shrugs and says "OK…why not…" and we take the state exam and score higher than expected, at least high enough to be accepted at the third three state colleges we checked off when choosing where our score should be sent. It's the only one we have never heard of: *Geneseo State*.

When he finds out we're going away to school, Sal Salute, our next door neighbor, starts singing this stupid song every time he sees us.

"Yer workin' yer way through college
Ta gain' a little knowledge
You'll probably never, ever use."

And then he chuckles and says something about how he wished he had stayed in school instead of running numbers in the Bronx, but we just nod and smile. What are we supposed to say? "Yeah…that sure was stupid, Sal. But then, you're not the swiftest Capo in the Borgata." If we had said that he probably would have put out a contract on us.

☞ ❏ ☞

By now I'm at a level of George's consciousness that makes it hard for him to deny me. Whenever an opportunity presents itself, I demand my release. Sister's at an overnight with friends. Mother and Father are with their friends for the evening. George is home all alone. Time to rummage through Mother's dresser or Sister's closet and soon I'm there. It's not exactly where I want to be, but it's more of an expression of me than usually possible. And when I'm feeling truly bold I go out for a walk, through the back yard and the vacant lot behind the house to the parking lot of the restaurant around the corner. I probably look foolish. I know what I'm doing isn't just sinful, but unlawful too. But none of that matters. What matters is that I'm out, shaking off the part that is George and being who I am. And that's what gets me in trouble.

In addition to the job at *Red L Foods*, George works nights in a record store in a strip mall. It's a dream job, at least insofar as someone seventeen years old in 1959 might consider it because we can listen to our favorite records and get them at a discount. This includes so-called 'Party Records' by comedians like Rusty Warren, Belle Barth, B.S. Pully, Redd Foxx, and others. There's jazz and rock and roll (a phenomenon in 1959) and sometimes we take the records home and tape-record them, then bring them back before they're missing. We were doing illegal downloads before there even was such a thing. And the job is fun.

The strip mall has a series of stores connected by a common basement, and soon the owner trusts George enough to give us the weeknight shift, coming in around 4pm and closing up the place at 9. When I realize that we're alone in the store after closing, I encourage George to explore the basement area further.

Records and other stuff are stored under our section and it has been made into a little room of sorts, with a couch, a dresser and mirror, and boxes arranged to cordon off the area. Maybe this is where the boss brings his mistress or perhaps it's just a place he goes to when his wife has had enough of him. No matter. George doesn't think much of it, but I begin to devise a plan.

The area between the stores is open, so we can walk from the basement of our store into the basement of the next store, and so on. And the shop next to the record store sells women's clothing. The first time we see that, we freeze in our steps and I take over. There's a ladder leading up to a trap door near the front door that opens into the store itself. Eventually I get George to climb up through the trap door and take me inside the store where I can "borrow" ladies underwear and dresses and the wigs off the mannequins, and bring it all downstairs to the little room where I can try them on. George feels it's a creepy enterprise, but I don't. I'm thrilled at the opportunity to get 'out' and I spend many evenings modeling various outfits.

Of course, George can't tell anyone about it. The priests and nuns made it clear that such behavior is an "abomination" and there's no way friends like Mitch or Maris or Skip would understand. George is convinced he's the only person with this awful desire. But given this opportunity, I'm compelled to pursue it, with no clear goal really, no objective beyond getting to that point where I'm looking at myself in the mirror and feeling that somehow George and I have reversed roles; that I have replaced him, that he is no longer in charge. It's a sense of deep relief and gratification.

But we are not thieves. So every evening, when it's time to go home, we sneak back into the ladies shop and return everything to where we found it. And that's good. Until one night, after returning everything (replacing the wig on the mannequin's head, the dresses on the racks, the underwear in the drawers) it comes to a screeching halt.

George is holding the trap door open above his head and stepping down the ladder to descend back into the basement and when he looks up, to guide the trap door closed, he finds we are looking straight at a policeman. He's standing outside the front door to the shop and there's no question about whether or not he sees us. But he doesn't move and so George slowly lets the door down and descends into the basement, returns back up the stairs that lead into the record store, and pokes his head outside, planning to go to the parking lot. *Maybe*, George is thinking, *he didn't see me. Maybe the light was in his eyes.* There are no police cars pulling up, no sirens, nothing to suggest a problem. So he locks up the store and takes the few steps around the back of the strip mall toward the lot…and there he is.

What happens then is a blur. Fast-forward to the police station where George is interrogated. They have searched the car and found nothing, so now they want to know where we 'stash the goods' and they go through George's wallet where, among other things, they find a school photo of a friend who has written what he thought at the time was a humorous message on the back: "Good luck, Sweetie."

"Is this your boyfriend?" the good cop asks.

They're putting things together to fit an established pattern of some sort.

"No…he's a friend."

"A boyfriend?"

"No."

And the interrogation abruptly ends.

In the jail cell, the only sleeping area is a wooden slab that hangs from the wall by two chains at either end; the only other thing in the cell is a commode, a stainless steel, seatless toilet.

Somehow we get through the night. George cries. The police knew what we were doing and called us names like 'fairy' and 'queer.' But soon it's six a.m. and one of them bangs on the bars of the cell and hands us a fried egg sandwich wrapped in wax paper and a styrofoam cup of black coffee.

Shortly thereafter, Father picks us up. We don't discuss any of it and later Father tells George that he's 'sick' and they're going to get him some kind of treatment. Out on bail, we're charged with a felony, despite the fact that we never took anything from the shop. The owner has told the police that she's missing thousands-of-dollars-worth of clothing.

At seventeen years old we've been arrested and charged with Grand Larceny, but when the case goes to the Grand Jury it's dismissed for 'lack of evidence' (not entirely accurate, since there is plenty of evidence to the contrary). How did we wind up here? Father swallowed his pride and hired a good lawyer.

The lawyer sends us to a *Catholic* psychiatrist. Father thinks psychiatry is voodoo medicine, but on the advice of the attorney he sends us to the shrink so that when the case goes to the Grand Jury he can say that George is already 'in treatment.' Furthermore, college acceptance comes through, so he can add that George is headed to college. With no prior record, the argument goes, "He's just a messed-up freaky kid who has some 'issues' he's dealing with" and the missing clothing can't be proven. And wouldn't you know it, the Grand Jury, for what is apparently one of the few cases at the time, refuses to indict us.

The psychiatrist's approach is to give us some tests—the Rorshock Ink Blots, of course, and the Thematic Apperception Test (TAT), which presents a series of pictures of people in ambiguous, creepy situations and asks us to create a story based on each picture. That's right up George's alley. George loves to make up stories, so he regales the man with delightful details that include anger and frustration and guilt and then the shrink explains to Father and Mother (and the Grand Jury) that we're simply immature, that this women's clothing 'fetish' is nothing more than a reflection of that immaturity, a kind of stunted growth.

All the while, George never mentions <u>me</u>. He's read enough Freud to know where that could take us. He simply talks about the 'dressing up' as if it's a curiosity about girls, about how they feel and act. And the psychiatrist concludes the final session with "Don't you feel terrible about it and don't you want to confess to your parents and apologize to them?"

At that point he brings in the parents and George tells them something that satisfies them and the shrink and everyone is happy. It's obvious the parents are embarrassed since there have been stories in the local newspaper and rumors are sure to be circulating. But it doesn't matter, because come that fall we will be off to college.

☜ ❏ ☞

This brush with psychiatry leads to an afternoon at the public library with George scouring psychology books looking for me. But not 'me' in the physical sense; rather, he's after the 'why' of me. And he finds something on multiple personalities. (We had followed The Three Faces of Eve, the case of a woman who had multiple personalities, but reading about it now, we sensed that I wasn't in that category. We know about each other, though at this point I certainly know more about George than he knows about me.) Then he finds a book about 'transvestites.' It defines them as men who dress in women's clothing for sexual pleasure. And there's a photo of a man in a dress. I have to say it's not very attractive. Neither of us thinks so. And there is a kind of arousal associated with it, but it's born of fear, not sex—the fear of being caught.

Fear?

Listen. George and I don't communicate the way individual people do. It's more like telepathy. I know what he's thinking and I can intrude on his thoughts with my own so that sometimes it's hard to tell who's who. I know who I am more than George knows who he is. The impact of the robbery, the arrest, and the psychiatric experience, with letting me out and then having to talk to a psychiatrist about it, is major. Despite the shrink reducing it to a kind of teenage fetishism, I know now that George is afraid of me. He's afraid that the pressure from me to be let 'out' could become so great that one day I might take over, that I might come out and stay out, and he might be pushed aside. He's worried and afraid that everything he's been told that he should 'be' would not, could not, be. Instead, he believes, he would be seen as some sort of pervert, dressing up in women's clothes and parading up and down the street, the subject of ridicule and a complete embarrassment to his family and friends. And of course, they would all reject him and he would be left to tumble down some rabbit hole of degradation.

And maybe he's right, but for now he doesn't realize that all I want to do is to express myself and I really don't know how best to do that without ruining both of our lives. So I stay back and do my best to calm those fears, waiting for I don't know what. Just waiting.

The irony in much of this is that we later learn that the only thing that got us into college was the fact that we have a penis. Why? Because until 1948, Geneseo was a *Normal School,* a school that trained women (almost exclusively) to be elementary school teachers. So when it became part of the state university system it became co-ed. But it was still regarded as a school for elementary education majors and that meant it was mostly female. The academic powers decided that had to change. As a result, just about any male applicant was accepted. And George qualified. And where, I wondered, does that leave me?

THIRTEEN
A Geneseo Freshman

COLLEGE CHANGED EVERYTHING FOR US – both intellectually and emotionally. The foundation for the change may have already been laid down, but we're left to wonder what might have become of us if we had <u>not</u> gone to college and we're sure there's no scenario where that turns out well.

It's September in the Genesee Valley about thirty miles south of Rochester in upstate New York. The trees haven't started to turn yet; the warm residue of summer lingers. At the top of the hill, turning off Main Street and onto Campus Drive we get our first view of the campus. From here the buildings look like the layout for a model railroad. The Main Building is in the center, its carillon tower dominating the quadrangle. It's weathered red brick is darker than the newer buildings and dark green tendrils of ivy twine up its sides. It's everything we've seen in movies and read about colleges—the ivy-covered halls and all that.

Father turns the car to the left, then turns again and pulls up beside one of the smaller buildings; the sign by the door says *Fraser Hall*. He turns off the engine and gets out, but George doesn't move. A part of him wants us to turn around and go home. And me, I'm terrified; wondering where I belong in this.

It doesn't take long to find out. I'm nowhere.

George is wearing the new outfit his mother bought for him: a navy blue sport coat, charcoal gray slacks, black loafers with a slightly pointed toe, a pink shirt and a narrow gray tie. Pink and gray are the 'in' colors this year. George thinks he looks cool, but then George never had a clue. This is not an outfit I would have chosen for hm. And worst of all, his hair is still slicked back in the Elvis-style called a D.A.—short for Duck's Ass).

The air here is different. Where the Long Island suburban air was more a mixture of the scent spilling out of people's homes and that stagnant odor of Air Wick which was always regurgitated into our neighborhood, this air is strange stuff. It's like the air from those morning cross-country meets in the city parks.

Father takes the bags out of the trunk and sits them on the curb, then slams the trunk shut. George is holding a brown shopping bag that includes, among other things, three sandwiches Mother made for George and Father to eat on the trip from Long Island. George grabs one suitcase with the hand that's already holding the shopping bag and grabs the other bag with his free hand. Father starts to walk away, then stops and steps in front of us and extends his hand.

George drops the shopping bag and suitcase and takes Father's hand and they do one of those quick business-like handshakes. George is the first in the family to go to college; the first to graduate high school. College, as Father saw it, was something you did so that you wouldn't have to 'work with your hands,' like he did. As a machinist, he had spent most of his later life around the monotype machines, operating those ungrateful behemoths that spit drops of hot lead on his skin until his arms looked like the surface of the moon, pitted and cratered and always cold. And now here was the result of that work—his son a college student. "The boy's" life, he hoped, would be better than his.

Then Father turns and walks away, steps back in to the car, starts the engine, and without looking back, drives off. We could wave, but instead we just stand and watch as the car becomes smaller and smaller and Father makes his escape. He has dumped us at last.

⤺　❑　☞

The Old Main Building rests at the bottom of the U-shaped quad; the arms on either side are formed by the Wadsworth Library building, the auditorium, and the theatre. The other arm is formed by a single building comprising three dorms: Sturges, Fraser and Blake. At the shoulder of the dorm arm there's a fourth section with two levels. The upper level contains the Student Lounge and snack bar; the cafeteria is located on the lower level.

Behind Old Main the Genesee valley cradles two new L-shaped women's dorms. A few years later a new student center, cafeteria, and gymnasium will take up their places down the hill, but for now, it's just the quad above and the valley view below.

We walk up the steps of the dorm named Fraser. The front door is open and there's a welcome sign, so we put the bags down and George takes the envelope of papers from his pocket, sorts through them, and finds the one that says what room we're in. Then he picks up the bags and we walk inside where there's an older student, dressed in a tee shirt, athletic shorts, and tennis shoes, seated at a desk. He smiles at us.

"Do you know what room you're in?" he asks.

"One-twelve."

He points down the hall. "Second to the last door on the left."

We pick up our stuff and move down the hall. The door to Room 112 is open and someone is standing inside, his back to us, looking out the window. The suit he's wearing is too small; his socks and his wrists are exposed. (I notice these things, but don't share them with George who is in a strange state of mind—

afraid, sad, anxious; all bubbling excitedly.)The stranger at the window seems unaware that anyone else is around, so we wait, but he doesn't move.

"I'm George."

The roommate turns and extends his hand. "Charles…but call me Dutch."

We step forward and shake hands, then step back, grab the suitcases and shopping bag and stop at the center of the room. To the left there's a set of bunk beds; to the right, there are two wooden desks and two chairs. A matching chest of drawers is tucked into the far corner and another chest of drawers stands at the end of the bunk beds.

Dutch is a big guy. George is about 5'8" and 135 pounds while Dutch is at least six feet tall and probably seventy-five compact pounds heavier than George. He has a crew cut and a round face and his skin seems chapped. (Mother would have called him "ruddy.") And his head seems out of proportion to the rest of him, smaller, and sort of cartoonish. Maybe it's just the suit

"Top or bottom?" he says.

George blinks.

"Bunk…"

"Oh…" We look at the beds and consider the prospect of Dutch's ass curving into the sagging mattress above us. "Top."

"I hope you got some warm clothes in there," Dutch says. "It gets pretty cold here. Not like Long Island."

How does he know where we're from?

"Oh. Where are you from.?"

"Camden…north of Syracuse" He snickers and shakes his head. "You're down by the city," he says. "I'm up in the woods."

George smiles.

"I think that makes me the Country Mouse," he says, and you…."

George finishes the sentence. "…the City Mouse."

☜ ❏ ☞

There is no tuition at any State University of New York (SUNY) school. And like George, most everyone in our class is the first in the family to attend college. We are the last of the innocents—the last to "pull pranks" rather than "stage demonstrations," the last to "do" alcohol rather than drugs, the last to pursue commitments rather than 'relationships' and 'hook ups.' Scientists call what happens over the next four years a "paradigm shift," a change in the set of basic assumptions we reference when making decisions. It's 1960 and the stuff at the core of what we believe is being challenged by a new view of the world.

That shift comes at us in two ways. The first shift is from the inside out. The professors make it a point to challenge our basic assumptions. There are just three rules—question everything, don't take anything for granted, and take a hard critical look at yourself. In our classes the notions of what's right and what's wrong, what's true and what's false, are pulled apart and reassembled into a logical framework and then further ripped to shreds in the dorm or at one of the uptown bars late at night.

The shift from the outside in is driven in part by the modern civil rights era and Rock and Roll, which has taken root, after sharing space for a while with folk music. The free speech movement is afoot in Berkley, Cassius Clay will become world champion and change his name to Muhammad Ali. And monks will set themselves on fire in Viet Nam while films like *One Flew Over the Cuckoo's Nest* and *Dr. Strangelove* tweak our views of sanity and the cold war. And we read books like *Lolita*, *Naked Lunch*, and Twain's *Letters from the Earth*. Everything we see and hear tells us it's time to change. The bus is leaving and we can get on and take the ride or get left behind. And most of us jump on.

☜ ❑ ☞

The fall semester is a whirlwind. After having made the effort to come out, I get shoved farther back than ever. I sleep in while

George goes to classes and on the week-ends I do my best to stay awake, but George has discovered drinking and while he's excited about what's happening in classes, he's still following the old high school pattern—lay back and don't act like you care.

We have a five-and-a-half-day meal ticket—three meals Monday through Friday, breakfast and lunch on Saturday and none on Sunday. Saturdays there's often a keg party somewhere. So George goes and gets drunk and Sunday morning he throws up, doesn't feel like eating and that takes care of the one-and-a-half days off.

He's also into dating. The female-to-male ratio is eight-to-one. For the first time since his timid High School days, George has no trouble getting a date and soon overcomes his timidity. He and Dutch date on the weekends, sometimes trading off one's date from one night with the other's date for the next night. It's party time all the time. And the result is predictable. By the end of the semester, George's GPA is 1.4…an F, three D's, and one A.

But don't blame me. I'm sitting back quietly watching another episode of *The Many Loves of Dobie Gillis*, knowing exactly where this bus is headed and making sure my seat belt is strapped on. He knows where I am if he wants me.

In the Spring semester, Dutch does not stay on as our roommate. Instead, he is replaced by Bill Desmond, a short, feisty guy known as Desi, who doesn't want to be in college. He wants to be in the Navy, but his parents insisted he go to college, so he did. And now he concentrates on doing whatever it takes to get out. That means flunking. So, like George, he begins the Fall semester on Academic Probation.

Desi spends most of his time in the pool room in the student lounge. And he's pretty good at it, winning more than losing and sometimes making a few bucks from it. He has a girlfriend back home, but he dates some of the college girls, with motives that are generally dishonorable. He's a likeable guy and a pretty good roommate and he has a guitar he can't play, so George buys a chord book and teaches himself some of the basic chords.

More important than the guitar are the events that turn things around. First, there's the Spring musical. The show this year is *Guys & Dolls* and one evening George and Desi go to the dormitory rec room where they find Barry Kaplan, a third year student and drama major, rehearsing to audition for the show's main character, Nathan Detroit.

The show is based on characters created by Damon Runyon, a newspaperman and writer best known for his short stories about prohibition era gangsters in New York City. They all have the unique Brooklyn accent. The *Damon Runyon Theatre* show ran on radio in the forties and so we grew up hearing the language there as well. Runyon's story "The Idyll of Miss Sarah Brown" was the basis for the Broadway musical. Here's an example of the Runyonesque dialogue:

There is very little action of any kind in town with the high shots gone, and one night I run into Feet Samuels in Mindy's, and he is very sad indeed. He asks me if I happen to have a finn on me, but of course I am not giving finns to guys like Feet Samuels, and finally he offers to compromise with me for a deuce, so I can see things must be very bad with Feet for him to come down from five dollars to two.

So we go to the audition and George gets the part of Nathan Detroit. George has never acted or ever been on stage. (I don't count the lip-synch number we did for a *Catholic Youth Organization* talent show back in Elementary School.) We don't know anyone connected with the Drama Department or any of the other performers, so it's all new.

But what is significant in all this is that there's an unspoken hierarchy of actors and roles. A Freshman cannot get anything more than a place in the chorus or as a stagehand. A Sophomore might get a part with a few lines or maybe, if he or she is especially talented, a supporting role. But by Junior year, one can expect to get a leading role. George, a Freshman, with no experience, gets one of the leading parts, never realizing that the person who expected to get that part is Barry Kaplan, and he's furious, especially because he and Sherry Dorf, another Junior got together over the previous summer, got copies of the script and music, and rehearsed it all so as to guarantee they get the leads. But no; George gets the part Barry feels is his.

And me? There is no way for me to appear in any shape or form—no clothes to try on when the rest of the family is gone, no time to fantasize about what it would be like to trade places with George, no chance of being me at all. But, the introduction to theatrics opens another window for me: a chance to learn about make-up and costumes. So while George has his guard up, making sure he gives no indication of being interested in these things, I am taking notes and storing them away.

The show is well-received. George becomes known and the stage is set, so to speak, for the second life-changing event (yet to come). There is a Junior named Kimber Hasselriis in the show. (He plays the role of Nicely-Nicely Johnson.) Kimber and George hit it off (and for what it's worth, I find him especially engaging as well.) One of the traditions at many colleges at that time is Freshman Hazing; all incoming Freshmen are required to wear beanies and the Sophomores are allowed to demand various things of them: fetch lunch from the cafeteria, shine their shoes, carry their books to class, etc. It's all in good fun and following a conversation about it, Kimber recommends that George be given the 'directorship' of hazing of the incoming fall freshman class. And George accepts.

The third event comes in the form of another upperlcassman named Frank Kraat. His persona is that of the older, wiser Korean war veteran who enjoys sitting in the lounge in his trench coat and beret, entertaining questions from the Freshmen. Nearly everything he says is with a smirk, giving the impression that he doesn't take anything seriously, especially himself, but at the same time his comments seem 'deep.'

He lets George in on some of his 'jokes.' "I told that little kid in your dorm that I'd pay him $100 if he let me crap on his chest," Frank says. George laughs and Frank continues. "He thought about it," he says. "He actually thought about it."

So it's with that same anachronistic delivery that one afternoon over coffee he tells George he needs to change his style.

Style? My ears (also George's ears) perk up. "What do you mean?"

"You like it here?" Frank asks.

We nod. "I love it," George says.

"Well, if you want to stay you're gonna have to learn to act the part."

Not sure what that means, we ask "What part?'

"The college part," Frank says. "Act like every word the professor says is so important you have to write it down in case you might forget it. And sit up front and ask questions. Find something in the reading or work you turn in to ask about."

We nod again.

"Drop that pseudo-tough-guy posture. It's obvious you can act," Frank says. "So act like an intellectual, a bookworm, a guy who wants to learn. Figure out what the professor wants and give it to him." Frank pauses and looks us in the eye. "If you want to stay, that's what you've got to do."

The words ring true and once more, George nods. "I know you want the $100," he says, "So I have to convince you that I <u>really will</u> shit on your chest."

Listen to him, I whisper. *He's on to something.*

And so it is that we pull out of probation, earning a 3.2 average for the second semester, making it possible for us to return in the Fall.

FOURTEEN
A Geneseo Sophomore

THE SUMMER BETWEEN FRESHMAN AND Sophomore year we are 'trapped' back home and manage to get a job as a 'counselor' at a Day Camp. This means riding a school bus to a state park with a bunch of pre-teen kids and helping to supervise things like field games and swimming. The field games are uneventful, but the swimming is another matter. George never learned to swim; he has a major fear of the water, and of course, if he were to drown, so would I, so I was equally afraid.

But since George was twice the height of the kids he had no problem being in the water with them—it was over their heads, but only up to George's waist. He pretended to be entirely comfortable with the situation (more acting) and organized 'swim lessons.' He taught the kids to swim and at the end of the summer one of the parents gave him a $20 tip and thanked him profusely for having taught her son. Until this summer, she explained, he had a great fear of the water, but George had helped him overcome it.

Another job we had for a short time that summer was at a kiosk in a local mall, selling hot dogs and soft drinks.

☙ ❏ ☞

At first, coming back to Long Island the summer after the first year of college is a huge relief for me. We are back at home and the opportunities to push George aside and dress up also are back. But nothing has really changed. I'm still feeling trapped, a woman stuck inside a man-child, though not so much physically as a personality that's the prisoner. Rather than being free to be completely himself, which is also to be me, George is still terrified of being identified as a sissy, effeminate, unmanly—so he makes a special effort to be George. He reminds himself that men don't cross their legs at the ankle or at the thigh or that the simple act of looking at one's nails must always be done by turning the hand over and curling the fingers inward. And his father's voice still booms: "Be a man."

So by the time the summer is over we are depressed and agree that we must find a way to stay in Geneseo year-round. And the answer is "summer school," which we always had to attend due to the poor grades in high school. The parents are so accustomed to George having to go to summer school to make up failed courses that the next summer and every one after that he has no problem convincing them that he has to stay and take college classes.

September can't come too soon, but rather than driving the eight hours to Geneseo, Father puts us on a charter bus taking students from Long Island to Geneseo. And when the bus stops at a major rest area where liquor is sold, he and two of the other boys chip in to buy several bottles of pre-mixed screwdrivers. I know this is a bad idea. It's times like this I'd like to know who paired me up with him and apply for a transfer. I can promise you, if that had been me on the bus what happens next would not have happened.

Within the hour, George is feeling the effects of the vodka/orange juice combination and before long his head is hanging out the bus window, looking back at the highway, vomit spewing onto the outside of the bus windows. It's just enough of an event to change his notoriety so that once back at Geneseo he becomes *the guy who threw up on the bus.*

☜　❏　☞

Back at Geneseo, Desi has achieved his goal and is gone to start his career in the Navy and George has a new roommate, Ben Codispoti, a stocky fellow of Italian descent. When they meet and shake hands Ben mentions that he's from New York City, then, pushing his glasses further up his nose, he squints at us and murmurs "Aren't you *the guy who threw up on the bus.?*"

☜　❏　☞

We're taking more interesting classes this year, including British Literature and Psychology, which gives us an opportunity to study our 'condition' without raising too much suspicion. And as Director of Freshman Hazing and being an organizer (a talent of mine he has heretofore untapped), he jumps into it with both feet, getting 'summonses' printed up, to be handed out by sophomores to freshmen who refuse to perform their assigned tasks or who, in the eyes of the sophomore, do not perform the task adequately. The summons requires the ticketed freshman to appear at a 'Kangaroo Court' which is scheduled in the college auditorium on the second Friday night of the school year.

George has planned the court as a scripted show. The members of the Kangaroo Court are seated in a row on the auditorium stage, behind the main curtain. One seat in the middle of the row is raised on a platform. The students who have received summonses must line up outside the auditorium and wait for the doors to open. A pre-recorded tape of Rock and Roll music is playing and sophomores have been enlisted to patrol the aisles, telling the freshman where to sit.

At last the doors are opened, but there is no line—just a large crowd shoving their way forward. Students with and without summonses come rushing in and somehow get seated. When everyone is seated and the lights dim and 'the show' begins.

The curtain slowly opens to reveal the members of the court. The music and the theatre lights fade and then, suddenly, George comes running down the aisle from the back of the auditorium. He's wearing a cape, has a whip in his hand, and is chasing a freshman who is wearing the required beanie and a torn T-shirt with streaks of fake blood.

The freshman runs onto the stage and falls at the feet of the court. George cracks the whip and sits in the elevated center chair and begins to read off the student's alleged violations. *"Failure to bow to an upperclassman! Disrespecting the authority of a Senior! Appearing on campus without a Freshman Beanie!"*

But then, suddenly, the attendees begin shouting—booing and hissing. More students join in, shouting epithets and then stand and starting to walk out. Within seconds it morphs into a rebellion. They're rushing for the doors now. The students are shoving one another, pushing at those by the doors, which are slow to yield, and yelling.

George tries to bring it under control, but it's too far gone. All we can do is stand and watch. Some students get trampled; others are shoved to the floor. Fortunately, no one is seriously hurt, but George's reputation has dropped another notch.

☜ ❑ ☞

The Freshman Uprising of 1961 becomes a legend and the hazing tradition is discontinued; however, we've both had a taste of public drama over and above the rehearsed sort. A seed has been planted. Maybe the uprising prompted it or maybe something else, but it gives me an idea which I slip into George's consciousness. He takes the hint and 'pitches' a column idea to the editor of the school paper. The paper accepts the column and so begins the shift away from bus puking notoriety to campus satirist. And the column converts Desi into an icon of sorts.

The columns, called *Me & Desi,* consist of conversations between George and his former roommate. It's a rhetorical device that lets him make humorous observations about college life. The critical comments are always Desi's and George, as the narrator, simply 'reports' them so that any offense is laid on Desi who, fortunately, is no longer around to defend himself. Desi is a Student Lounge pool playing regular and an artist for the paper comes up with the drawing on the left to run with the column.

The Desi Character

The columns substitute comic names for the fraternities and sororities. Phi Sigma Phi becomes Signa Phi Nothings, Delta Kappa becomes the Deekays, the Agos became the Egos, and so forth. It's hard to measure my contribution to this, but I see it as more of a collaboration than something that solely belongs to George. That's a moot point, I suppose, since he's the only one with a name.

Fraternities and sororities are a big part of Geneseo life where they generally control most social activities. There are three fraternities: Phi Sigma Epsilon, Delta Kappa Tau, and Prometheus. 'Phi Sig' is regarded as the 'artsy' frat; the 'D K's' are the athletes and 'party animals.' (The movie *Animal House* does a good job of illustrating what DK was like.) The Prometheus fraternity was formed by Korean veterans and so many of its members are going to school on the GI Bill.

George has decided he's most suited for Phi Sig. Most of his friends 'rush' that 'frat,' but because of his poor first semester grades (a 1.4 average on a 4.0 scale) he's not eligible, so he plans to rush the following year.

But I have a problem with this. As I see it, the fraternity thing is more of George's efforts to shut me down and be 'one of the guys,' (even if these guys aren't the alpha males on campus.) I'm pretty much out of the picture as it is. There's little, if any, opportunity for me to show myself. The only time I enjoy is when George is dating and I get to consider his date's femininity. I watch her walk, listen to her talk, see how she relates to him. I'm going to school too, you see, but my curriculum is very different.

When sophomore year rushing season comes, George is encouraged by his Phi Sig friends and attends the early rush parties, which consist mostly of macho male chatter and drinking. And it's in the middle of that chatter that we learn that Barry Kaplan, a senior member of the fraternity, has never forgiven George for taking the part of Nathan Detroit in *Guys and Dolls*. He makes sure George does not get in.

During fall of that sophomore year, George is sitting at the counter of a luncheonette on Main Street. The entryway has inlaid tiles which spell out the word 'NORMAL.' This is a reference to the fact that SUNY Geneseo was originally a 'Normal School' (the original term for a school or college that trains teachers). The luncheonette is called George's (named for the owner, George Scondras, a chubby, cheery Greek who takes great pride in his work. My George learns that George Scondras is looking for someone to work a couple hours every night to help clean up and close. My George applies and is hired.

The work isn't hard. Most nights we arrive around 10:30 to mop the floors, clean the grill, wipe down the counter, and do whatever else has to be done to get the place ready for the next day. A couple of nights a week, after the shop closes, George Scondras makes ice cream and we get to watch. He tells us how much better his ice cream is than anything sold anywhere else. "It's the butterfat content," he explains. "In most ice creams it's about 10%, and in the premium ice creams it can be as high as 13%. This" George adds, handing us a dish of vanilla fresh from the hopper, "is 16%." And he's right; it's incredible. Imagine eating the thickest, freshest whipped cream. We love it.

When Spring comes, so comes Easter and the chance for George Scondras to show off his talent as a candymaker. Each Easter season he makes chocolate bunny rabbits of the kind they still sell but, as with the ice cream, George's are made with better ingredients. And his *pièce de résistance,* a giant chocolate bunny, a good three feet high, gets displayed in the store's front window.

The bunnies are made from a tin mold that is in two halves which are clipped together, then filled with melted chocolate. The mold sits for a few minutes in the walk-in refrigerator, then it's removed, turned upside down, and the chocolate is poured out. Some of the chocolate has solidified on the inside of the mold, so when the clips are removed and the mold gently taken away, a chocolate bunny (with a hole in the bottom) remains.

It sounds easy, but the larger the mold the trickier it is. George Scondras tries every night for a week. He makes the small bunnies first and puts them on the shelves in the walk-in. He saves the big bunny for last. Most nights he fails. The bunny cracks or just falls apart when he opens the mold. But eventually, he succeeds. It's art. Watching him work is one of our favorite jobs. It's not about gender identity, being me or being George, or anything other than ice…cream…bunnies.

George Scondras likes to joke around and is known for his quick wit. If he knows you, you can always count on him for a wise crack. So it is that one day when a Geneseo co-ed shows up at his soda fountain and he can tell she has been crying, he tries to cheer her up. He leans over and pats her hand and says "There, there. That's OK honey. Everybody is a little late once in a while."

And George Scondras hit the nail on the head. The co-ed jumps down from the stool and runs outside, her hands over her face, sobbing hysterically. The days of political propriety and harassment concerns haven't arrived yet. So the next day when she comes back, he gives her a free pint of his homemade chocolate ice cream. Ice cream and bunnies, I believe, will cure anything. And when it comes to Easter, they're better than church.

☞ ❑ ☞

During that sophomore year a dog shows up at the Phi Sig fraternity house. We name him 'Phiggy' and sneak him into our dorm room and steal sausages from the cafeteria for him. Sometimes when he sits with us we clean out the crusty matter that collects at the corner of each of his eyes and over time, we start calling that 'stuff' *phiggies*.

Phiggy is all dog. And as all dogs do, he acts on instinct. Unlike humans, who establish 'norms' and set standards for behavior and presentation, animals are only expected to be that animal. In the words of Walt Whitman:

> *They are so placid and self contained;*
> *I stand and look at them long and long.*
> *They do not sweat and whine about their condition;*
> *They do not lie awake in the dark and weep for their sins;*
> *They do not make me sick discussing their duty to God;*
> *Not one is dissatisfied—not one is demented with the*
> *   mania of owning things;*
> *Not one kneels to another, nor his kind that lived*
> *   thousands of years ago;*
> *Not one is responsible or industrious over the whole*
> *   earth."*

So it is that sometimes George would have wished to be more animal and less human.

Do you think some day they will discover a transgender dog?

⊱   ❑   ☞

Faith isn't something George or I had much of to begin with, but there was probably some residue left over on our Catholic plate. One spring afternoon in a conversation with another student named John Heim (also a 'lapsing Catholic') about various religious matters we are to the question of Satan (aka Beelzebub, the Prince of Darkness, Beetlejuice.)We share the classic image of the guy in red with a pointed tail, a pitchfork and horns and joke about it and somehow that develops into a more serious question concerning the devil's existence. So we decide that we'll ask the local priest at St. Mary's, the Catholic church down at the end of Main Street.

We walk the four blocks and when we arrive at the church we seek out Father Know-it-all. (It would make a much better story, I'm sure, if I could say we found him with an altar boy behind the sanctuary, but nothing of that sort happened…so far as we know.)

We snag the good father on his way into the confessional, asking if he had a few minutes to settle an argument.

"Father," George begins, "we have been discussing the existence of the devil. You know, the guy with the horns and a tail and a pitchfork?"

Father nodded. "And what have you concluded?" he asked.

"Well," George went on, we have concluded that while people may have an inclination to do wrong and there's clearly evil in the world, that image, of a creature, with horns and tail and pitchfork who tempts and possesses people is just a metaphor for that evil. I mean…" (he hesitates) "There's no <u>real </u>creature like that. Right?"

Father Know-it-all takes a deep breath and sighs mightily, then shakes his head. "My son," he says, in that fatherly tone priests love to use when they're pontificating, "one of the greatest victories Satan has won is convincing people that he's not real."

George blinks. I blink. John Heim blinks. George and John look solemnly at each other, then at father Know-It-All, who is about to continue his sermon, but before the conversation can go on any further, we turn away, George tosses a "Thanks, Father" over his shoulder at the priest, and we go back to the campus.

And that marks the end of our Catholicism.

🐦 ❏ ☞

Guys & Dolls made George a theatre person. And his new mentor is theatre Professor Bob Sinclair, who appoints George to write a show for homecoming weekend. So we create (for my hand was certainly in on it too) a series of skits (a precursor of comedy writing days to come). They end with a spoof of the Busby Berkeley musicals, replete with a medley of patriotic songs like *Yankee Doodle Dandy*, *She's a Grand Old Flag*, and *God Bless America*, during which a cutout of the Statue of Liberty is wheeled out from center stage where it has been behind a curtain.

Standing behind it is fellow student Lewis Kaem, who is nicknamed "Spastic Lew." We're not sure why, but Lew is subject to minor spasms which are most evident when he walks or gestures. So midway through the statue's entrance, it falls flat on its face on the stage to reveal Lew, looking sheepish and subsequently being berated by everyone in the cast.

The skit was wrong on at least half a dozen levels, the least of which is not Lew's nickname, but remember, this is the sixties, before political correctness put a damper on mean-spirited comedy. We had no problem making fun of Lew's reputation as 'spastic' and to Lew's credit, he had no problem going along with it.

🐦 ❏ ☞

The short-lived roommate Desi left a guitar behind. He wasn't interested in learning how to play it, so George starts fooling with it. He buys a chord book and some sheet music and though he can't read music, we can figure out how to play each of the chords based on the diagrams and muddle our way through.

This is for fun, mostly. It's still the folk music era and those songs are fairly easy to play—*Michael Row the Boat Ashore, Sloop John B, Tom Dooley*. We can't play notes, but we can play the chords and sing along. Rock and roll music isn't difficult either. There are four chords (C, Am, F, and G) played in succession at various rhythms that work for dozens of songs like *Teenager in Love, Silhouettes,* and *Twenty-Six Miles.* Learning them would pay off later.

GEORGE WILKERSON

FIFTEEN
The Evil Mr. T

GEORGE IS MORE COMFORTABLE ASKING girls for a date or even striking up a conversation with them since the male-female ratio is so lopsided. But if I stick <u>my</u> nose into it (so to speak) it is still a struggle. Because one thing I was always doing (whether George realized it or not) was sizing up the girls' styles and outfits and secretly trying them on in my imagination. And since that was his imagination as well, he tried to fight it. Sometimes a girl would catch him staring at her and not realize that it was me and I was simply considering how that dress or blouse would look if I wore it.

So George fumbles along, stuffing my fantasies into the darker caverns of his brain. After all, if I dated the girl that must mean George has lesbian tendencies. George's sexual orientation was clearly directed at females and though I wasn't part of that population, I was part of <u>him</u>.

Does that confuse you? Then consider what it did to <u>us</u>.

The confusion grew in the Spring of 1961 when George begins to spend time with a girl named Gale, another Freshman. As he is becoming "the writer on campus," wearing the labels of "creative" and "witty" that would stay with him through his college years, Gale becomes a comfortable companion. Not especially popular or attractive, but with a nice figure and petite frame that some would call 'cute;' she spends most of her social time with a couple of girlfriends in her dorm who tag along on some of their dates.

George doesn't like it, but I revel in the situation. If I had been able to appear as myself I'm sure I would have just been another one of the girls. But that sensibility makes the situation even more discomforting for George.

What is really happening is driven by the evil Mr. Testosterone. George seems to have a constant erection. Mr. T pushes me aside and plows his way to the foreground and that just about drives me crazy. Gale and George 'make out' anywhere and anytime they can. But she is 'a good girl' and though she lets him reach under her sweater to feel her tiny breasts and she puts her hand between our legs and rubs George's penis until it's about to explode, she backs off whenever George tries to move things farther. "I don't just want to be your bed partner" she says, sounding like Annette Funicello in a beach party movie. And George, still being held to his residual Catholicism, declares that he is not at all interested in that sort of relationship. ("You are such a liar!" I whisper at him, but Mr. T. immediately clamps his hand over my mouth and reminds me who is in charge.)

☞ ◻ ☞

Gale lives in Youngstown, New York. Her father is an executive at Union Carbide and the family lives in a charming, rustic house on the banks of the Niagara River. Her father, a kind and sad man who says very little and doesn't fit the stereotype of the corporate executive, says that when it freezes in the Winter you can walk across the Niagara river to Canada. This is the extent of his attempt at a conversation.

Gale's mother is an aristocrat, or believes she is. Our mother would have accused her of "putting on airs" but they never met and if they had and Mother had made such a comment it would have been ironic since Mother was generally guilty of putting on airs herself.

George and I visit Gale in Youngstown that summer between Freshman and Sophomore years. We pick her up from her job at Old Fort Niagara. She has to wear a period costume that makes her look like a milkmaid; she works in the souvenir shop. (I'm fascinated by the milkmaid costume and wonder if there might be an opportunity to try it on sometime, but that never develops.)

Gale and George have frequent arguments. I can't remember what any of them are about since I usually back away from them, but one in particular stands out. It happens on an evening when George is drunk. (Oddly, no matter how much George drinks, I remain sober, in the background, observing and recording. Those are very difficult times, since he becomes incoherent and is prone to foolish behavior that I would never tolerate.)

George and Gale are in the dormitory lounge, shouting at one another, and then she storms away and George calmly walks to the front door and punches his fist through the window. ("Are you crazy?" I scream at him because I can feel the pain even more than him, but he tells me to shut up.)

His hand is badly cut and one of the other guys in the dorm who has seen the event walks him up the hill, off the campus, to a doctor who sews up the cut hand, with George mumbling all the while how thankful he is to be drunk since it would surely hurt otherwise. Lucky George—unlucky me.

The next day we talk about it. The best way to explain how that happens is to say George mulls it over and I play back the events from my perspective. He sees the argument, considers the relationship, and considers ideas that I put forth, though he hears them as his own. And ultimately, we decide the relationship is over.

☜ ☐ ☞

Back at Geneseo, there are other forays into theatre. George wants to play Big Daddy in *Cat On A Hot Tin Roof.* (I want to play Maggie the Cat, but we know what that would entail, so George quickly shut me down.) He tries to talk Sinclair into letting him try out for the part, arguing that he can wear a fat suit and dye his hair grey. (Of course, I know there's no way he can do it, but when he gets his mind set on something, no matter how bizarre, I cannot change it.) He winds up playing Reverend Tooker, a small part, that of a weasely southern preacher.

☞ ◻ ☞

One of the best things about Geneseo for someone like us is that it is easier for us to explore George's interests than mine. This is not to say I don't find his pursuits interesting, but I know that if I were to take the lead in matters, I would not pursue most of them. And George would not be interested in what I would be .

In the spring George gets a radio show on the college station. It's on once a week and Bob Barone is his co-host. They call it *George and the Pygmy* (because of his height, that is Bob's nickname.] They play music and ad-lib stuff they think is funny. In one of the bits, George is the interviewer and Bob is a guest who is introduced as a visiting musician.

> *"What's your main interest here at Geneseo?"* George
>   asks.
> *"I'm a bibliophile,"* Bob replies.
> *"AH...so you are a Library Science major."*
> *"No,"* Bob says. *"I play books...dictionaries....*
>   *encyclopedias...novels; it all depends on the type of*
>   *music."* He pauses then adds *"I did an album of songs*
>   *for kids ...I played comic books for that one."*

The show is the last one on the air; it goes off at midnight and there is a script that has to be read that goes something like...

> *"This is WGSU signing off. WGSU broadcasts on 1270*
> *FM from the State University of New York at Geneseo.*
> *Thank you for tuning in. We now conclude our*
> *broadcast day."*

They were then supposed to play the national anthem. But instead they played *Dixie*. And that may be why the show didn't last long. Or it might simply be that no one was listening.

∾ ❏ ☞

George and I also have now begun to write short plays, one-acts influenced by the theatre of the absurd—Albee's *Zoo Story*, Beckett's *Waiting for Godot*, Feiffer's *Crawling Arnold*. At the same time, Mr. Sinclair establishes a small performance space in the basement of one of the classroom buildings and starts producing some of those one-acts and some of George's scripts and those of a couple of the other writers on campus.

In the fall of sophomore year, due in some part to the positive "creative" image we've produced among the faculty, George's submission of poetry to an annual campus contest, earns him the Mary A. Thomas Poetry Award. We both know this is something of a sham, given that he's not a true poet. Yes, he plays with words, but he lacks the poetic spirit. And while I may be a muse of some sort, I play no part in this effort. (One of the 'poems', about a friend of Gale's, contains this line: *If Trudy would giggle less and bang more she would be a lot more socially acceptable.*

So now, George, they guy who threw up on the bus, writes a newspaper column and wins a poetry award gets better known as the campus poet and playwright.

GEORGE WILKERSON

SIXTEEN
The Hoax

GEORGE'S STINT AS MANAGER OF Kangaroo Court and his starring role in the Spring musical is probably why Peter Gregoire came to the dorm room one night that sophomore year, shortly before Thanksgiving, and made a classic offer—one I knew he couldn't refuse.

Peter is a popular student, a member of the soccer team, a Phi Sig fraternity member, and had an unassuming, charming air. Tonight, though, he has a silly grin on his face, as if he'd just sneaked some Oreos out of the cookie jar, twisted them open, licked out the icing, put them back together, and back in the jar. He hands us a sheet of paper that has the college logo neatly printed at the top along with the Dean's name, title, and address. This is clearly an "official" document; it's a statement announcing that "due to unforeseen circumstances" Thanksgiving vacation would begin one day earlier than usual.

"Is this real?" George asks.

Peter chuckles. "Cool, huh?"

"Where'd you get this?"

"Never mind that," Peter says. "I need your help. Are you in or out?"

He knows George well enough to know the answer. "In...of course."

"'Great. Now here's what I want you to do..."

And Peter goes on to explain that he also has the master key to all of the student mailboxes at each of the dorms. The plan is for George to act as a distraction while Peter sneaks to the mailboxes and stuffs them with the bogus announcement.

"What sort of distraction?" George asks.

"You'll think of something," Peter says. "I'm sure."

The next evening Peter arrives with a briefcase filled with the bogus announcements and we're off.

Please understand that I am not an accomplice. I know that madness lies down this path, but I'm not able to intercede. Too often, George has a mind of his own. And when it comes to crazy shit, I let George take his own bowel movements.

Each of the dorms has a common area with a piano and couches and easy chairs. George's roll is to dash in, sit down at the piano, and do his best Tom Lehrer imitation. (Mr. Lehrer, an undergraduate student at Harvard University at the time, wrote comic songs to entertain his friends. He later put out an album of the tunes which had titles like "Poisoning Pigeons in the Park" and "The Old Dope Peddler"). A crowd gathers and, as planned, Peter is able to sneak in and stuff the mailboxes.

The routine is repeated at all of the dorms and everything goes smoothly so that by the next morning the word has spread and students are frantically changing bus and plane reservations, calling parents, and gleefully talking about the extra day off. But that is short-lived. By the end of the day a new announcement is circulated from the Dean's office declaring the whole thing a hoax and asserting that there is no extra day off.

But what of all of those changed reservations and vacation plans? Students were outraged and that evening, there's a march on the President's house, where hundreds of students demand that the extra day be granted anyway.

The President is new to the job, having been selected just two short months earlier, and he strikes a compromise: school will not close down a day early, but anyone missing a class on that day will not be penalized.

But there's more to the story.

☞ ❏ ☞

During their planning, Peter and George agreed that in the event of an accusation they would completely deny everything; neither would ever admit to being part of it. (I tried to point out to George that he would be the only one who could be identified as being present at "the scene of the crime," but I was wasting my time.) So it is that the next day a messenger appears at our door with a notice for George to come to the office of the Academic Dean: Dr. Lawrence Park.

Dean Park, a pinch-nosed off-sized academic whose shirt collar is a little too tight (though not tight enough that the next size wouldn't look too big), is a tall man and probably wears glasses for effect, taking them off as we walk through the door to his office. He immediately stands up so as to tower over us. (I immediately look for an unoccupied space in George's mind to hide out. George's immediate response is to cringe and gasp.)

The Dean begins: "We know you were in on this, Wilkerson… You were seen at the dorms when the notice was distributed."

George flashes to that day he and Maris faced the high school principal.

"We know you had an accomplice," the Dean adds. So you'd better come clean right now."

To my astonishment, George turns into Edward G. Robinson in *The Last Gangster*:

"YOU CAN'T PIN THIS RAP ON ME COPPER! I'M INNOCENT, I TELL YA! INNOCENT!"

Actually, George says "You can't do anything to me. You don't have any proof."

"If you don't want your college career to go down the drain, I suggest you cooperate." (We may as well be in a windowless room with a green lamp hanging over our head.)

The Dean leans over his desk, his beady little eyes drilling a hole into George's brain. (I wonder if he can see me.) "I don't

121

need any proof," he says. "I can throw you out of school just because I don't like your face."

Now George switches to the role of innocent victim. He scoffs at the man. *I am indomitable*, he's thinking. (*Are you crazy?* I ask, to which George reminds me of the 'arrangement': deny everything.)"Oh yeah?" he says, sneering. "I doubt that."

The Dean leans back, places his elbows on the arms of his chair and leers at us for a moment, smirking now, enjoying the experience. Then he points to the door.

"You're out," he says. "Pack your things and be off this campus by noon tomorrow."

George's gulp is loud enough for the secretary in the outer office to hear.

"You heard me," the Dean says, shaking a pointing finger. "Out...now!"

George rises, walks to the door, and leaves. In just a few minutes he has morphed from the indomitable innocent victim to the defeated Cyrano with the windmill laughing at us as we leave the Administration building and cross the quad.

Back at the dorm, he collapses on his bed just as Ben comes in.

"What's the matter with you," Ben says. "You're as white as my maiden Aunt's privates."

"I've been kicked out of school," George says, then recounts the story of his brave stand against the evil force of the college administration and his subsequent fall.

"What are you gonna do?" Ben asks.

George shrugs.

"There must be somebody you can talk to?"

We think for a moment. Then...yes...there is someone. And we run down the hall to the phone and call Bob Sinclair. After all, this is high drama and who better than the director to tell us how to play the next scene.

"Did you do it?" Sinclair asks after George finishes describing the incident.

"Do I have to answer?" he asks.

"No," Sinclair says. "I think I know the answer. You just sit tight; don't do anything. I'll call you back in a little while."

We go back to the dorm room and wait. An hour. Two. Three. And then the phone."

"George?"

"Yes." (It's Sinclair.)

"That scene in the Dean's office?"

"Uh huh."

"It never happened."

"But... .he said..."

"You're not hearing me George. It never happened. You just go back to your classes and forget about it."

"But..."

"It never happened."

And just like that, we're off the hook. The next morning, we go to classes and noon comes and goes and nothing happens.

Well...almost nothing. Because there's a third part.

☜ ❏ ☞

Thanksgiving vacation is over and everyone is back at school and one evening Peter and John Meuser, the dorm counselor (aka Resident Advisor) walk into our dorm room. John is Captain Goody-Two-Shoes. He is admired as a serious scholar, a straight arrow, and adored by the girls as a big teddy bear. He's a good dorm counselor, especially when in the role of Father Confessor to rowdy underclassmen.

Peter gets right to the point. "I couldn't handle it anymore, George."

"Handle what?"

He sighs. "The guilt. It was driving me crazy. I felt so bad about it."

I'm not sure what's going on, but I already have a bad feeling about it. And so does George.

"He told me the whole story," John says. "The Thanksgiving hoax, how you distracted people while he stuffed the mailboxes."

I'm screaming. I'm losing it. But George is repressing it. The whole thing is crashing down around us, made especially worse since we had escaped expulsion and won our freedom, but George's primary urge right now is to kick Peter squarely in the nuts.

But he doesn't. Instead, he calmly looks at John and blinks a couple of times. "Hoax?" he says in his best innocent voice, "I had nothing to do with any hoax. I don't know what he's been telling you, but…"

Peter interrupts. "Come on, George. We need to stand up to this, accept our punishment…"

Suddenly, George is Edward G. Robinson again. "YOU DIRTY RAT!" he's thinking. "YOU RATTED OUT ON THE MOB!"

"They'll probably just suspend you for a semester," John says. "You can probably come back next fall."

"Suspend me….a semester…".

And then Peter starts to laugh.

"What's so damn funny?" George asks.

"You," he says, then turns to John. "Look at him."

John is smiling. And George and I both are thoroughly confused.

"How do you think I got the Dean's letterhead stationary?" Peter says. "And the mailbox key?"

John, the Teddy Bear, Father Confessor and Goody-Two-Shoes has an evil grin on his face and he's nodding at us. "You?"

"Uh huh."

Peter is slapping us on the back. "You should have seen the look on your face," he says.

"We sure had you squirming," John adds.

We take a deep breath. "You sure did."

[We later learn that the new President at the time of the hoax, the one who negotiated the compromise, inherited Dean Park from the previous administration and couldn't stand the man. Bob Sinclair knew this and spoke directly to the President on George's behalf, saying something like "Do you know what that ass Park has done now?"

We never kept in touch with John or Peter except for once, when John was a Dean at Finger Lakes Community College in New York and George, a Dean at Austin Community College in Texas, came to the Finger Lakes to explore a job possibility. John was just the way we remembered him; still the unlikely cohort; still one of the sweetest guys ever.

As for Peter, the likelihood of exacting revenge for that night in the dorm room when he and John worked us over like scared rabbits is not likely. It is one of those events that made me wish I wasn't part of George, but looking back, it gives me an odd sense of pleasure at having lived through it.

The full story behind the hoax remains a secret for more than twenty-five years, until it is told at a class reunion, sponsored by the college and attended by the President of the college (not the same one) who comments that he wishes the problems he faces now are as minor as that hoax.

GEORGE WILKERSON

SEVENTEEN
A Geneseo Quinceañera

IF YOU'RE WONDERING IF GEORGE had sex with me, consider how that would be possible. I'm a figment of his mind, or he is a figment of mine. On those occasions when I get to express myself and he sees me in the mirror, he gets aroused and satisfies himself. Does that constitute a sexual relationship? I leave that to the experts in such matters to settle, though now, as then, there are no experts.

When college is in session, the population of Geneseo doubles. The few businesses on Main Street include the Hotel, George's Luncheonette, the drug store, the Big Tree Inn, a movie theatre, and a small restaurant. Having contrived ways to remain in Geneseo all year long, George takes at least one course, works at the luncheonette, and lives in town.

In the summer of 1962, Dutch and George are both still virgins. Neither has had sex and both will soon turn twenty and that is an unseemly state of affairs. So they set out to correct the situation.

So Dutch proposes that whoever loses his virginity first will pay the other one-hundred dollars. But that's a deception, because Dutch is actually 'going steady' with Glenda, the woman he would later marry, while George is unattached, having broken up with Gale the past Spring. Nonetheless, George sets out to find a candidate and given the number of girls on campus, that's not a difficult task.

George is enrolled in an English Literature class which meets in a classroom consisting of tables and chairs, rather than desks, with three of the tables arranged in a U-shape, with the open side occupied by the teacher's desk. Sitting directly across from us is Bonnie Woodworth, a girl with a campus-wide reputation as being easy. Some would call her a slut, or even a nymphomaniac, those being the fantasies of most of the males on campus.

Bonnie is a Library Science major, two years ahead of us, a Senior. She's not especially pretty, but she's intelligent and has a nice figure. She wears her hair in the classic librarian's bun and dresses conservatively in loose clothes and drab colors. But none of that matters. George has never had sex and at this point would find a girl who resembles a slobbering St. Bernard, sexy.

When the first class meets, there she is, sitting across from us, and though we have never had any conversation with her outside of the classroom, she immediately begins to send glances at us in ways that suggest (to George's horny mind, at least) an invitation.

That invitation becomes clearer on a day when she's wearing a tank top and a short skirt and very calmly, but deliberately, uncrosses her legs and allows the skirt to slide to one side so as to provide a clear view of her crotch. This causes nothing less than a hormone raging tornado to touch down between George's thighs. (And frankly, it causes quite a wind storm in mine.) I can hear George's breathing (panting, actually) while I strain to determine the color of her panties. But that's useless because in George's now rampant imagination, she isn't wearing any!

Does anyone else in the class notice this? Do they not hear George's heavy breathing, his heart pounding against his ribs, the waterfall of sweat spilling from his forehead? No matter. Everything else is blocked out.

And then we start a conversation. *You're misinterpreting everything*, I tell him. *She doesn't know what she's doing.*

No matter, he says. *It's like the Native Americans riding their horses bareback. Do the horses care?*

Huh? (Sometimes George's metaphors have no basis in logic.) *Just shut up,* he says. *This is the real thing.*

But when class is over, he makes no attempt to follow up on it. He's sure of what he saw, but I can tell he doesn't have the courage to follow through.

The fates are on his side though. That very night we are sitting alone at The Hotel and she walks in and George is thrust into a bar in Morocco. (*Of all the gin joints in all the towns in all the world, she walks into mine.*)

Bonnie spies us and sits down at our table and we're tongue tied. So she asks questions: "Do you like the class? What're you majoring in? Where are you from?

George's addled brain finally struggles to answer. He offers to buy her a drink, but she declines. "Let's go for a walk," she says, and stands up, knowing we will follow her like a smitten puppy. We leave The Hotel together without saying a word and walk down Main Street, turn left down Ward Street and then to Wadsworth Street, to the end where we arrive at a rooming house. This, she says, is where she lives.

The rooming house is one of those old Victorian style homes and after a brief comment ("I have a room upstairs.") she motions to George to come inside with her to a 'sitting room' just off the entrance with a dim view of a long staircase leading up to the bedrooms upstairs. Except for the light from a small lamp resting on a doily at the end of the couch, the room is dark and as we sit down, Bonnie turns off the light so that there's only the pale glow of the street lamp coming through the window.

Our eyes adjust and we can see the outline of her body as she slides close to us, takes George's hand, and rests it on her thigh. He follows her lead and lets her guide him to the smooth area between her legs and starts stroking it, but she slows him down and leans over, rests her head against his cheek and begins to slide her panties off.

Suddenly there's a clatter at the door and voices. Two of the other girls who live there have arrived. One snaps on the entryway light as Bonnie frantically pulls her panties back up and motions to us, with her finger to her lips, to be quiet (a struggle for George who is panting like a woman giving birth.) I help him hold his breath as the girls scurry straight to the staircase without glancing into the sitting room.

Once they're up the stairs, Bonnie stands and says, in her best librarian voice "You need to go."

We both want to cry—George because of a lost opportunity and me because I want to know how this all works, from the woman's perspective. I want to know what a vagina looks like. (Yes, I've seen photos, but that's not the same.) And I want to figure out my role in all of this.

George fights back the tears and follows her as she leads us to the door, leans over and kisses him on the cheek, and gently shoves us outside.

☜ ❏ ☞

One night, a week or so later as George is heading back to The Hotel for a beer, his nascent Catholicism kicks in, in the form of a guardian angel. It's the one Sister Thomasina told him about, except the angel is an alcoholic. He's a perennial nineteen-year-old kid who got killed when he drove into a tree and in his last moments of consciousness made a "sincere act of contrition," which is akin to a governor's pardon (assuming the governor is Catholic). This angel is now making up for his besotted life by serving as a spiritual guide and even though it's probably against the rules, he is taking pity on George's lack of success in his efforts to get laid.

(Were the angel truly there and not just the work of George's Catholic upbringing, I'm certain he would want no part of me. For one thing, I don't fit anywhere within the tenets of Catholic doctrine, and for another, I'm not the sort that Catholic boys would find attractive.)

So then, on this holy night, this boy-angel has guided George to The Hotel where Bonnie Woodworth awaits, sitting alone at the same table, unmoving, like a Baglione chiaroscuro painted in the shadows of the barroom. She is reading a book. So we go to her and sit down at the table in the seat directly across from her.

At first she acts like no one is there, so we wait awhile, figuring she's engrossed in the narrative and will acknowledge us when she reaches the end of a chapter, but after turning five pages, we realize that's not going to happen.

George clears his throat. "You want to take a walk?"

She says nothing, closes the book, puts it in her purse, stands up and walks toward the door and then stops and turns and looks at us.

George's reaction is somewhere between a young Jerry Lewis in *The Bellboy* and an old Woody Allen in *Manhattan*. He jumps up, skips across the room to stand alongside her, and the three of us walk out together.(Two of us are conscious. I'm there, but for them, I'm not, though later I try to push myself into the picture because I'm thinking that Bonnie just might be the sort of girl who would understand me, and I urge George to let her know. But it's not the right time.)

We walk until we arrive in front of the rooming house, site of the previous bad encounter.

Bonnie turns to us. "Wait here," she says, then walks into the house. When she emerges, she motions for us to follow her and we walk further, around the corner, to Court Street and shortly we're in front of a small apartment house consisting of just four apartments.

Bonnie hands us her purse and again, she says "Wait here." She walks to the building's entrance, pauses for a moment, then steps inside and disappears.

Within a few minutes, she's back, but now she has a bottle of Jack Daniels in her hand. It's about two-thirds full. She takes a swig of it and hands it towards us.

George waves it away. "No," he says. "No thanks."

She shrugs, says "Suit yourself," then takes another swig and says "C'mon."

The walk is longer now, and uphill. We continue up Court Street, back across Main, where Center becomes North Street, then all the way up North, to Temple Hill, the location of the Wadsworth Estate.

The Wadsworth family originally owned about 2,000 acres here, including farmland and what eventually became business property. In the 1870's they organized "the Genesee Valley Hunt." A pack of foxhounds and hunters in full regalia gallops across the valley chasing a poor fox raised solely for the exercise and though they give up the hunt in 1917, a later Wadsworth following in the grandfather's footsteps, reorganizes the event, and declares himself "Master of the Genesee Valley Hunt." It continues to this day. George knows how the fox feels.

Bonnie slows down, guiding us between a row of long poplar trees. The estate itself is visible at the corner of South Street and Temple Hill, but when we emerge from the other side of the trees we're next to a stable. It doesn't appear to be in use, though it may have been where the horses were brought in and kept for the annual hunt.

We're walking gingerly now, as Bonnie has made it clear that we don't want to be seen or heard. We come around the stable and there we find a swimming pool. Bonnie takes George's hand and walks us to the far side of the pool where there's a long row of lounge chairs and lays down on one of them, leaving a space beside her, patting it, and waving for us to join her.

George obeys, lying down beside her as she takes another swig of the Jack Daniels, then puts the bottle on the ground beside her and turns to face us. She smiles and we smile back and some heavy groping begins. I can tell that George is now in over his head and I'm feeling like a Sunday school teacher trapped in a porn theatre. (I suspect that situation isn't all that uncommon.) Parts that have never been touched are being fondled. Hands glide this way and that, interrupted only by an occasional pause for a drink. At times it seems we're kissing the bottle and the taste is unusually sensual, but then it mixes with the night air and the slight scent of chlorine coming from the pool and then we become a hound chasing after the fox.

Gradually, George maneuvers himself next to Bonnie so that they are side-by-side, facing each other and then, in an awkward attempt to be suave, he rolls over, intending to get on top of her… but the chair collapses and we slam onto the poolside concrete.

I believe I can hear the guardian angel chuckling. The sound of the collapsing metal of the chair and the 'oomphs' as the wind is knocked out of us reverberates across the water—a canon fired, a car crashing, fireworks.

Almost immediately, Bonnie is on her feet, rescuing the Jack Daniels. She takes another swig, then a deep breath, and now strips off her clothes, leaving her in only her bra and panties.

"Come on," she says, arms extended, waving her hands at us.

George is dumbfounded, still lying on the collapsed chair, out of breath and trying to decide if any bones are broken.

Bonnie shakes her head and then points at the water. "In the pool," she says, grinning.

"Uh…uh…uh…" George is stammering and blinking, but nothing intelligible is coming out.

"The pool," she says, pointing now, the Jack Daniels still in her hand. "In…the…pool."

And George blurts out his embarrassment. "I….uh…I can't swim."

"Jesus Christ!" she says, takes another swig, and dives into the pool.

And George is now certain that he must be destined for the priesthood. All of the events of our shared life converge at this moment as a sign from god, or at the very least, an illusion created by the drunken angel.

This is suddenly replaced by a vision, of Bonnie, drunken and hitting her head on the side of the pool and drowning and George, unable rescue her, leaving her there since he's certain no one saw them that night. And now wondering if he should call the police and try to come up with some sort of credible explanation.

"I can't swim officer, and…"

"You can't swim? You came up here with this girl and you can't swim?"

George nods, holds out his hands, ready for the officer to put on the cuffs, when the vision bursts. Bonnie is on the steps in the corner of the pool. She seems calmer as she walks toward us, puts down the bottle of Jack Daniels, goes over to the defunct chair and picks up her clothes, then comes back, takes George's hand, and guides us into a little building at the other end of the pool.

It's a cabana—a dressing room, with shelves of towels, a few folded up beach chairs, and, best of all, a soft floor made of some sort of spongy material. She puts down the bottle, motions to George to undress, lies down, and finally the task is complete.

I am not a part of this. I remain in the shadows, and watch as the guardian angel cheers. For somewhere there are sins, I murmur, and somewhere there are sinners, but on this night in uptown Geneseo, there is, at last, satisfaction.

EIGHTEEN
Mary Catherine, Liberal Arts, and a Gale

BOB SINCLAIR (OUR DRAMA TEACHER) shares the summer musical production duties as director along with music teacher Daryl Hanson. It's a major event due to the inclusion of a "star." (The word is misleading; a professional actor with a recognizable name is brought in during the final week of rehearsal.)

The show, produced in the summer between our Junior and Senior year is *Finnean's Rainbow* and the star is Arnold Stang. Stang has done a lot of minor TV and film roles, but at this time he is best known for being in a Chunky candy bar commercial. ("Whatta chunka chocolate," he intones in his high-pitched, adolescent voice, after taking a hefty bite.)

We spend a portion of that particular summer at Sinclair's house, a funky place filled with antiques. Sinclair is out of town for much of the time on acting gigs, including the role of Alfred Doolittle in a touring production of *My Fair Lady*. Sinclair is adamant about George getting to his classes; so much so that very early one particular morning, after passing out on the couch, we are awakened to the near-deafening sound of Kate Smith singing *God Bless America*. Arnold Stang and Kate Smith…we are truly blessed.

☞ ❑ ☞

Phil Bracchi, a classmate of ours, is the person in charge of the house when Sinclair is gone and there are frequent parties with a variety of folk in attendance: theatre people, athletes, townfolk and out-of-towners. Much of what goes on there is lost in a drunken blur. I can access those memories, but they're like something written in another language.

One scene that comes through has George lying on a mattress in Sinclair's attic. There's a television at the foot of the mattress and the Johnny Carson show is on. George is seeing a double image of Johnny and there's no sound. Lying beside him is Mikki Brandt. She's a year behind us and she has no chin. (Of course, she has a chin, but in profile it's as if her jawbone narrows down to a curve that disappears into her neck. And in the cruelty that is rampant in those times, jokes are made about this behind her back.)

George's mind is not on her chin, as Mikki turns to us and we kiss and she takes George's head in her hands and guides it down to her crotch. "Kiss me there," she murmurs, but George's nose bumps into something—a Tampon.

Later, when retelling this story, George adds that he replied "Hey...kiss me <u>here</u>," and points to our ass, but that didn't happen. What did happen is that he passed out and awoke the next morning alone.

༺ ❏ ☞

In 1963 the college adds Liberal Arts to the curriculum and begins offering the Bachelor of Arts degree and John Collinson, the chair of the school's Philosophy department, is appointed as the college's interim Director of Liberal Studies. (He becomes the 'permanent' Director in 1964.) His daughter, Mary, is a sophomore and George is a Junior and they date.

Mary is a bright girl. She and George get along intellectually... discussions over coffee, walking and talking, that sort of thing.

She is not especially attractive. That should not matter, but it does to George. And to me as well because I have a need to know what things a girl has to do to make herself attractive—things like hair and make-up.

Mary has big thumbs...overly big. Years later, reading Tom Robbins' *Even Cowgirls Get the Blues,* I discover his description of Sissy Hankshaw's thumb:

> *It is a thumb. The thumb. The thumbs, both of them. It is her thumbs that we remember; it is her thumbs that have set her apart.*

One Fall evening that year, George takes Mary to Rochester to see Allan Sherman, a comedy writer, best known at the time for an album of song parodies (*My Son, the Folk Singer*). He takes well-known folk songs like "Jump Down, Spin Around" and writes comic lyrics. (Most of them satirize Jewish culture. He's not an especially good singer and his accent is very New York and Yiddish.)

> *Gotta Jump Down, Spin Around*
> *Pick a dress of cotton*
> *Gotta Jump Down, Spin Around*
> *Pick a dress of wool*
> *Grab those bargains off the racks*
> *Who needs Bergdorf, Who needs Sax*
> And so on.

The show concludes with Sherman sitting on the front edge of the stage, lit only by a single spotlight and waiting for the theatre to get very quiet, then launching into *Somewhere Over the Rainbow,* which most of the audience recognizes as the same thing Judy Garland did at the conclusion of her live shows.

We drive back to Geneseo having had a couple drinks at the theatre so George is drunk by the time we get to Mary's house. It's late and she is attempting to enter quietly (George trailing along behind her) when her mother appears at the top of the long stairs leading to the second floor of the old Victorian home. She's scowling and says something like "Mary Catherine…do you know what time it is?" (The 'Catherine' part makes her anger clear.) But before Mary could answer, George steps forward and looks up at her mother, scowling down at him in her nightgown. "Mrs. Collinson…please," he says in full-on puppy-dog fashion, "It's my fault. I'm sorry. And besides the night is really very young…and…" (he pauses and sighs) you are so beautiful."

I can't believe he said that nor do I know where it came from, but what's more astonishing is that Mrs. Collinson falls for it. Her demeanor suddenly does a one-eighty. Her expression turns from a scowl to a blush and she dashes down the stairs, muttering something about it being chilly and that we should sit down while she makes us some hot chocolate. And she is grinning from ear to ear.

Nonetheless, despite the clever conclusion to the evening, that is our last date with Mary— not because she and George didn't get along, but other matters got in the way. Do you remember Mikki? She's the girl George slept with in the attic at Sinclair's house. Very shortly after the date with Mary, a scandal involving Mikki and Mary's father emerges. The word on the street is that they were having an affair and Mary's mother was filing for divorce. The official word from the college was that Dr. Collinson was stepping down and planning to leave the college. So long Mary.

∽ ❏ ☞

Consider this: you're a serial killer, and though you understand the vile nature of your actions and have a strong desire to confess your sins, you just can't help yourself. That's how George often feels about me. Maybe it comes from the Catholic upbringing and the sense of sin associated with his gender confusion and the relief surrounding confession. But looking at it from where I stand, there is no gender confusion. We are one and two at the same time, but only able to express ourselves as one and our physiology as well as the social milieu demands the male be the one 'out there.' So I know I have to lay back and let that persona dominate. But make no mistake about it—I am just as much there as he is.

☞ ❏ ☞

"Worn out phrases and longing gazes…won't get you where you want to go," Momma Cass sings in the Beatles song "*Words of Love*," so in the fall of that year, George and Gale become engaged.

George is playing out the American love scenario from a sense of what one does (as opposed to what one wants to do). According to the screenplay in his mind (not one that I wrote, you can be sure), you find the girl, you get engaged and then married, struggle for a while at a low-paying job, but eventually work your way up the academic ladder to a position as a Supervisor or Manager and you earn some respectability. You buy a house in the suburbs and you have two children, a boy and a girl, and you belong to the P.T.A. and the Junior League, and you sell Girl Scout cookies for your daughter, and coach your son's Little League team.

When it first comes to George's mind, this scenario makes me laugh, for as much as he believes in it, I can't see him in any of it. He is already too far outside the norm to fool anyone. And moreover, what would he do about me?

But the girlfriend Gale is sure she can bring him around. She plays the forecast game with him, tells him how she is saving her virginity for marriage, how her parents have property right across the street from their house and will foot the bill to build a little castle for them to live in, and how she will cook dinner for him and bear beautiful children. It's pure Disney, but without *Herbie* or *The Shaggy Dog*.

Then Barbara pops up.

NINETEEN
The Beginning of Barbara

S HE POPS UP IN A theatre class called *Stagecraft* and George loses it. (I prefer to think that he came to his senses, but you have to understand that neither he nor I had much control over the testosterone.) She sits next to him and just as I'm noticing her pretty red dress with the flared skirt and the hemline just above the knee and fantasizing how it would be to wear that and spin around and have that skirt flare out... George shuts me down. His eyes shift to her legs—like those of the mannequins in Macy's window—perfectly proportioned with tiny feet that slither neatly into a pair of plain black flats. This is long before Viagra, but those legs should have carried a warning: *If these cause an erection lasting more than four hours, contact your physician.*

It isn't long before they begin to meet outside of

REHEARSE — The Experimental Theater at Geneseo State will present three one-act plays written by George Wilkerson of Hempstead, a recent graduate of the college, in the College Cave from Monday through Saturday of next week. Rehearsing one of the plays are Barbara Wilkerson, wife of the author, and Cal Culver of Holcomb.

Barbara acting with Cal Culver in one of George's plays

141

class. Gale is off doing her student teaching. And she is no competition for Barbara. In the cafeteria, the student center, the hallway after class—Barbara listens as George talks about his dreams, his frustrations, his infatuation with words and sentences. No one we spoke to before had seemed interested. And I liked her too. I sensed that it would be OK for George to tell her about me. She was open to different ideas, to different ways of looking at things. She certainly wouldn't have a problem with me. And I'll bet we even wear the same size!

But no. If anything, George's infatuation precludes sharing anything that might put her off. He still sees himself (or me, at least) as a freak of nature, a threat to his chance at a normal life. And as much as it pains me to say it, I can't blame him. Would Dr. Jekyll ever tell the woman he loved about Mr. Hyde?

☜   ❏   ☞

But then, Gale returns to campus and the reports from her friends are confirmed. She springs them at us.

"I know about Barbara," she says.

"She's just a friend," George replies.

"A girlfriend," she says with a snort.

"No," George says, his voice lowering. "A girl who's a friend."

Gale smirks and fumes. "A friend who you've been fucking."

Wow, I mutter. *There's a word we don't hear often.*

"What?"

Gale already has the engagement ring off her finger and is holding it out to us. "Here."

"Listen," George says, about to explain. "She's just..."

WHAP!

The slap comes out of nowhere and without a pause, George slaps back.

WHAP!

The moment is frozen in time. On film it would include one of those rotating shots where we get to see the people from all sides. Seconds pass like minutes. Then Gale reaches up to her cheek, now red from the impact, drops the ring to the ground, and turns and walks away.

George remains, his face flushed and a momentary vision of Father slapping us. And I see it too. It's just a tiny, violent nuisance, but it's not like anything George can handle. I can feel him deflate, like the air slowly passing from a leaking balloon, as we both pull back from the world and realize we are together and yet alone.

☜ ❑ ☞

That same year the theatre department mounted a production of the Bertold Brecht/ Kurt Weill musical *Threepenny Opera* (adapted from the 19th century ballad opera, *The Beggar's Opera*, by John Gay*)*. George gets the lighting assignment along with Barbara and a girl named Mary Lou Fatimo. Barbara and Mary Lou works the spotlights from a booth at the back of the theatre and George runs the stage lights from the wings.

The most famous song from the show, *The Ballad of Mack the Knife*, as performed by people like Bobby Darin and Louis Armstrong, doesn't really reflect the tone. The show is actually one of the more depressing theatre experiences in musical comedy. Nearly everything about the story is depressing. For example, one of the songs goes like this:

If first you don't succeed
Then try and try again
And if you don't succeed again
Then try and try and try
Useless, it's useless, our kind of life is tough
Take it from me it's useless, trying ain't enough

143

Hearing songs like that, night after night, through six weeks of rehearsals would get anyone depressed. At the end of the show the audiences didn't leave humming the tunes because most of them were preoccupied with considering suicide.

Working the lights is a physically demanding operation. The stage lights are operated by a bank of large levers which control the rheostats which slowly raise and dim them. To get a quick blackout, both hands and feet are needed. George has to reach across two or three of the levers in order to slide them down simultaneously as fast as possible.

Up in the booth, the spotlights Barbara and Mary Lou operate are called 'carbon arcs' because the source of light is created by the tips of two carbon rods being brought together. The tips of the carbon rods start to heat up more and more, and eventually reach the point where they produce an extremely bright light. There is no match for the power of arc lamps which are about 200 times more powerful than filament bulbs. A lot of heat is generated and there isn't much ventilation in the spotlight booth. As a result, Barbara and Mary Lou often work the lights wearing nothing but their bras and panties. Barbara and Mary Lou communicate with George via hardwired headsets and to coordinate the light cues.

Once, during one of the blackouts, Barbara's voice comes through with something of a strain. "Can you come up here?" she asks.

"Not really," George says, as he is in the middle of setting up the levers for the next light cue.

We find out later that Mary Lou is putting moves on Barbara and Barbara is not comfortable with it. But nothing comes of it until a few nights later at one of the gatherings of the cast and crew at the Big Tree Inn, where Mary Lou proposes a 'Light Staff Threesome' which would include George in the fun. This isn't appealing to George, but I have to admit to trying to persuade him otherwise. And though I'd like to say he went for it, since that would make for a far more interesting story, he didn't.

Mary Lou was notorious for other reasons. George often brought his guitar to the parties and gatherings of the theatre folk and soon discovers that if he plays the song *Just Because* (made popular at the time by Elvis Presley) Mary Lou, with no encouragement whatsoever, will hop on a nearby table and perform a striptease.

I found it was easy to get George to play the song, even after it reached the point where the room would clear after the first few bars. It became trite. George played, Mary Lou stripped, and everyone yawned. But not me. The whole subject of lesbianism loomed even larger as I considered exactly how the sexual activity would play out. (It generally consisted of repeated images of labia, penises, breasts, and lips played out like a series of flash cards in a sex education class gone bad.)

After a while, Barbara takes George home to Schenectady to meet the parents and we find they are nothing like ours. Her father is a strong, silent muscular type; her mother is an energetic, talkative woman whom we conclude usually plays dumb and naïve because that's what men of that generation find attractive.

On the first evening, we go for a walk. George and I are in love…with Barbara. It's spring and we get caught in one of those light showers that dissolve the minute the raindrops touch the ground and just as we get to the driveway of her house, we look back and there we see not one, but two rainbows, side by side in one of those moments that is just too perfect to be real. If we hadn't enrolled in the Fuck-god School we might have called it 'a sign.' "Hey…you two. Don't get any dumb ideas. You belong together" the voice from the heavens would say. And we probably should have paid closer attention. Many years later the meaning will be clear.

GEORGE WILKERSON

TWENTY
Drowning with Professors, Fraternities, and Sororities,

BY SENIOR YEAR WE ARE in awe of our professors. Sister Thomasina, still beating our head against the blackboard in sixth grade, and the English teacher at Oceanside High School, were the standards against which we measured teachers, but these college professors change all that. They, more than the college itself, point us in the direction of intellectual inquiry, curiosity about life's mysteries, and the opportunity to express oneself through the arts.

Bob Sinclair mentors George's entry to the theatre, casts him in a couple of the school's productions and encouraged his interest in playwriting by giving him the opportunity to have his work produced. Sinclair is Mr. Drama, onstage at all times. When he arrives at the Big Tree all activity stops. And when he leaves it is always 'stage right.' He's a master at executing the perfect exit, delivering a dramatic farewell statement just before turning and leaving.

☜ ☐ ☞

By contrast, there's *Alice Austin*, a woman with the hard life she must have led etched into the folds of skin on her face and the stoic posture she always maintained. She is the head of the drama department and a campus legend. (Rumor has it that she keeps a bottle of scotch in her bottom desk drawer and doesn't hesitate to use it to reinforce her legendary status.) She lives with and cares for her elderly mother, having given up a promising acting career to do that.

A story is told that one day when she is lecturing she places her hand dramatically on her chest, leans her head back, and declares that she *lawfed* and *lawfed* and could not stop *laffing*. The point of the story, of course, is meant to attack her as being pretentious as revealed by her speech inadvertently slipping out of the aristocratic accent into that of a commoner. (Poor Alice. Were I living this life instead of George I could very well wind up like her)

☞ ❑ ☞

Daryl Hanson, head of the music department, is rotund like a latter day Orson Welles and very nearly as dramatic as Sinclair. He tries to break out of his professorship via a musical play called *The Water Babies,* based on a book by that title, published in England in 1863.It had already been made into a musical theatre version in London in 1902 and in 1973 there was an animated film version. The Hanson show never got beyond the Genesee Valley.

☞ ❑ ☞

William 'Bill' Orwin teaches foreign languages and his brother teaches at Geneseo as well. In our last year, when we switch from being an Education major into the new Liberal Arts program we have to take a year of a language, so we sign up for Russian, figuring it's far enough removed from the romance languages that we won't get confused. It will be a whole new thing. But as luck would have it, the class meets at 8:00 in the morning. This means George can get up at 7:45 and roll from bed to class in one fell swoop. (And I get to 'sleep in.')

Those are the times when it's nice to live in the background. George gets up and goes about his business, but I stay asleep, except that within moments of George taking his seat in class he dozes off and Dr. Orwin quietly steps over beside him and sighs. "Mr. Wilkerson," he says, his soft, gentle voice tinged with pleading," please...get up early...have some coffee... take a nice walk around the campus." To which George smiles and nods and then proceeds to try and translate Pushkin.

> *I have outlasted all desire,*
> *My dreams and I have grown apart;*
> *My grief alone is left entire,*
> *The gleanings of an empty heart.*

Beautiful, really, but it has very little effect on either of us since it's punctuated by yawns and eye-rubbing and 'uhs' and 'ums;' however, Ron Cicoria, who sits next to us, is completely absorbed by it—not so much because it's Russian love poetry, but because he is in love with the girl who sits on the other side of him. Only someone with an Italian heart could be as smitten as him—totally, madly, insanely in love. It was clearly a case of the Pushkin tsarists abdicating to the Italian fascists.

And there's *Dr. Lucy Harmon,* whose American Literature II class George wouldn't have taken were it not for the advice of Whitey Offchess, an upperclassman who, on hearing we will be staying at Geneseo for the summer, tells George to sign up for her class and "Stick with me and we'll get easy 'A's".

Long before Prince established it as his preference, it is widely known on campus that purple is her favorite color. "Do you have a purple shirt?" Whitey asks before the first class meeting.

George shakes his head.

"Get one," he says. "And wear it often." We did. And Whitey's advice paid off.

Dr. Harmon is the Emily Grierson of SUNY Geneseo. (She's the main character in the William Faulkner story *A Rose for Emily*.) To paraphrase Faulkner, Lucy Harmon is "a tradition, a duty, and a care…a sort of hereditary obligation." She is an old fashioned 'lady' who makes sure we all know her status from the first day of class, when she shows us slides of her trip to Stratford-on-Avon and tells us that she never left her hotel without her gloves. George enjoys her, but I like her even more. For me, she embodies the kind of femininity to which I secretly aspire.

On the first day of class we take a seat beside Whitey (who got his name from his premature snow-white hair) at the back of the room and Lucy immediately takes note. When she calls roll Whitey replies with the usual "Here!" but immediately adds "and I want to introduce my good friend George Wilkerson. You may have attended one of his plays." Lucy smiles and welcomes George. She notes his attendance in her register and, pointing to Whitey, says "It's so nice to have you boys here." And from then on George is *In Like Flynn*.

This is never clearer than on the day she asks what the 'desire' refers to in the Eugene O'Neill play *Desire Under the Elms*. She pauses for just a second and then points back toward George, who already has his hand up. She waves it down and says. "I'm sure you know the answer, so please, just put your hand down," producing glares from a number of the other students, as she goes on to explain in hushed tones. "It wasn't their desire for the land," she says, grinning and winking, "it was….*sex*."

Later in the term, when Whitey and George both skip class on the same day, we learn from a friend in the class that when she calls the roll and realizes they aren't there she pauses, then asks sadly "Where are my two?" This report is confirmed when

Whitey and George return for the next class and one of the girls says loudly "Oh look…here comes '<u>her two</u>.'"

Lucy was nothing short of delightful.

One day when she's off on one of her regular tangents talking about her life, she says "When I was a young girl and I lived by myself, I would look around my room and check under the bed to make sure there wasn't some man hiding there and planning to have his way with me." Then she adds "Now…I come home and I look around the room and under the bed…and I hope."

The course is as delightful as Lucy herself and George isn't nearly as delighted as me. Lucy stands in such a sharp contrast to Alice Austin's sad and lonely existence. If I could be free to be me, Lucy Harmon is the me I'd be.

So then, while I sleep through the Russian language class, I never sleep in American Lit II because I relish every moment with Dr. Lucy.

In addition to Bob Sinclair, *Leo Rockas,* an English professor whose specialty was rhetoric and the Poetics, is a mentor. He's Greek and fluent in the language. He has us read Aristotle and Sophocles and takes us inside the minds of the playwrights and authors. He encourages George's creative writing, believing of course that it was all the work of George's imagination. George gives him scripts of one-act plays (often unknowingly inspired by me)and he critiques them, asking questions about the characters, the events, and so on. The questions are clearly meant to make us think about them. There are no prescribed answers. And he often lets us sleep at his house on the couch on his side porch. He gets us accepted into the Syracuse University Creative Writing program, despite George's weak GPA (around 2.5).

Rockas always calls George by our last name. "OK Wilkerson, would you like to explain to me why this piece lacks a plausible conclusion?"

❧　❑　☞

Walter Harding, head of the English Department and our advisor—is always kind and willing to listen to our interests and try to guide us through the maze of required courses. (He's a prominent scholar on Henry David Thoreau.)

❧　❑　☞

And *Jay Walker*, an African-American man whose presence makes us feel like we should kneel when he speaks. He is unique for his time—a black man who, after attending the City University of New York, earned an M.S. from Columbia and a Ph.D. in Victorian Literature from the University of Nottingham in England. He always stands straight and tall with his chin up and a royal demeanor. He has lectured at Tottenham College in London and when he leaves Geneseo he goes on to teach at Dartmouth.

Despite his impressive credentials, experience, and posture he is neither pretentious nor aloof. He is approachable and always open to questions. And he has a sense of humor which is demonstrated when it comes time to submit the final paper for the first term in American Literature I. George decided to take a very different approach to the assignment—one involving a good deal of risk. (As usual, I tried to warn him, but he didn't listen.) Rather than prepare the standard research and analysis paper on Hawthorne's *The Scarlet Letter*, George submits a script for a very silly musical version of the book. In the opening scene, the townspeople of Boston have formed a circle around Hester Prynne to present her with the red 'A' (the scarlet letter of the title) which she must wear to identify her as an adulterer. In George's version, Hester accepts the letter and sings (to the tune of *Carolina in the Morning*):

> *Nothing could be better than to wear a scarlet letter in the*
> *morrr...rning.*
> *Nothing could be better than a letter that is redder than the*
> *dawwww...awning.*
> *See the townfolk gather, round the jailhouse door*
> *Whispering little curses*
> *I long to hear once more*

And it got worse from there.

But when we come to the next class, Walker returns the paper ...with a red 'A' at the top and asks George to act it out for the class. Walker chuckles and applauds the entire time. (I made a brief appearance in the part of Hester Prynne, but George, fearing the exposure of his secret, made sure it was not all that convincing.)

🖎 ❏ ☞

And though he wasn't really an influence, *Robert Durkin*, a Physical Education teacher and very much the stereotypical coach, can't be forgotten. He is memorable only because he pronounces volleyball "*volla-ball*" and we have made up a limerick about him. It goes like this:

> *There once was a Coach named Durkin*
> *Who was always jerkin' his gerkin'*
> *His father said "Durkin!*
> *Quit jerkin yer gerkin*
> *Yer gerkin's fer ferkin' not jerkin'*

🖎 ❏ ☞

With the exception of Coach Durkin, the atmosphere generated by the faculty's attitude toward the students produces a mix of intellectual devotion and openness while allowing for experimentation and inquiry. The result is a 180 degree shift away high school pursuits. We are now in an academic world. We do more than mimic the scholarly institutions that we would never have been able to enter. We become.

The pursuit of a degree has been replaced by a need to learn and there are no boundaries. "Fuck god," Skippy Cortelyou said. "Fuck God" George said as he drank ever more from the well of knowledge. And I said "Fuck God" too.

TWENTY-ONE
Bless the Apostles, the House Party, and Big Joe

AND NOW AN ACCOMPLISHED GUITARIST named Ric Shaefer shows up; he can actually read music and play notes and asks if we're interested in starting a band. We jump on board.

We start a group, with Ric as lead guitarist, Joe Auriemma, our drummer, and George on rhythm guitar. For the first few gigs, Ric leans forward before we begin and shows George where to put his fingers and the chord sequence. We start to play and as we muddle through, somehow, we finish. Though George's fingers may be bleeding by the end of the song, he has learned the chords.

We play mostly for fraternity keg parties for $20 apiece and all we can drink.

Van and the Apostles [Van on mike and George behind him at a fraternity gig]

155

Our signature song is *Night Train*. After a while we add a second drummer and incorporate a 'drum duel' into the act. That works for a while until a freshman named Van Apostalou shows up. Van is a stubby little guy, maybe 5'4" and he's not too bright, but his voice is priceless. He sounds exactly like Ray Charles. Van is the mythical white guy who sounds black.

So here we are with a singer who sounds like Ray Charles, but he has a problem with lyrics. He can't remember them. And he isn't very good at the kind of improvisation that comes effortlessly to real blues artists. So George writes down the lyrics to each song on 4 x 5 index cards (in large letters since Van's vision isn't all that great either) and Van reads and sings. He sings exactly as the lyric is written, even down to the *Yeah, Yeah, Yeah, Yeah* of our trademark song, *Peanut Butter.*

VAN:*There's a food goin' round that's a sticky sticky goo*
BACK-UP:*Peanuuut, peanut butter!*
VAN:*Oh well it tastes real good, but it's so hard to chew*
BACK-UP:*Peanuuut, peanut butter!*
VAN:*All my friends tell me that they dig it the most*
BACK-UP:*Peanuuut, peanut butter!*
VAN:*Early in the morning when they spread it on toast*
BACK-UP:*Peanuuut, peanut butter!*
VAN:*I like peanut butter, creamy peanut butter, chunky peanut butter too! Yeah! Yeah! Yeah! Yeah!*

We call the band *Van and the Apostles*, a play on Van's last name and I push through the music to give George the idea of them wearing robes and sandals and adopting an 'apostle' style look. (I'm clearly the girl with genius marketing skills, but George isn't much of a visionary, so the idea never gets beyond the suggestion stage.)

Having Van helps the band some. We get a few gigs off campus, even playing at a ski resort and there's a story the drummer, Joe, tells that sums up the situation best. He was at a party once where a group of people standing beside him were talking and he overheard their conversation. One of the girls says she heard a band at a ski resort a couple weeks earlier and they were terrible. At that, Joe turns and asks her the name of the resort and when she tells him he exclaims: "That was us! I'm the drummer in that band!" The girl begins to apologize for the insult, but Joe immediately stops her. "No..no…it's no problem," he says. "We <u>are</u> bad. In fact we're pretty awful. You must not have had enough to drink."

Looking back on it now, I'd have to say he was right. But playing and singing for a room full of drunks was an odd kind of fun for both of us. I enjoyed watching George do his music thing. I sang along with him as he slowly became drunk and I was entertained by his slurred words as he sang backup, trying to help Van struggle with the lyrics.

And then the Beatles and Paul Simon and others came along and the music went beyond the simple four chord progression that had got us through the early days.

☞ ❏ ☞

In the spring of 1963 George shares a room with Joe Ridky, a Senior, in a house uptown. The little room has bunk beds—George is on the bottom, Joe on the top—and one day when a class lets out early we come home unexpectedly and find Joe lying on his bed, looking at a magazine, turning the pages with one hand and "pleasuring himself" with the other. When we come in, he hurriedly tucks the magazine away under the covers and he and George exchange some small talk without any reference to what had been going on.

Later, when Joe leaves, we can't control our curiosity and look around for the magazine. We find it under the mattress (not the most creative place to put it.) It's titled *Muscle Boy* and pretty clearly was not intended to arouse the interest of straight males. George isn't aroused by it and neither am I and to some extent this immediately soothes some concerns about our sexuality. I consider then that I must be a lesbian because similar photos of women get George and I both aroused. But how that will play out if I ever get out, I'm not sure. And it scares me.

⚡ ❑ ☞

At the end of each school year the fraternities and sororities rent houses on Conesus Lake for a week and host non-stop parties. In the summer of 1963 we spend a week at the Clio's lake house. Clio is the informal name of a sorority Barbara belongs to. There's plenty of beer and most of the time is spent hanging out; playing cards is a major pastime. The fraternity and sorority members visit one another's houses, swim, and play games.

Barbara and George become the house cooks. That means taking up a collection, going to the store for supplies, and making a big pot of spaghetti. But the more interesting aspect of the Clio house party is the relationship the sorority has with Big Joe Vitale, a short, stocky, very Italian man who is the owner of a local construction and demolition company. Big Joe frequently appears at the Geneseo Hotel and often shouts, in a deep, booming voice "*Give everybody a little touch!*" and then makes a sweeping gesture with his hand to indicate that everyone at the bar is included in his largesse.

To understand the Big Joe/Clio relationship we have to go into some history to a time in the late 1950's when Big Joe had an arrangement with a girl named Barb Husher, a Clio member who it is said provides escorts for Joe's clients who come to Geneseo to do business with him. In return for this, the sorority girls are given favors of some sort, though exactly what those favors were we never knew. The story says that Barb is Joe's mistress and that the relationship ended when it became too blatant and the college administration got wind of it and called in the officers of the sorority to tell them that Barb was 'persona non grata' and that they had to divorce themselves from her. And so she was 'drummed out' but she remained living in the area. (Additional threads of the story say that Joe put her up somewhere and that she had a child by him.)

That's the history.

But we come back now, to the end-of-the-year Clio house party on the lake, where we are relaxing and enjoying our time off between the regular year and the summer session. It's late one morning, we're all slowly waking up from the night before when one of the sisters discovers a half dozen cases of champagne at the end of the driveway, a short way from the entrance to the house. And there's no doubt about where they came from. They are immediately carried down to the lake, as that's where we keep beer and anything else cold, and all but one bottle is submerged. We leave that one back in the house and that morning we celebrate decadence by brushing our teeth with champagne instead of water.

I wonder during those times, if I were in a sorority which one would it be. And would I consider being a Barb Husher? Is that what worries George? I probe his part of our mind, but I can't get an answer because he's lying in bed with Barbara and there's a DO NOT ENTER sign across the entrance to his mind. He's nothing but George then.

The following summer the college begins an expansion program which includes buying up houses on Wadsworth Street (which runs along the upper side of the campus). Those houses include a number of fraternity houses and the Clio house. And Big Joe's company gets the contract to demolish them. (The story we're told is that he isn't charging for demolishing the Clio house.)

One lazy afternoon that summer, George and three friends are playing cards in the Student Union when someone runs in and announces that "Big Joe is tearing down Clio House!" Everyone immediately leaves the Union and heads up the hill to Wadsworth Street and sure enough there's the house, or what's left of it. Most everything of value has been stripped from it so that only the shell remains, but it is still the Clio House, with the Clio logo over the front door.

Protruding from the center of the house, and stretching out through the front windows is a series of cables which cross the street and meet in a single bunch knotted together and tethered to a large bulldozer. And seated in the driver's seat of that bulldozer is Big Joe. The members of his demolition crew are nowhere in sight. There is a small crowd and the only sound is that of the bulldozer engine and as we arrive, it starts to grind slowly away from the house, pulling it down slowly and deliberately. Thus it is that Big Joe wreaks his revenge on Clio for dismissing his girlfriend and ending the 'escort arrangement.'

But despite all of that history, Joe retained a soft spot for the sorority, for a while later, when the pharmacy located at the corner of Main and Center Streets burns down, Joe and his crew get the demolition contract and shortly thereafter boxes upon boxes of make-up, hair products, and the like appear on the porches of the residences where Clio members are known to live.

☞ ❏ ☞

Like the story of Big Joe and CLIO, there are stories that circulate which we hear second-hand. They may or may not be true, though like a lot of legends there's probably an element of truth behind them.

The Legend of Quizzes and Tests says that one day when students show up for American Literature I or Biology 101 or some other Freshman level course they are greeted with instructions to take their seats and put their books away. As the professor passes out the blue test books, Marsha (or Gale or

Elsie) in the back row raises her hand and when the professor acknowledges her she says "Excuse me, sir, but what is this?" The instructor grins and replies "This is just one of my little Quizzies." To which Marsha responds "Gee…if this is one of your little quizzies, I'd hate to see one of your little testes." (Rim shot, please, Joe.)

The Legend of the Apollo Landing is about Larry, the resident jock, and his girlfriend, Lynn who are known for their public displays of affection and are often discovered in this or that corner of the campus having sex. Larry lives in the Delta Kappa house and over a period of two or three days he appears to be very nervous. Then, one day, the phone rings and one of the fraternity brothers answers. It's Lynn calling. "Larry's not here," the frat brother tells her.

"Oh…well.." she says, "can you give him a message?
"Sure."
"Tell him *the eagle has landed.*"

The frat brother hangs up, knowing full well the meaning of the message, so that by the time Larry returns to the frat house there are signs on the front door, on the door to his room, in the common area, and anywhere else a sign can be posted, proclaiming in large letters *THE EAGLE HAS LANDED!*

A few years later, in July of 1969, when the Apollo 11 Lunar Lander sits down on the moon, the message sent to earth is *the eagle has landed!*

"Oh my god," I said to George. "The astronaut is pregnant."

TWENTY-TWO
Drowning in Politics

RON CICORIA IS SUAVE, GOOD-LOOKING, smart, and popular. He's the Skip Cortelyou of Geneseo and in our junior year, Ron and George have become friends, mostly by virtue of sitting next to each other in Dr. Orwin's early morning Russian class. One day after class Ron tells George he wants to be President of the Student Senate and asks if he will help. George says he'll get back to him.

Cicoria's polar opposite is Everett Hall—built large, a bear, always unkempt and always dressed in a dirty, oversized sweater or sweat shirt and baggy cargo pants. When not in class, he hibernates. The windows to his dorm room are covered by black drapes. The sole lamp in the room has a thirty watt bulb, and the bulb has been removed from the overhead light. And he's always on the Dean's List.

Everett is a Political Science major and George goes to him to talk about the structure of campus politics. The way it has always worked is that the fraternities and sororities get together and create 'tickets' consisting of candidates selected from their membership. The elections are essentially a competition between the Greeks. You might not be sure who will get elected, but you can be sure it will be a Phi Sig or DK as President and an Ago or a Clio as Secretary. The majority of students, even though they may not even belong to one of those groups, goes along with 'the system'. But as George and Everett size up the situation, they reduce it to one question: "Where are the greatest number of votes?"

The answer is that in 1963 the majority gender at Geneseo is still female and the majority of those students do not belong to a sorority. The greatest number of votes belongs to the unaffiliated female. They far outnumber any other single group. And so that becomes the target population.

George and Everett form the Independent Student Party and they create a slate of four candidates spread out among the Greeks. The presidential candidate is Ron (he belongs to Phi Sig), the Vice-President is Lynn Stein, Bob Schultz is Treasurer (Lynn and Bob are in D.K.), and Brenda Dockery (she belongs to Ago), is Secretary. Once their commitment is assured, we go to their organizations.

What we tell them is this. We are running Ron, Lynn, Bob, and Brenda for these offices on our ticket. We want the fraternity or sorority to contribute $100 to the campaign and support our candidates, but not publicly. We explain this as part of our 'pitch.' Our people are going to run regardless of what the Greeks decide. And they're going to win. We're simply giving them the opportunity to be part of the operation.

I'm surprised at how comfortable George seems with this conniving. He has got everyone to agree to it and each of the candidates has made the commitment that they will run whether or not they have the backing of their group. That's a win-win situation for us. If the group agrees to our terms, we win. If they don't agree, we have even greater credibility as an independent organization.

We tell the candidates that they are to make no public appearances in conjunction with their organizations. Don't wear the fraternity or sorority blazer. Don't wear the fraternity or sorority pin. Don't hang out in the group's usual section of the Student Lounge area. In short, don't do anything to connect yourself to your group. The image we want to project is that of a renegade organization, taking on the insiders and running 'regular' students for office.

Independent Student
Party Logo

And the Greeks buy into it.

One of the most successful parts of the plan is a nighttime march and rally around the campus. To pull this off, George tells the fraternities and sororities (many of whose members live in their organization's houses) to plant members in the dormitories on the night of the rally.

"If you have a friend or know someone who lives in the dorm, find an excuse to drop by and visit…and don't wear your group's jacket or sweatshirt or pin," George says.

Then, George and Everett form a little group at the top of the campus and begin marching up and down the sidewalks in front of each of the dorms. George has composed lyrics to the song *Marching to Pretoria*, substituting the words *Marching for Cicoria*.

> *You vote for him and he'll work for you*
> *And we will work together,*
> *And we will work together,*
> *And we will work together,*
> *You vote for him and he'll work for you*
> *And we will work together,*
> *As we march along*
> *We are marching for Cicoria, Cicoria, Cicoria,*
> *We are marching for Cicoria, Cicoria, Hooray!*

As we come to each dorm, we stop for a bit and wait for students to come out to join in the fun, encouraged, of course, by the friends who have 'dropped by.' So by the time we reach the 'back campus' we have two or three hundred students singing and clapping. Then Ron gets up and makes a speech and introduces each of the other candidates and the next day the event is the talk of the campus.

Then comes a moment of unplanned and unexpected synchronicity. The Saturday night following the march there's a concert by *The Highwaymen*, a popular folk singing group of the time, in the Wadsworth Auditorium. It's part of the school's regular concert series and the auditorium is packed. It's all going along just fine until, about halfway through the show, the group launches into their rendition of *Marching to Pretoria*. But to their dismay, the audience joins in with George's lyrics…and the performers stop singing, but continue to play and stand back and listen to *Marching with Cicoria*. And that's when we know we've won the election.

We retire from politics while we're still ahead.

☞ ❑ ☞

Daryl Hanson has collaborated with Bert Stimmel, a Columbia University professor, on a number of shows (*Happy Prince, Christopher Columbus*, and *Waterbabies*). Over the summer of 1963, with some persuasion from Bob Sinclair, he agrees to collaborate with George on a show to be based on Milton's *Paradise Lost*. The idea comes from an offhand comment Sinclair made as a joke. The show is to be presented as part of the 1963Homecoming Weekend.

So that summer Hanson lets us live at his house and we work on the songs every day after our summer classes. And this is one of those situations where I am heavily involved in the creative process. George has a sense of theatre by now, but once I let <u>my</u> imagination loose, my ideas take precedence. There are three of us collaborating, but since I have no name yet, I'm not on the credits. This is not a time to let George's cat out of the bag.

The show we write is called *Paradise Misplaced* and the premise is that following a nuclear holocaust only two people are left, a man named Adam and a woman named Eloise. Given the chance for humans to start over, Satan sees an opportunity to repeat his initial triumph. But it's not what it seems. While Eloise is in favor of it, Adam doesn't want to start over. That's when Satan appears with a band of devils disguised as a survivalist Boy Scout troop, and Gabriel, the archangel, shows up with a band of angels (disguised as Girl Scouts), to counteract Satan's efforts; however, God intervenes and a battle ensues.

❧ ❑ ☞

By Spring Semester of 1964, SUNY Geneseo has a new gym with a swimming pool and college policy now requires that every student take a one semester swimming course. As Bonnie Woodworth knows all-too-well, George has never learned to swim. This shortcoming I attribute to an episode that occurred when we were about six. Father attempted to teach us to swim by carrying us on his shoulders into the ocean at Jones Beach and suddenly tossing us at the largest incoming wave. The results were disastrous. We nearly drowned and had to be dragged onto the beach shivering more from fear than cold. Mother complained, but Father insisted that that's how he learned, despite that the Green River in Livermore, Kentucky, had no waves, was continually muddy, and was only four feet deep. As a result, George and I share an abiding fear of drowning, for if George dies, I die too.

So we go to our first class and begin the slow process of trying to overcome our fear. (I'm curious to know how I might look in a swimsuit, but fear trumps curiosity at every turn.) After some time practicing the usual business of putting our face in the water and blowing bubbles, the teaching assistant assigned to George begins a routine with a long pole, which he places in the water and has George climb down, hand over hand, until he reaches the bottom, and then climb back up.

After a couple of weeks, the routine moves on to having us jump into the water alongside the pole and when we reach the bottom, grab the pole and climb up. It's scary, but we do it, closing our eyes as we glide to the bottom, then opening them and moving up the pole. It's all going swimmingly...until the teaching assistant decides we're ready for the next step, which is to remove the pole just after we jump in so that when we reach the bottom there's no pole to climb up.

No pole? Frantically, we're searching, but there's no pole. What now? Death by drowning; we are both convinced this is how it will all end. I'm feeling sorry that I will never be able to <u>be</u>, never to take the foreground, while George is oddly at peace. *We are going to die*, he thinks. *Ah well*. Goodbye George.

<u>Splash!</u> Within seconds there's a hand around our waist and we soar to the top of the water and get lifted out.

"What the hell are you doing?" the teaching assistant asks.

George, after a deep breath, says: "Drowning?"

"You got that right." The teaching assistant hands us a towel. "All you had to do was float up," he says. "Push off the bottom and float up."

We shrug.

The teaching assistant is shaking his head.

And we skip the swim class for the next few weeks.

But shortly before the end of the semester, we run into the teaching assistant.

"Hey."

We smile.

"You know if you don't come back you get an 'F.'"

We nod.

The teaching assistant sighs. "Listen," he says. "All you have to do is come in and swim one lap, the length of the pool. Dive in at the deep end and climb out at the shallow end and I'll give you a 'D.'

"One lap?" George reiterates.

The teaching assistant nods. "It's actually half a lap."

"Dive in at the deep end and climb out at the shallow end and I get a 'D'?"

The teaching assistant nods.

We consider the offer, then nod back. The teaching assistant extends his hand and George shakes it.

"See you tomorrow."

And the next day we walk to the gym, downstairs to the locker room, and change into swim trunks, then upstairs to the pool. *This has to happen fast*, George is thinking. *Don't think about it...just do it.*

Can I stay here? I ask.

We spy the teaching assistant at the far end of the pool, the shallow end.

"Hey!" George yells.

The assistant looks up and George immediately jumps into the water and begins splashing frantically, gasping for air, arms flailing and legs kicking so much that some seated on the nearby bleachers stand and point.

Progress is slow, but it's progress nonetheless, and gradually we make our way to the other end, standing up in the shallow water in front of the teaching assistant. He looks at us and smirks.

"I didn't think you'd make it," he says.

"A 'D'" George says. "You promised."

The assistant nods. "There's an advanced class next semester," he says, but he knows damn well we won't be there.

Another feature of the Spring semester of senior year is that George has decided to take the dorm rent money and instead of living in the dorm, he'll live out of his car, a 1950 Ford painted only with primer, which is much the same consistency as a blackboard and soon people have taken chalk from classrooms and writing messages on it.

Barbara is sharing a room in CLIO House with Linda Trabert, the Sorority president. The house is on the ground floor and frequently (especially on cold nights) George sneaks in and sleeps in their room. This nearly comes to an embarrassing halt one evening when the house mother comes into the room. Fortunately, George is in the bathroom and when he hears her he immediately steps into the shower/bathtub—just in time, as the house mother comes into the bathroom and sits down and pees.

The jumble of emotions bubbling up at this moment are almost unbearable. George is holding his breath, daring not to move, while I am torn between laughter and panic. The girls are talking to the house mother as she does her business and George and I are now about to do some business of our own.

At last the house mother is finished. The toilet is flushed, providing a short opportunity to gasp, as the house mother leaves.

TWENTY-THREE
A Geneseo Senior — A Geneseo Resident

I T IS FEBRUARY 4, 1964. Everyone is huddled in the living room at Clio House watching the Ed Sullivan Show. We sit through performances by Georgia Brown and Oliver Kidd, then Frank Gorshin, and then Tessie O'Shea. (There were quite a few Brits on the show.) And then...*The Beatles!*

Television is still in black and white and half the time the cameras are focused on the screaming, tear-streamed faces of teenage girls. We can barely hear the music over the din. Everyone watching the show is quiet. We know that something special is happening. We can't define it, but we feel it. The world, <u>our</u> world, is changing.

☜ ❑ ☞

Because we switched from majoring in Education to Liberal Arts we have to take two additional classes in the summer session of 1964. So once again, it's summer and we are in Geneseo, sharing an apartment with two guys. The apartment quickly becomes *Party Central,* serving as a beer stop for some and a crash pad for others. Rent parties are frequent and Barbara and George cook a lot of spaghetti to feed whoever is around. Beer collections are common and more than once the town cop (the only cop) comes banging on the door frame (the door is always open) and passes along complaints from neighbors.

Once someone slapped the cop on the shoulder with an unused tampon; that was the last straw. Shortly thereafter, a state trooper arrives, checks the ages of those at the party, and inquires about an "alleged feminine hygiene product." George begins an explanation that revolves around a stopped-up toilet and not having a plunger and one of the other partygoers manages to produce the unused, though now very wet, tampon. Displaying the unused tampon evidence makes the trooper visibly disturbed, but George pursues the subject, illustrating with wonder the amount of moisture said tampon has absorbed.

In the meantime, Barbara, to her credit, has curled up in a corner and gone to sleep. And so had I. And George has passed out.

❧ ❑ ☞

Barbara still has a year to go before graduating, so George finds a job teaching Junior High School reading at Letchworth Central School, about 25 miles from Geneseo. George moves into an apartment on the third floor of a house in town. He shares it with Bill Ryan, a free spirit much like D-Day in Animal House. He rides a Harley and says very little, but like so many friends we have made, he likes George and I have to wonder if he would like me, too.

We have no experience or training to qualify to teach reading and George is not certified to teach at a public school. But this is another case of things being synchronous without a plan. There's a 'loophole' in the state's teaching requirements that allow a school district to hire anyone they can get when they have been unable to find a qualified person and the school year is about to begin. And George is the best they can get.

As for the reading part of it—the school has purchased an 'out-of-the-box' kit which requires no skill or knowledge on the part of the teacher. Students take a test that puts them into one or another category, then work through a series of booklets, each concluding with a test they must pass before moving on. The routine is simple and we are thankful.

With the teaching job comes the opportunity to buy a new car and we jump at it. Before we even start work, we go to the bank and present the letter from the school district and that afternoon we drive away from the car dealer in a 1964 Poppy Red Convertible Ford Mustang.

Life is good…for a minute.

TWENTY-FOUR
The Father of the Bride

I DON'T RECALL GEORGE PROPOSING, THOUGH I was there during the hours he and Barbara sat around talking about their plans for the future, names for their babies, adoptions, Roy Rogers, and so on. It didn't become real until one evening during dinner at the Zechners when George simply announced it.

I never saw it coming. You would think that hanging out in someone's subconscious would give you a "heads up" in matters like these. But then I realize that George never planned it. As the words come blurting out I realize he is as surprised as I am.

"We're gonna get married," he proclaims during a lull in whatever conversation is going on.

Nothing.

Mrs. Geroge Wilkerson

WILKERSON-ZECHNER Barbara J. Zechner, a senior at the State University College, Geneseo and George Wilkerson, a graduate of State University College, Geneseo, who teaches at Letchworth Central School, were married Jan. 23, in Schenectady. Best man was Charles VanRy of Geneseo. Ushers were William Ryan, Oriskany, Robert Barbee of Batavia and Richard Barron of Mineola. Maid of honor was Nancy Zechner of Schenectady. Bridesmaids were Mary Kay Waggoner, Attica; Diane Opdyke, Newburgh and Gail Zechner of Newport, R. I. The couple will reside at 18 Prospect St., Geneseo.

Marriage Announcement
(Note the spelling of
George: Geroge)

Then her mother begins blinking…repeatedly…repeatedly…blinking.. blinking... blinking…as if George had poked her in the eyes, like Moe did to Curly.

Then her father belches, slides his chair back, gets up, drops his napkin on his plate, turns and walks to the back door, reaches out to the coat rack at the top of the cellar steps, puts on his jacket and hat, and leaves.

A few weeks later, Barbara is at home, sitting at the kitchen table, when her father walks in (probably wearing the same jacket and hat) and he drops a large sample book on the table in front of her.

"What's this?" she asks

"You want to get married," he says.

 "You're gonna get married. Pick one out."

The book is filled with sample wedding announcements. Her father has kicked the process into gear. He tells her he has leased the *Gwan Ho Ha Rod & Gun Club* for the reception and has hired a band.

"You wanna get married?" His voice echoes in her head, "You're gonna get married."

The wedding is set for January of 1965 at St. Gabriel's Church, just down the road from the Zechner home. Preparations are made and when the day arrives a major blizzard hits the area. Undaunted, everyone forges ahead. After all, this is upstate New York. Blizzard shmizzard.

Cut now to the scenes that stand out. The first is with the directions given by the priest at the obligatory pre-Cana conferences. Lying comes easy as George swears they will not practice birth control. (Fingers crossed—Barbara is already on 'the pill.') This is the same who will marry them and at the conclusion of the last meeting, the priest warns that they need to be prompt on the wedding day because he is leaving town to go on vacation and has a plane to catch. "No reception line at the church," he says, "and no damn crowd outside. Just walk down the aisle and drive away." This is all said as the good father's false teeth wildly slip from side to side, causing him to drench them in spit as he talks. And given these moist instructions, George promises that they will make a hasty escape immediately following the ceremony.

A few weeks later the wedding ceremony turns out to be brief, but it is followed by an hour-and-a-half long high mass, during which the bride and groom have to kneel at the altar for an ungodly amount of time. And now George is starting to itch and it is an itch that comes in the worst possible place, an itch that must be nature's way of asking why we're doing this. And finally, when George cannot stand it any longer, he reaches around and digs his fingers deep into his butt, scratching until he is satisfied, but then realizing too late that everyone in the church can see him. Muffled chuckles echo against the high ceiling as the priest's ill-fitting dentures spritz on the bride and groom:

*In sickness...s.ss...***(sptritz)** *and in health, 'til* **(sptritz)** *death do you part.*

At last it is over and George takes Barbara's hand and dashes to the church doors, stepping outside into the snowy daylight. He looks around and sees his new father-in-law's car, engine idling and parked directly at the bottom of the church steps. Bill Ryan, an usher, mutters something about how thoughtful Barbara's father is to do this and opens the rear door for us to get in, then runs around to the driver's side, climbs in, and speeds away, down the road toward the *Gwan Ho Ha Rod & Gun Club.*

❧ ❑ ☞

And where am I in all of this? Am I getting married? I don't think so. But I'm in the wedding and feeling George twist and squirm and sweat while I wonder how it would be to be wearing that wedding dress. I wonder how it would be to be prepared by the ladies of the family, coiffed and fitted while George must suffer the suit and tie. So I am in the car too, but as all so often, I'm just along for the ride.

❧ ❏ ☞

Guests are already at the club, but before long we learn that the waiting car Bill commandeered was not for us at all. Barbara's father had driven it up and left it running to go inside and get her mother. Without that car, her parents had to walk down the road, through the blizzard, back to their house, where her Dad had to load her mother into their pick-up truck and drive themselves to the club, all while her father is mumbling "She wanted to get married."

When they arrive, the reception line has already formed at the *Gwan Ho Ha Rod Club*. Guests pass by each member of the wedding party, introduce themselves, exchange pleasantries, and when they get to the groom, hand him an envelope of money. George's best man, his former roommate, Dutch, who is better known for his irreverence than his tact, is standing behind the wedding cake, a multi-tiered traditional iced cake with the little bride and groom dolls at the top and just as Toto and Bruna (just two of the Zechner friends with names like characters created by the Brothers Grimm), reach that spot, Bruna, who is wearing the standard little black dress, leans over to congratulate the bride and groom and comes away with a neat dollop of white icing on the tip of her left breast, to which Dutch exclaims: "Hey! No problem, lady! Just stick the other titty in there and no one will notice!"

❧ ❏ ☞

But there's more, for George has told everyone he is planning to fulfill one of his lifelong dreams; to sing at his own wedding. (Mind you, I was not part of that dream.) Given the questionable success of *Van and the Apostles,* he was feeling confident that this would be nothing less than a spectacular show of his talent. Never mind that he was warned solemnly by the father of the bride that were he to perform, and thus embarrass his father-in-law in front of friends and family, it would not end well. But George does not process these things very well…especially when alcohol is involved.

An hour or so into the reception, the band goes on their break and George goes to the bandleader and tells him of his wish.

"Sure," he says. "You're the groom! Here!" and he hands George his guitar whereupon George turns to the band members and asks if they're familiar with the Buddy Holly song *That'll Be the Day.* They all nod. George replies "In C," then slips the guitar over his shoulder, and begins to play a la Michael J. Fox's *Johnny B. Good* in the first *Back to the Future* film.

He has barely begun when I spy the new father-in-law at the back of the room, his face flush with anger and his fists clenched. And he is making his way toward us.

George playing guitar at the wedding reception

I try to warn him, but George holds his ground. He has had enough to drink that his courage is insanely greater than mine. *"That'll be the day"* he chants, *"When I die!"* Prophetic words? The irony of the lyric is not lost on me as I shut my eyes tight and wait for the inevitable.

But nothing happens. I wait, but I still hear George singing so I open my eyes and look around, but the father-in-law is nowhere near us. George finishes the song, bows to the applause, hands the guitar back to the bandleader, and steps down from the stage. I wonder if he realizes we have looked death in the eye and death has blinked. Only later do we learn that, as the father-in-law made his way toward us, friends were slapping him on the back and congratulating him on having such a talented son-in-law, so that he had no choice but to acknowledge the praise and act as if it was something he knew all along.

～ ❑ ☞

When Barbara and George return from Schenectady to the third-floor apartment in uptown Geneseo on Prospect Street, Barbara has a semester to go to finish her senior year and George has the job teaching reading at the Junior High School in Letchworth.

Bill Ryan shares the apartment with us. George and Bill had shared that apartment in the fall and Bill had plans to move out when Barbara moved in, but he can't find another place to live, he stays.

We're on the third floor. There's a rear bedroom at the back with an outdoor stairway down to the back yard, so Bill can come and go as he likes without disturbing us. Bill rides a motorcycle and is what people of the day call 'cool.' (He would probably be considered 'cool' even today.) Actors like James Dean and Marlon Brando established the image. In some ways he is George's male role model, though George knew he could never be him (and I certainly had no desire to go that route, except maybe as a rider hanging on to Marlon Brando's back).

One of the unique features of the apartment is the shower. It's squeezed into a corner where the roof of the house slants, so the shower stall is at an angle. Ryan likes it because the shower hits him in the chest and he can smoke and shower at the same time.

George must get up early and drive to Letchworth each day, but Barbara and Bill, both still students, get up later and Barbara gets to climb on the back of Bill's motorcycle for the ride down to campus. As they're leaving they wave at the two little old ladies who live in the house next store. They peer out from behind the curtains and shake their heads, probably conjecturing about three-ways and orgies and whatever else.

In the late afternoon, George returns home from the teaching gig and when we walk in the door Bill sticks a beer in George's hand and we would join the party that is already underway.

🐟   ☐   ☞

In the spring of that year, Barbara moves back to Schenectady to do her student teaching in Amsterdam and Bill and George (and I) stay in the apartment. George goes to Schenectady on the weekends and drives back to Geneseo on Sunday nights. On one of those nights, as he is driving, the hourly newscast reports a 'drug bust' in Geneseo at a "certain Prospect Street address." *How interesting,* I think. *I wonder which house it was.*

When we arrive home the house is empty. The door is unlocked, but that's not unusual. A number of friends have keys to the place and when we're gone they use it as a kind of 'love nest,' often leaving alcoholic gifts like a six-pack in the frig or a bottle of whisky on the counter. But this night there are no presents, just a messy house. So we assume there has been a party and crawl off to bed.

The next morning we are off to Letchworth Junior High to try and teach pre-pubescent kids to read when, about halfway through the morning, the Principal appears at the classroom door and motions to George to come outside. He asks him to go to his office and stays to watch the class for him while he's gone.

When we arrive at the office we discover the Sheriff. He extends his hand, asks George his name, and asks if he lives at 18 Prospect Street in Geneseo. George nods 'yes' and the Sheriff gestures for him to sit down. What follows is a polite series of questions concerning our whereabouts over the weekend, activities for the past couple of weeks, and our relationship with a student named Tom Hermann.

Tom Hermann--folk-singer and math major. Heck of a nice guy. And one of the Prospect Street key holders. But George doesn't mention that last part. We find out that Tom has been arrested for drug possession (marijuana) and that the arrest took place at our house, which they had searched without finding anything. The Sheriff thanks George and we return to class considering the value of teaching pre-pubescents to read.

Sometimes I wish George would just back off and let me take care of the details. That's not to say some of my anal retentiveness doesn't seep into George's behavior, but at other times it's just not enough.

Such was the case for Barbara's graduation. The graduation ceremony is held at the new gym and each graduate is allowed two tickets. George is gracious and when the question comes up about who will get those tickets he says "Sure…your parents, of course."

Unfortunately, when graduation day comes, George has put them in his jacket pocket and drives off to the *Big Tree Inn,* to drink, while the parents head down to the gym, expecting the tickets to be waiting for them there. I know where the tickets are, and where they ought to be, but once again, all I can do is watch and wait for the proverbial shit to hit the fan, driving another nail into George's coffin. Indeed, there never seems to be a shortage of metaphors when it comes to George's life.

Fortunately, a friend of Barbara's is working the door and upon learning that George did not pass on the tickets, she lets the parents in. And the warm and loving relationship between George Wilkerson (the shit) and John Zechner (the fan) continues.

But the best is yet to come.

GEORGE WILKERSON

TWENTY-FIVE
Universitas Syracusana*

L EO ROCKAS, A SHORT, ENERGETIC professor who can actually speak Greek (because that's what he is) and is steeped in Aristotle is one of George's English professors at Geneseo. He teaches Creative Writing and lets us sleep on his sun porch in the summer. He critiques George's work and through his contacts at Syracuse University he gets George accepted into their Creative Writing Masters degree program.

So it is that in the summer of 1965 we are in an apartment in Syracuse University's Married Student Housing. It's essentially a set of old Army barracks—wooden shacks. There are four units to a building and each unit is probably no more than 600 square feet. The buildings are adjacent to an area known as Skytop, which is rumored to be a military intensive training center for foreign languages that employs Syracuse University language professors.

⬿ ☐ ☞

Also at Married Student Housing is Doug Brode, who graduated Geneseo in 1965 (Barbara's class). He's short too, and Jewish, and quite full of himself as a fledgling writer. While at Geneseo he and Bob Root (also in Barbara's class) and George hung around together. They were "the" writers on the campus. Doug is a movie aficionado and whenever he has an idea for a story or play he decides on the title first.

[* The Latin form of Syracuse University as it appears on the Masters Degree]

The Viet Nam war is heating up and legend has it that when Doug's draft notice came, his mother went to the draft board and told them in no uncertain terms that her 'baby boy' was not going into the Army, that he would be going to graduate school, and that was the end of that. We wondered how Doug got into the program at Syracuse; maybe his mother was behind it.

Doug is married to Sue and they live a block away. We never had a conversation with Sue or heard her say more than a few words, probably agreeing with whatever Doug said. (Another rumor is that before they were married, Doug gave Sue a list of 100 books he expected her to read.) Sue is shorter than Doug and is pasty-faced. The reason, we're told, is that as a teenager she was attacked by a dog and there is a massive scar on her face which she hides under a thick layer of make-up. We don't know if it's true, but whether it is or not, we expect it to show up in one of Doug's plays or stories. (Doug will go on to have a career as a film critic at the local Syracuse TV station and as a teacher at the local community college. He also taught at Syracuse U. and wrote a number of books about films.)

One day there's a knock on our door and when George opens it Doug is standing there looking sheepish. Before George can say anything, Doug explains that he needs help with something and would we come down to his place. So we follow him to their barracks/apartment and once inside Doug points to the ceiling and flips the wall switch. The light doesn't come on and when George asks him if he has checked the bulb he says something we aren't surprised to hear—he had never changed a light bulb.

So we changed it for him.

☜ ❏ ☞

In addition to having Doug around, we meet Vaughn Bode. Vaughn is a popular cartoonist; he writes a strip for *The Daily Orange* and later will do a popular underground strip called *Cheech Wizard* for *National Lampoon*.

That fall Vaughn draws some original pieces for the advertising for plays George writes as part of his graduate program. One of the drawings is for a piece called *Solitaire*.

Solitaire Poster

Another friend we make is a film major, Ric Sternberg who later is part of the 'goes around comes around' *Solitaire* history. Sternberg will make the skit into a short film and George will convert it into a rhyming piece for *Esther's Follies* in Austin, Texas.

But I'm getting ahead of myself. Ric and George hit it off right away. George finishes his Masters degree, but Sternberg doesn't graduate, due in part to the fact that his fraternity was banned from the campus after an incident involving sexual exploits with the daughter of one of the University's administrators.

For a Master's thesis George writes a play about Mark Twain's daughter, *Suzy*. It's not very good; probably because he lost interest in it about halfway through. And honestly, I never cared much for it either. I had no part in its development. As part of the research, we go down to New York City and meet with Hal Holbrook, who is appearing on Broadway in a revival of his one-man show, *Mark Twain Tonight*. Holbrook's rendition of Twain is excellent, but during our time with him backstage he tells us that the motive for this revival is financial. He is well-known for his portrayal of Twain, but has a hard time getting roles on stage or in film and needs the money. He's sick of Twain, so he's not a very helpful resource. (I'm pleased to say that he did manage to escape the Twain trap, but at this writing I learned he's on the road doing Twain again, though now he doesn't need as much make-up.)

About three-fourths of the way through the Masters program, the department chair tells George that he's not considered a good candidate for the Ph.D. program (which is where the Masters is supposed to lead) and offers him the option of taking the Masters degree and calling it a day. And he accepts, thus leaving us in Syracuse without a job. Barbara has been working at a number of low paying jobs, having quit teaching in one of the city's high schools after a lack of support from the school's administration and the grueling work of trying to teach kids who don't want to be there gets to be too much to bear.So we begin searching for work and find (and get) a job teaching at Cortland High School (about 30 miles south of Syracuse). Barbara is hired as well. For the first time there will be some decent money coming in. Double-income. No kids. Here we come!

Sometime during this time period we decide to attend a class reunion at Geneseo and we hook up with old friends Dick and Katie Barron, and Bob and Linda Barone. We agree to share a room at the *Big Tree Inn*, which is almost in the center of town and just uphill from the campus. Everything will be within walking distance. And we begin drinking immediately upon our arrival.

We have a room on the second floor overlooking the roof of the Inn's front porch. Built in 1886, the Inn is quite old and not in the best of shape. (It had been purchased by the College's Campus Auxiliary Services and been refurbished, but still needed some work.)

The room already has two beds and after we request an extra bed and get a rollaway there's not much room left to move around. There's a sink in the far corner and a common toilet down the hall. Nonetheless, we three couples (and me) arrive and get along just fine, reminiscing over drinks and taking turns getting 'dressed up' for the alumni dinner and dance which is being held in the newly constructed Mary Jemison Cafeteria.

At the dinner/dance we visit with other alums, dance a bit, and very shortly find ourselves 'under the weather.' Barbara and George both agree we aren't up for any more partying and excuse ourselves to go back to the room and 'crash.' And shortly thereafter we are joined by Dick and Katie and soon we are all asleep, when…

SLAM!! The door flies open and the overhead light flicks on as if a meteor just crashed through the roof. Standing there, carrying an industrial-size pot (each holding one of the handles on either side) are Bob Barone and another alumni, Bill Weitsman. Standing behind them, clearly unamused, is Linda Barone, shaking her head and apologizing. "I'm sorry. I really…"

"Party Poopers!" Barone exclaims.

We sit up and rub our eyes, watching as Barone and Weitsman squeeze their way to the center of the room and drop the pot onto the floor.

"Party Poopers!" Barone exclaims again. "You poopers pooped, so we're bringing the pooping party to you!" It's amazing that he can say that while in his condition. He reaches into the pot and lifts out a large (also industrial-size) ladle and offers it to all of us. "Punch with a punch," he says, grinning.

Dick Barron, our perennial peacekeeper, smiles and says "Thanks, Bob, but you know it's kinda late…"

"Late? Kinda late?" He turns to Weitsman. "It's late?"

Weitsman shakes his head and looks at his watch. "Two o'clock."

"There you go," Barone says. "The night is young!" and he holds out the punch-filled ladle. "C'mon…I got a whole bottle o' vodka in here."

Now Linda steps up. "I told you this wasn't a good idea," she says and motions toward the door. "C'mon."

"C'mon?!" Bob exclaims, waving his arms frantically. "You want to c'mon?"

Linda reaches for his arm. "Bob."

The ranting and raving escalates and then, the climax. As Linda is about to leave, Bob slams the door shut. "I don't think so!" he says.

It's a loud slam, meant to punctuate his exclamation, and it works. It works so well that it results in the door knob coming apart. The spindle, the part needed to make the latch turn when the handle is turned, falls outside, into the hallway, and all that's left inside the room is the handle. The door cannot be opened and we are trapped in the room with a mad man.

"I'm leaving!" Bob shouts, waving the knob at us. "Let me out of here!"

Weitsman reaches out to calm him. "You broke the door, Bob."

"Fuck that," Bob says, and throws the knob on the floor. "I don't give a shit. Fuck you," he says, to no one in particular. "And fuck you, too. Who has a razor?"

Linda now tries to calm him down. "Sit down Bob."

"I'll slash my wrists," he yells. "Right here, right now! Who's got a razor?"

Dick Barron, relatively quiet until now, reaches into his suitcase, grabs an electric razor, and hands it to Bob.

Of course, the joke goes over Bob's head. He rejects the razor and turns to Linda and grabs her arm. "C'mon," he says. "We'll drive the goddamn car into a tree."

Linda pulls back. "<u>You</u> can drive the car into a tree," she says. "<u>I'm</u> staying here."

In the meantime, Weitsman has opened the window overlooking the porch and is about to climb outside.

"What are you doing?" George asks.

"Can't stay here," Bill says, stumbling out and onto the porch. "Hey! Anybody down there?"

Perhaps he was heard. Maybe someone came up and opened the door and Bob and Linda left. But if they did, they didn't drive into a tree. They stumble away. Somehow we all escape, alive, and the Big Tree had another legend to add to its history. George and Dick and Bob remain friends, though the incident is never mentioned in any conversations afterward.

〜 ❑ ☞

That Christmas George gets a Volkswagen Microbus and at vacation time a crowd of people wanting a ride home pack into the VW and rather than drive the New York Thruway to Schenectady we take what's called the Ridge Road (Route NY104) to avoid the Thruway tolls. A snow storm a couple days earlier left the roads, though mostly plowed, still dense with the white stuff and the high drifts on the sides of the roads made some of them into bobsled runs.

Part of the fun of the VW was that it doesn't have a lot of horsepower, but if everyone lunges forward together it seems to help get it up the hills; however, going downhill requires more care. Halfway home we come over a hill leading down to a small town where there is only one traffic light situated at the bottom. Instinctively, George steps on the brake, but George's instincts are wrong. Within moments the VW starts to skid. He slams harder on the brakes (I try to tell him what a bad move that is, but he is too scared to listen to me). The bus begins to spin and as if in slow motion it spins and slides down the hill, but it stays on the road. (Devout Christian readers will affirm it was the hand of God, but I can promise you, He was busy with other matters right then.)

Everyone in the bus chants "Shiiiiittt" as if on some carnival ride, until we finally come to rest directly under the lone signal light. The only sound is that of everyone panting, their gasps ringing against the walls of the little bus. I swear, if I didn't know him better, I might think George is trying to kill me.

☜ ❏ ☞

In the Syracuse summer of 1967, shortly after George begins coursework in the Masters degree program, a notice comes in the mail. "Greetings," it begins, but we already know what it is— the draft board is inviting George to come in for his physical.

One of our ongoing fears, going all the way back to the gym showers in high school, is that someone might somehow identify us for what we are. Unfounded? Probably, but they are wrapped up in that package of worries and concerns we always carry around. Be careful how you cross your legs, George. Be sure to walk like a man. Don't act too emotional. Avoid all things that might give away <u>my</u> presence.

So having to get totally undressed and stand in a circle with a couple dozen others in the same condition is beyond intimidating and as the doctor walks around behind each of us and examines our feet, our legs, our rectums, all we can do is strike the most masculine pose we can conjure up for the occasion. "Who do you think you're fooling," I whisper to George. "Do you really want to wear boots and carry an M-16? This isn't a Hopalong Cassidy western and that guy next to you isn't Jimmy Jingles."

To no avail. We're now told to step into the next examining area. Only it isn't an examining area. It's a seating area and everyone there is given a pen and forms to complete....while completely naked.

We dutifully answer questions on a variety of subjects, including family history and physical and psychological health. And that's where <u>the</u> question jumps out at us, though it's actually one of a series of choices on a list following the question *Have you ever experienced any of the following?*

Irrational Fear ☐ YES ☐ NO
Unexplained angry outbursts ☐ YES ☐ NO
Voices in your head ☐ YES ☐ NO
Mood Swings ☐ YES ☐ NO
Homosexual tendencies ☐ YES ☐ NO

Whoa! Cue the bells and whistles and fireworks. Nothing else on that list or on any of the other forms even comes close. Are we homosexual? No matter. If having me there with George isn't somewhere in the mix of that phrase then nothing else is.

☑ **YES** we check with a shaking hand.

Shortly after that, the sergeant in charge comes by and picks up our papers and has us form two lines to take the eye exam, but by then, thank goodness, we have put our clothes back on. George stands up to the examiner's wooden box and we press our face against a metal plate which has cushioned openings for our eyes.

"Read the first column," the examiner says.

"E, F, P, T, O, Z, L, P, E, D

"Now read the middle column."

"A, O, E, H, L, A, N, T, C"

"Now read the column on the right."

"On the right?" we ask.

"Yes."

George chuckles. "There is no column on the right."

"Hmmm," the examiner mutters, followed by a soft, clunking, sliding sound.

"Now?" the examiner asks.

"Oh...yes..." George says, and proceeds to rattle off the third column's letters.

Another soft, clunking, sliding sound.

"Gone," George says. "The third column is gone."

"Close your left eye," the examiner says.

"Oh!" Somewhat shocked, we open and close the left eye and the third column appears and then disappears.

The examiner makes some notes, then tells us to step back. "You need to see an ophthalmologist," he says and motions for George to follow the others who have returned to the seating area.

One by one now the potential draftees names are called and they are taken to the exit and sent on their way until, at last, George's name is called. But we are not guided to the exit. Instead, we are taken to an office just outside of the seating room. A man in uniform sits seated behind a wooden desk and as soon as we are seated he extends a familiar page of paper and points to the YES checkbox.

"Do you understand this?" he asks.

For the first time, someone is opening the door to my existence and I hesitate. I don't want to go to war. I know something awful will happen to me, and to George, if I go. He may not get killed or wounded. He may not be a complete failure as a soldier, though he's pretty sure he wouldn't make it through basic training. But he very well may be forced to deal with me in ways that have always frightened him. So I step back.

And George nods.

The officer continues. "Do you want to explain why you checked that?"

"Sometimes…" George stammers, "Sometimes…I…."

"Go ahead," I whisper. "Tell him."

He takes a deep breath, sighs, and then: "Sometimes I dress in girls clothes."

The officer pulls the paper back and jots a note on it, then looks up at us. "And what do you do then?"

George shrugs. "Just…you know…hang out."

"Do you go out in public?"

George shakes his head. "No sir."

"Is there anyone else around when you do this?"

Again, George shakes his head. "No sir."

The officer jots down another note. "Do you believe you are homosexual?"

George pauses, then replies hesitatingly. "I don't know."

Another note gets jotted down, then the officer looks up at us—a long, hard look—then motions to the door. "You can leave."

Without hesitating, we walk to the door and step into the seating area which is now empty. All of the others have left. The exit sign on the opposite side of the room beckons and we make a controlled dash for it.

It will be close to twenty years before George ever openly discusses our relationship with a psychological professional.

GEORGE WILKERSON

TWENTY-SIX
Blackboard Jingles

L ATE IN 1968 BARBARA AND George are hired to teach at Cortland High School. As with the job at Letchworth, the school can hire them because there are no state certified teachers available. We move to Cortland, rent an apartment, and begin teaching—George, English and Barbara, Speech.

The Civil Rights Movement continues and the war in Viet Nam has heated up; the mood of the country is tense. Peace marches, love-ins, and pot smoking are the order of the day and the Wilkersons are joining in.

The only local problem is with the high school's principal, a man named John Gee. He rules with an iron fist and soon George and Barbara are ranked high on his shit list. They're obviously hippies. George's hair is too long (though I reveled in that) and Barbara's skirts are too short (and George reveled in that). As a result, a particular kind of student likes us—the kind who challenges authority and relishes the new age thinking. And it is also why we hook up early on with Anne Ash (another English teacher) who recently moved to Cortland from Muncie, Indiana where she completed a Masters degree in Education and been involved in theatre. Spotting kindred souls, she immediately reaches out to us, invites us to dinner at her place, and fills us in on Mr. Gee and the culture of the school.

Another teacher we connect with, though not so much as Anne, is Bob Van Gorder. He is also an English teacher. He graduated from Cortland High and had gone into construction work, getting into the operation of heavy equipment—giant back-hoes, earth moving vehicles, and the like. It paid well, but he had always wanted to teach, so he left that work and returned to college and completed a B.S. in English Education at SUNY, Cortland and then went to teaching at Cortland High School.

Bob is the classic down-to-earth guy. He has a large family (six kids) and has us over to dinner on a couple occasions. Once, at the end of the meal, he leans back and comments that he is satisfied with the meal, but now he has to go to the bathroom, then goes on to say he is so full he can't get up, so he asks his four year old son to go for him. And sure enough, the boy dutifully rises and leaves the room, only to return a few minutes later, tears in his eyes, to apologize to his father because he wasn't able to do it. Considering the episode later, we decide that it is either child abuse or the funniest parent-child interaction we ever witnessed.

In many ways, Anne is what is described in those days as an *Earth Mother*. She is in tune with things, is very well read, extremely articulate, and does not tolerate fools. (She can finish the Sunday New York Times crossword puzzle in about one hour in ink.)

She married early to a man who was in the military and treated family members as if they were part of his platoon. He would order the children (as well as his wife) to 'police the area' and assign them duties like KP. He could be extremely violent, so during one of his extended drunken disappearance, she moves to Muncie, where her only sister lives, divorces him, and goes back to college.

The year at Cortland is a strange mixture of madness and color. The students, by and large, are great, despite Mr. Gee's attempts at establishing the Cortland High School K.G.B. George accepts an assignment as teacher of the dumb and troubled, but they're neither. They are the students who have been assigned to that category because school just doesn't do a good job of capturing their spirit. These students are much like George was, only without the more stringent controls of the nuns. (Mr. Gee's efforts pale by comparison.)

In the classroom, George arranges seats in a circle and encourages the students to say whatever they feel. Having been given an expurgated version of *A Tale of Two Cities*, George waves it in front of the class and says "You don't deserve to be cheated out of the good stuff," then marches everyone to the book room and swaps out their book for the complete version. And that creates the first notation on his teaching record.

Undaunted, while the weather is warm he takes the class outside and they sit on the grass and read poetry. And later, he lets them pick topics from the syllabus and take turns teaching.

Strike two.

Now George is told to get a haircut, as the school rule is that all boys hair must go no farther than the top of their collar. So he gets a haircut that barely complies. And in the meantime, Barbara gets sent home to change her clothes because her skirt is too short. (Mr. Gee has a habit of stopping girls in the hallway and making them kneel down, the rule being that any skirt that does not touch the floor when one is kneeling is too short. Barbara did not have to kneel down. She shops in the petite section. Miniskirts are in and I'm missing out.)

❧ ☐ ☞

On a particularly nice day after school a knock comes on the apartment door. Three of George's students invite themselves in and present a gift—about five gifts actually, all neatly rolled to about four inches long, twisted at the end, and ready to be smoked. This has to be the best student/teacher relationship one can have, though Barbara is frequently looking out the window to see if the police have arrived.

That year is as packed as the VW microbus. The *Sergeant Pepper* album is released, we set off a nuclear bomb in the Mojave desert, Mohammed Ali is indicted and sentenced to five years in prison, Evel Knieval jumps his motorcycle over 14 cars, Thurgood Marshall becomes the first black Supreme Court Justice, the Smothers Brothers TV show begins and our Father nearly has his second heart attack as William Shatner and Nichelle Nichols of *Star Trek* share the first interracial kiss on American television

When the end of the school year comes, Mr. Gee sends out a message saying that although final grades are due by Tuesday, teachers must come to work on Wednesday, Thursday, and Friday. This is announced at a faculty meeting held in the cafeteria at noon on Tuesday.

Bob Van Gorder raises his hand and the Principal calls on him.

"There's nothing to do the rest of the week," Bob says. "This is stupid. What happens if we don't come in?"

"You don't get paid," the Principal replies.

"Screw that," Bob says. "I can go drive a dump truck on those days and make three times what I get paid for being here."

The veins on the Principal's neck start to puff out. "You don't get paid," he repeats. "And you don't have a job here next year."

Bob picks up his briefcase, steps away from the table, and says "Fine by me" and walks out.

Subconsciously, the faculty applauds. But in reality, we all sit quietly. *It's just another sign*, George thinks, *that public school teaching is not a good career choice.* And this time, I agree with him.

That afternoon, when the mail comes, there are two notices, one for George and one for Barbara, stating simply that their contract for the next year will not be renewed. As for Bob, he doesn't come back either. He packs up the family and heads to Wassila, Alaska. (In 1996 Sarah Palin becomes Mayor there and later, the Governor, but Bob stayed there nonetheless.)

Near the end of their time in Cortland George and Barbara decide to move to New York City so George can write the Great American novel or the Great American play or the Great American screenplay. Ric Sternberg is already there and he encourages George to come. It's early summer, 1968, the summer of love. They get a fourth-floor walk-up on Ninth Avenue, around the corner from the Chelsea Hotel and jobs in Greenwich Village, Barbara as a clerk at the Capezio shoe store and George as a clerk at the Marboro Book Store, around the corner from each other. They work late shifts, from mid-afternoon to late in the evening. Their days consist of mundane chores like shopping for groceries or, on weekends, getting the New York Times right after it has been thrown off the delivery truck and then going to a deli for a midnight sandwich.

Do I have a voice in any of this? No. I am a ghostly spirit, waiting for Scrooge to knock on the door and see me, only I'm starting to think George will never knock on <u>my</u> door, never let <u>me</u> come in. Apart from playing 'dress up' (a depressing activity since Barbara wears clothes that are way too small for me), I can only keep my distance and try to restrain myself.

Within a couple weeks of our arrival, four of the students from Cortland show up and ask to hang out with us. They're free spirits, spending their days panhandling, their afternoons in a nearby park ('scoring weed'), and their evenings roaming the streets and hanging out with others their age, usually in the Village, sometimes stopping into the book store to say hi. One weekend they pile into the VW bus and we all go to Jones Beach. They have never seen the ocean and it's worth the trip to watch them play in the waves and build castles in the sand.

One of the nicer aspects of their visit is that they panhandle for as much money as they need to eat for the day, then give the remainder to one or another of the older, established panhandlers, starting anew the next day. This is the hippie era and there are hundreds of kids just like them—boys with shoulder-length hair and girls wearing tie-dyed bandanas and tank tops—the images that become clichés, but at the time represent a dramatic mood, a warmth and affection among people that is unlike anything before or since. They stay for a couple weeks and one of them writes to George a few times, but the letters stop within a few months and we never hear from them again.

Ric Sternberg and his wife, Terry, have an apartment in the Village. Ric somehow got a deal working as the superintendent for the building (there are only four units) and has a daytime job as a news cameraman at CBS television. During this time, George and Ric collaborate on a short film, a version of the piece George wrote while at Syracuse—*Solitaire*. Ric has managed to get some black and white film CBS is discarding because now they're going to broadcast in color and he makes arrangements to get the use of an empty loft. Meanwhile, George contacts a Geneseo friend named Mark Limerick who, while at Geneseo, was openly gay, though given his extreme feminine behavior most people would have guessed it.

Solitaire is a strange sort of sketch. I thought it was clever, but when I pushed it to the forefront of George's consciousness, he had no idea where it came from. The only connection in George's experience is with Grandfather Cook, who spent hours at the kitchen table playing the card game. He taught George how to play, passing along tips like 'get your aces out early.' (Maybe there's a metaphor in that somewhere.)

It involves three men, each playing solitaire, and a fourth dressed in a vest and dealer's eyeshade who periodically runs onstage screaming madly, wielding a dustpan and broom, who sweeps up the players cards and then runs off. Each time he does this, the players produce a new deck of cards and start over. And each time, they chant:

Of all the games we play or dare
The only game is Solitaire

As the skit progresses it becomes evident that the sweeper's actions are being initiated by one of the card players (the last to enter) who creates trash first by taking a sandwich from his pocket, unwrapping it, and tossing the paper over his shoulder then, following the sweeper's onslaught, producing a candy bar from another pocket, removing the wrapper and throwing that over his shoulder, and finally, taking an apple from another pocket and, after a few bites, tossing that over his shoulder as well. At this point, two of the three men go to the third man, lift him out of his chair, and throw him offstage. They then resume their game until a wicked laugh signals the entrance of the man just thrown off who is now dressed in the sweeper's vest and eyeshade and who comes onstage and sweeps away their cards.

George and Ric are making a film of that script and so Mark Limerick flies in from wherever he's living at the time and we go to the loft and launch into it. George plays one of the parts,

Mark another, and a couple of Ric's friends play the remaining two characters.

Looking back on it, I now realize that it didn't work. I had a clever idea, but George's script just didn't work. Years later, though, writing for *Esther's Follies* in Austin, Texas, George drags out the piece and I'm immediately struck with the solution and coach him in rewriting it as a rhyming piece, with that recurring phrase:

> *Of all the games we play or dare*
> *The only game is Solitaire*

But not now; the version we're filming now gets shot in 16mm and a sound track is later dubbed in, as if we're hearing the thoughts of the characters. Ric adds music to it, but it never really works.

☜ ❏ ☞

In the Winter of 1968 we are still living in the fourth floor walk-up on Ninth Avenue and barely eking out a living, cursing the bitter cold winds blowing through the Manhattan canyons when George sees an ad in the Sunday *New York Times* for an instructor position at a community college in Virginia. The ad says the Dean will be in New York to conduct interviews. So he signs up, takes his resume to the hotel where said dean is conducting interviews, and spends an hour talking to him. A couple weeks later he gets a letter with a job offer. And we take it.

The school is John Tyler Community College and it's located about thirty miles south of Richmond. George and Barbara pack up as much as possible, scrape together enough money for plane tickets, and head off for Virginia.

"Look at those birds," George exclaims, pointing out the window when the plane hits the runway in Richmond. "Why haven't they flown south."

Barbara sighs. "This is the south," she says.

TWENTY-SEVEN
Y'all Come Back Now, Ya Hear?

AMONG THE FRIENDS GEORGE MAKES at the college is John Butler, a former elementary school principal now teaching college English. He's tall, in his fifties probably, and carries himself with the stature of a statesman. He has the demeanor of a gentle giant, and yet, the man is devious. He is calculating and controlling, but only in self-defense. "*Phenomena is hostile*" is his mantra. It's a way of seeing things we have never encountered. And he offers George career advice of a sort he hasn't heard before.

"Don't blow your own horn." he says. "Indirect compliments are the best. You want someone to be flattered by you? Get someone else to tell that person that you said you think he's brilliant." John Butler will soon demonstrate the efficacy of his world view.

Community colleges in the sixties are a fairly new phenomenon. Their 'open door policy' operates in sharp contrast to colleges that use S.A.T. scores and formal applications to enroll students. Most of the older faculty don't understand what's going on. They want to be *'professeurs'* and, as John Butler explains it, "They want to stand at the podium and speak *ex cathedra*." But the newly appointed, younger president of the college wants that to change and he finds the mechanism in a consortium run by a federal program of education laboratories. A team of 'trainers' is brought in from the lab and they conduct workshops on writing course objectives and using testing methods that do away with grade curves.

George is the youngest person on the English faculty and the new ideas appeal to him. He sees the approach as a way to get the games his teachers played out of the classroom, a way to 'level the playing field.' It suits his rebellious personality, though if he truly wanted to rebel, I wonder, why not rebel against the gender patrol. Open up and let <u>me</u> loose. You want rebellion? *I'll* show you rebellion. So maybe he's just redirecting <u>my</u> desire to rebel as a way to push back when I push to move forward. But I let it go; this sort of psychoanalysis just gives me a headache.

The faculty don't embrace the new ideas and George often vents his frustration to his new friend, John, who smiles and says "Maybe you should be department chairman."

George laughs. "Not likely," he says.

John laughs. "How about it," he asks. "Would you like to be department chairman?"

"Sure," George says.

John nods knowingly. "Consider it done."

And within a few weeks the president of the college announces a reorganization of the administration that creates a Humanities Department that includes English, Speech, and Foreign Languages, and George is named chair.

I'm as flabbergasted as George is. What did Butler do?

George names John Butler as his assistant and sets about conducting interviews for a secretary. And here's where I come in, but not in a good way.

Among those who interview is a young woman whose sense of style is not very elegant, but I envy her. Miniskirts and cleavage comprise most of her wardrobe and I want to see more of that. "Hire that one," I whisper, and this time he listens.

As you might expect, the new secretary is more interested in doing her nails and fixing her hair than she is in secretarial work, but I could watch her all day and I take mental notes for the time when I get to come out. This puts George in another one of those struggles between his logical self and his feminine self—me. And I win this one.

☜ ❏ ☞

In addition to the secretary, George has to hire an English teacher to take his place on the faculty and his thoughts immediately jump to Anne Ash. He contacts her (she's now living in Vermont) and tells her that if she applies he will do his best to see that she gets the job. And she applies and along with the application form and other paperwork, she submits the name and address of her previous employer: that's John Gee from Cortland High School. Remember him?

The college's Human Resources people follow the standard practice of requesting a reference from the former employer and very shortly the 'employment packet' arrives on George's desk and in it there's a letter from Mister Gee with the following sentence.

"During Mrs. Ash's employment, she and two other employees (George and Barbara Wilkerson) were a constant source of aggravation and disruption. I strongly advise you to contact me further if you are considering hiring her or either of them."

George and I both enjoyed what George did next.

"Put down the nail polish and take a letter," he said to the secretary, and once she took out her steno pad he began to dictate: "*Dear Mr. Gee*" he wrote, "*Thank you so much for the information concerning Mrs. Ash and her associates. I will most certainly be careful in that regard. Sincerely, Mr. George Wilkerson, Chairman, Humanities Division, John Tyler Community College.*"

☜ ❏ ☞

Before they got married, Barbara and George agreed that they wanted to adopt. They had seen stories about Roy Rogers and Dale Evans, who had formed a family that included a Native-American girl, a boy who was a victim of child abuse, a girl from an orphanage in Scotland, and an orphan girl from Korea. So they decided that they need not adopt a child that looked like them, but a child that might be considered unadoptable, a child from a foreign country or one who is handicapped.

And at the end of the first year in Virginia, they pursue the idea. Barbara has quit 'the pill' a year earlier, but has not become pregnant. When they look into adoption they learn that mixed-race children are very hard to place, that white couples aren't interested (especially in Virginia) and neither are black couples.

My role? I am rarely a participant in matters like these, though I am just as interested in them, as I know it can cause a major change in <u>my</u> life. I watch and listen intently, but what sort of advice can I offer? I know George thinks it might actually keep me further suppressed, that him being a father will somehow diminish my importance. But I know that it would be just the opposite. The fact that I have a feminine perspective, a motherly point of view, just adds another angle to the discussion.

The adoption agency we are referred to in Richmond is run by the Quakers and they have more than one-hundred infants available. After a series of interviews and background checks (which takes about six months) we are called in to see the babies. What an amazing situation!

We're brought into a room with rows of cribs and infants ranging from two-weeks to two-months old. We pass a dozen or so cribs before pausing at one of them to look down at a ten week old little tan-skinned girl who is lying quietly, her enormous dark eyes looking up at us. George reaches out to touch the baby's hand and without a moment of hesitation, she grabs his index finger and squeezes it. George looks at Barbara and she smiles. "This one?" she asks. And George nods and within a week they bring Jennifer home.

Barbara, George and Jennifer at 12 weeks.

Adoption proves to be the winning ticket. Jennifer is the kind of child who cries when she sees Moe poke Curly in the eye, scolds George and Barbara for their liberal ideas, and voluntarily makes her bed every morning before leaving for school.

John Freeman, a young Ichabod Crane look-alike George hired to teach English at John Tyler comes to the office one day to announce there's a march protesting the View Nam war being organized. It's happening in Washington, D.C. He invites us to go along with him. Shortly thereafter, Anne Ash says she's definitely going, so George makes arrangements to stay in D.C. with Bruce and Carol Godsave, friends from Geneseo who are teaching at Gallaudet University (a college for the deaf).

Row after row of buses and cars jam the highways into the city and it takes hours to get to the Godsaves little apartment, but we arrive OK and the next morning we're up bright and early and heading off to Pennsylvania Avenue. All around us there are people walking in the same direction, chattering and smiling and introducing themselves. We're all heading off to the Capital to stop a war. It's not just 'hippies,' which is how the media has represented it, but people of all ages and 'stripes.' An elderly woman tells us of her memories from the 1950's protests at the U.N. against the development of nuclear weapons. 'Ban the Bomb' was the slogan. Others talk about traveling south to participate in civil rights marches.

I now feel like part of that legacy, a tiny piece in an enormous jig saw puzzle, square in a colorful quilt representing a people and a cause. (Years from now, George and I will be in Pride marches and visit Washington, D.C. to lobby congress on behalf of LGBT health.)

We arrive at a point where there are organizers arranging people into groups. The march has already begun and after a little while we gradually begin to move forward, shuffling our way down Pennsylvania Avenue, nudging each other, passing by army tanks positioned at street intersections or stopping in front of soldiers standing stoically outside Federal buildings. Some of us offer them flowers.

Then, as we turn a corner, George looks up. We're in front of a government building, one of many in the city—thick massive squares of stone with flat roofs. And there, at the corner of the roof, we see sandbags strategically piled to hide what's behind them, but they don't completely hide the barrels of rifles poking through spaces between the bags of sand.

Suddenly, the image of the Kangaroo Court disaster in Geneseo comes to mind. One mistake, one misunderstood gesture or error in judgment and the entire scene will change. We will become rioters and the soldiers will take action. Our soldiers could very likely shoot us—not the soldiers of an invading army or a terrorist organization, but our own American soldiers. In an instant, it could all go bad, very bad. I can feel the chill creep its way down George's spine.

But nothing comes of it. Everyone is well-behaved. There are tiny incidents in places where the marchers make a wrong turn, go down a street they shouldn't or try to climb onto one of the tanks. Anne Ash and her daughter get caught in one of those. Tear gas is fired and though some of the protestors are 'rounded up' most, including Anne and her daughter, get away safely. And Anne is appalled. "They gassed us!" she exclaims later.

Our world is no longer comfortable.

GEORGE WILKERSON

TWENTY-EIGHT
Wait A Minute, Mister Postman

I FIND IT'S EASY TO COMMUNICATE with George through his dreams. That's where the blinders come off and I can act out my role in private. In those dreams, I'm the main character; people accept me without prejudice, I do 'girly' things, and I have a female body (though my penis stays intact. Even in adulthood, I subscribe to the 'girl with a penis' view of myself.)

George tells Barbara about some of these dreams, expressing the view that it's the reflection of some sort of subconscious desire, and Barbara agrees to help by letting him try on clothes, curl his hair, and even try some make-up. But instead of it liberating me, it turns George into an awkward and clumsy clown. And Barbara is not comfortable with it, so at George's urging, I back off and George agrees to see a therapist.

Unfortunately, the therapist we go to doesn't have a clue as to what's going on.

"These dreams," he says. "How long have you had them?"

"All my life."

"Really?"

George nods, but hesitates to go into much detail. He doesn't mention the nights as a child when he prayed for a gender change or the times he rifled through the hamper in the bathroom to find a bra, a dress, or a skirt and top to put on. Instead, he talks about his parents, about being bullied, about being raised Catholic.

And I whisper to him: *Tell him about me, the 'girl with a penis',* but he doesn't.

The psychiatrist subscribes to Freudian theories and so eventually tells George that his father's abuse created a fear of castration. To that, I tell George that he has nothing to fear, that his father didn't want to cut off his penis, and that the psychiatrist is probably the one with a fear of castration. Together we decide that this therapist isn't much different from the Catholic psychiatrist Father sent us to and they should have paid <u>us</u> since we probably taught them more about us than they ever learned in psychiatry school.

☜ ❑ ☞

So then, to my name. Shakespeare was wrong; just ask any transgender woman.

> *"What's in a name? That which we call a rose*
> *By any other name would smell as sweet."*

No, Rose is a much better name than Brunhilda.

Caitlin Jenner struggled over what name to choose for herself. Unlike her, and much like a lot of my life, my name was purely accidental.

Had it not come about as it did, I would have picked something else. But I had no choice. George picked it. And he didn't even realize what he was doing.

One of the faculty members at John Tyler, Bob Goldman, is a drama teacher. We later learn that he got his job by claiming a doctorate from Vanderbilt University and producing a long list of invented credits and references which may have had some kernel of authenticity, but for the most part were bogus. How he got away with this we never knew, but eventually it all caught up with him and so he had to leave town.

Bob's wife, a very pretty girl named Parthenia ('virgin' in Greek), at least twenty years younger than him, was taken in by his sly pretention and pompous behavior. A short, stocky man with balding curly hair and a basketball size paunch, Bob is great at promoting his legendary status. He didn't teach drama; he <u>was</u> drama. But when he had to leave he came to George and asked him for a favor. Would he pick up his mail from his box at the local post office and forward it to him?

George agrees and so Bob leaves us with his mailbox key and some empty envelopes with a forwarding address. George dutifully checks the mailbox every other day and except for the mail that is clearly junk, he slips everything into one of the stamped envelopes and forwards it.

On one of those days that I get a brilliant idea. But it relies on George's efforts to find out more about me. He has made visits to pornographic book stores (strictly for research purposes, of course…right?) and found magazines with names like *Female Mimics,* which are aimed at crossdressers. Some of them have ads from people seeking to meet others like themselves.

There is no safe way to meet others or find out about the transgender phenomena. There is no Internet. In fact, the term transgender has not been adopted. Terms like crossdresser and transvestite are the common designations. So an ad in a magazine, even if the magazine is pornographic, is just about the only way to meet others with the same "affliction." (The only other way is through underground organizations which exist around the country, but whose contact information is not readily available.)

So I share my scheme with George, i.e. to use Bob Goldman's mailbox for <u>my</u> explorations into the trans-world. To test it, George sends a letter to one of the advertisers in the magazine and uses *Bobbi Williams* as the name along with the return address. We use *Bobbi* because it's close to Bob and he figures the post office people won't notice, and uses Williams because it's close to Wilkerson, but more common.

Thus begins a period of surreptitious outreach and thus my name.

◦ ❑ ☞

George and I are inseparable. My name is only a matter of necessity; it puts a label on my identity. Regardless of whether we have names, we share the same nervous system. My strain becomes his. And much of the time it's just one more rider on an already overloaded bus somewhere on a dirt road in South America. George is the driver, careening around the curves, speeding through the mountains as chickens and goats scramble to get out of the way and I'm tied to the top along with the other baggage. I would really like to get off, but I'm not the driver.

This new position of George's as Department Chair might be the bus. George is struggling to keep it steady, but he is only 27 years old. All of the other faculty are older than him and now comes word that he must evaluate them and make salary decisions. So George concocts a plan that inadvertently speeds up the bus.

His plan is based on new notions of education coming from the trainers at the education laboratory, ideas about specifying concrete statements about what students are to learn (i.e. what they expected to be able to do at the end of a course) and designing tests that measure those expectations. It appeals to his sense of fair play and honesty.

Here's how it works: each teacher will create the objectives for their course and prepare two comparable tests on those objectives, one to be administered at the beginning of the course and one at the end. The success of the teacher is then measured based on the average degree of improvement between the two tests and salaries as well as bonuses are assigned on the basis of the relative success of each teacher. In this way, George believes, the subjectivity of evaluation will be removed. The traditional evaluation method of going to a teacher's class and observing him or her "in action" and recording their attendance at faculty meetings and completing other faculty obligations becomes unnecessary.

Please understand that none of this is my idea. I'm the muse, not the academician. That kind of thinking is a part of us that is all him. All I can do is sit back and watch it unfold, as if it's a Michael Moore documentary and cringe. But George? His enthusiasm knows no bounds.

❧　❑　☞

As soon as the folks at the education laboratory hear of this scheme, they swoop down on George and begin to publicize his plan. He gets invitations to speak at other colleges around the country, describing the plan as if it's a *fait accompli*. It's reported in the *Chronicle of Higher Education*. He's a celebrity.

The president of the college gives George three years to institute the program and the first year serves as a testimony to George's naiveté. The faculty go along with it, but it soon becomes clear that they are out to undermine it. The trainers from the learning lab come to the campus to teach the faculty how to write their objectives and tests, but to no avail. A common response is that "the idea is good and will work fine in everyone else's subject, just not in mine." The project soon becomes unmanageable and George becomes unmanageable as well. He's off on a headlong crusade to correct all the wrongs in the world of education while I could care less. I have my own crusade to deal with.

But then the clouds open and the *deus ex machina* descends. One of the Lab's consultants is on the faculty of U.C.L.A. and the former Lab Director has taken a position as head of the Community College program at the University of Texas in Austin. (Not coincidentally, that's where the president of John Tyler went to school.)Soon George is invited to both schools to consider pursuing a Ph.D.

At U.C.L.A. the consultant tells George he should move to California and enroll in the higher education program there and once he has begun the consultant will try and get him some financial support. But the former Lab Director offers George a Fellowship—he will be a Kellog Fellow—free tuition and books, low cost housing, and an opportunity to earn some money 'on the side' as a consultant with the state's Higher Education Coordinating Board, and all the free Cheerios he can eat (milk not included.)

We travel to Los Angeles to check out U.C.L.A. and find California is much like Long Island, with its freeways and ranch houses and fast food joints. It's intimidating and all the while George is thinking *Texas...with tumbleweeds, Roy Rogers and Dale Evans, Ken Maynard, Hopalong Cassidy, the Cisco Kid.* And maybe even Jimmy Jingles.

☞ ❑ ☞

George accepts the Texas offer. He loads up the Volkswagen station wagon and tosses three-year old Jennifer in the back, on top of the pillows and blankets he has piled up, and they head off to meet Barbara, who is flying to Austin.

And <u>my</u> things—dresses, wigs, bras and panties, stockings, shoes—the things George has secretly hidden for those occasions when he has time alone and I can come to the fore, when George lets me get dressed and 'be.' Some of the things are in a bag in a crawl space under the house; others are in a storage locker rented specifically for that use. They can't be retrieved and packed without raising questions. So I'm naked and wondering: *Does he think he can leave <u>me</u> behind?*

Thus far, George has not gone away when I come out. His feelings and attitudes are right there along with mine. He may be uncomfortable with me. He may not understand me or know what (or who) I am, but he knows that I need my time and he has to give it to me. He has tried to deny me, but it never works. All it does is raise the discomfort level for both of us. I think of it as a Hulk attitude. *I need to come out*, I say. *'Cause if I don't come out I will be extremely agitated. And you don't want to see me when I'm agitated.*

Sadly, though, the only option we have when moving (and we move a lot) is to throw away the accoutrements or donate them to Goodwill (which is where we got many of the things in the first place.) That means that when we want to rebuild the collection of "things" we have to go shopping and that is excruciatingly awkward. We go to Goodwill, not so much for the prices as for the fact that the clerks appear disinterested and so it's not quite so uncomfortable for George to pull a dress off the rack and hold it up to himself to gauge how it will look on me. And it's highly unlikely that there will be anyone of George's friends or colleagues shopping there.

The Department stores, on the other hand, present a different challenge. Holidays are the best, a good time for "I'm looking for something for my wife."

"Oh? What size is she?"

This is a tricky question. Women's sizes are not as simple as men's. There are Ladies, Womens, Petite, Girls, Plus, and more.

"She's about my size," is the stock answer. "But thinner," we add.

Over time we sort out a lot of this and George learns where to take me and what to look for. (He leans toward the conservative. *I'm not your mother*, I tell him. But then, I lean toward the glamorous to which he says *That's slutty*. Another struggle.)

It's an ongoing cycle of gathering a collection of clothes, hiding them away, discarding them because of a move or a risk of being discovered, and then acquiring a new collection. In the early days, discarding the clothes came with a pledge to quit the whole thing, to get rid of me somehow (fat chance), and become the man he has been told he's supposed to be. But neither of us has any idea of how that's supposed to be accomplished. There are no acceptable role models. There's just the two of us and as we head down the highway to Austin, Texas, we quietly hum an old song:

Wherever we go, whatever we do
we're gonna go through it together.
We may not go far, but sure as a star,
wherever we are, it's together.
Wherever I go I know he goes.
Wherever I go I know she goes.
No fits, no fights, no feuds
and no egos, Amigos, together!
Through thick and through thin,
all out or all in.
And whether it's win, place or show.
With you for me and me for you,
we'll muddle through whatever we do.
Together, wherever we go.

["Together"/ Music by Ray Henderson; Lyrics by Buddy G. DeSylva and Lew Brown]

TWENTY-NINE
Into the Heart of Texas

I N 1969 TOM HATFIELD, THE president of John Tyler
Community College, has resigned. He has left Virginia and
returned to Texas where the former head of the education
lab, John Roueche, has become head of the Community College
Education Ph.D. program. And in May of 1971 George follows
them to Austin where he becomes a Kellogg Fellow (Yes, the
Cheerios company) at the University of Texas.

Roueche is a master manipulator. He is also the master
of George's graduate work. We spend that summer living in
Roueche's home while he is away. George and Barbara wait for
an apartment to open up in the University's Married Student
Housing. When an apartment becomes available we discover
they're not much more than a set of converted Army barracks,
an intellectual ghetto for graduate students with children. It's a
far cry from the Roueche home with its modern conveniences—
air-conditioning (a must in Texas), inter-coms between the
rooms, swimming pool. But the low rent makes it possible to hire
a housekeeper/babysitter and for Barbara to pursue a Masters
degree.

෨ ❑ ☞

The Community College Leadership doctoral program is under
the University's educational administration program which
trains school administrators. Classes begin shortly after we

arrive. There are fourteen people in the program and during the summer they meet as a single unit (a cohort) for about eight hours a day, on Monday, Tuesday, and Wednesday.

Charlie Tesar and his wife Sheila are in the program. Charlie is bigger than life, a Zorba the Greek crossed with Wreck-It-Ralph—the type of man who will slap you on the back, shake your hand, and convince you that the used car he's showing you is the best one on the lot and maybe the best in town. Charlie doesn't think much of people who take themselves too seriously. He and George joke in class a lot, pass notes, and make offhand comments of the sort that immature adults do. When one of the professors, who is from Georgia, makes a reference to the police by calling them the PO-LEESE, Charlie raises hand and asks: "Excuse me, sir. Are you talking about the campus PO-LEESE or the city PO-LEEESE?" (If there was a Principal's Office the professor would have sent Charlie there, but he just disregards the question and mentally adds Charlie to his shit list.)

George joins Charlie on that list when one day the same professor distributes an article dealing with the subject of Student Counseling and asks for opinions. George responds that it is one of the more poorly written pieces he has ever seen, adding that it is full of the 'pompous jargon' criticized by our SUNY Geneseo writing mentor, Leo Rockas.

"Is that so?" the professor asks. "And what would you say to the author of this piece?"

I realize what's going on before George does, but it's already too late—George had not bothered to look at the name at the top of the article. It was the professor's.

We already made the list.

❧ ❑ ☞

Billy Best is another student in the program. And he is angry. Visiting professors lecture us on the history of community colleges. They talk about the best way to design a campus and how to create a budget. Meanwhile, Billy Best mumbles about what's wrong with the world and how Richard Nixon is a crook and Billy wants to know what community colleges can do to bring justice to the downtrodden in America. Caring about such issues actually may be what got him recruited to the program, given that everyone there had a similar view of the community college as the salvation of higher education, with its open-door policy and the dream of higher education for all. We were to be the new leaders in education, building this great equalizing institution, bringing salvation to a corrupt America. But as it turns out, Billy is a bit too radical and it culminates one day in class when the subject is the role of the college counselor. The class has barely begun when something clicks in Billy and he jumps up, shoves his chair back until it falls over, and exclaims "Fuck that!"

Silence.

"What about Attica?" Billy says. "What about the men Rockefeller killed?"

More silence.

Billy continues. He's talking about a riot at the Correctional Facility in Attica, New York. Prisoners demanded better living conditions and when they got no response, about 1,000 of the 2,200 inmates seized control of the prison. The governor, Nelson Rockefeller, refused to meet with them and sent in the state police and when it was all over at least 43 people were dead.

"What are we doing for them?" Billy asked. "Who's counseling them? What are counselors good for if we can't bring justice to Attica!?"

But no one answers and Billy, true to the moment, picks up his chair, grabs his gear, and leaves. And he is never heard from again.

Justice is served though, in a way, because Charlie's and George's names are moved down the professor's shit list as Billy Best's name takes the number one slot.

❧ ▢ ☞

Being at the University provides an opportunity for George to do a little more research on us. One of the things he finds is a study that says Male-to-Female may be tied to the BSTc portion of the hypothalamus. The stria terminalis (or terminal stria) is a structure in the brain consisting of a band of fibers. The BSTc is the stria terminalis located in the central subdivision of the stria terminalis. During interactions between the developing brain and fetal sex hormones, the study says, this brain region, which is essential to sexual feelings and behavior, can misfire and result in female differentiation in a genetic male.

Well, now, I mutter. *Isn't that interesting? But so what?*

❧ ▢ ☞

While we were in Virginia, Barbara went off 'the pill' and George assumed it would just be a matter of time before she got pregnant. But that doesn't happen. So, after being in Texas for a year, they go to a doctor to find out if there's a problem and the Doctor has George 'donate' some sperm.

"Use a mayonnaise jar or something similar. Put the sample in the jar and be sure to keep it warm."

"Warm?" George asks.

The doctor nods. "You can put it under your armpit. Just someplace warm."

So George masturbates into an empty mayonnaise jar and carries it under his arm to the doctor's office. (I can tell he feels like a felon running from one of the priests in Catholic school who has caught him in an 'unnatural act' and is shouting at him: *"Onan went in to his brother's wife and wasted the semen on the ground and what he did was wicked in the sight of the Lord, and he put him to death!!"*

At the receptionist' she fumbles for words.

"Can I help you?"

"I…er…" He places the jar on the counter and the receptionist holds it up, examining the contents.

"A semen sample?" She says in voice a megaphone would have put to shame. "Yes?

"Yes," George says.

"And your name?"

Make something up, I whisper, but that's not necessary, as he hands her his driver's license which she takes, jots down the information, and says. "The doctor will be in touch with you."

A few days later we're with the doctor and he describes the problem. "Low motility," he says. "There's plenty of sperm…they just aren't very good swimmers."

No surprise. Flashback to the pool at Geneseo. "You're not much of a swimmer," the teacher says.

☜ ❑ ☞

So there is no pregnancy. George is in the Educational Leadership program and Barbara enrolls in the Masters Degree in Media program… and that's when she gets pregnant.

Is she now the model expectant mother? All brightness and sunshine? Glowing? No. She is miserable, always uncomfortable, always cranky, always complaining. So George gets a vasectomy. It's a deceptively simple process—a shot of Novocain in the scrotum, a small incision through which the deferens can be popped out, a quick snip of each tube, and one stitch and it's over in fifteen minutes.

But it's not <u>all</u> over. Not really. Because a subsequent infection causes the testes to swell and become super-sensitive and a week-long regimen of antibiotics is needed to recover. George spends the next few days on the couch, suffering whenever he has to move and wincing whenever Jennifer, now two, comes bounding over and jumps up to sit by him.

And me? For once, I do not watch or even listen. For this I have receded to the farthest reaches of our space. I may join in on his orgasms, but I want no part of this aspect of George's life, except that I point out to him that having the vasectomy pretty much washes away the notion of a castration complex.

🖛 ❑ ☞

In the eighth month of Barbara's pregnancy, over coffee one afternoon, Charlie Tesar tells us of an initiation rite. We must visit the Chicken Ranch. It's a house of ill-repute whose closure later results in a Broadway musical and a movie, both titled *The Best Little Whorehouse in Texas*. Would he have taken us if he knew <u>I</u> was going along? I think he would, but as usual, George didn't have the courage to tell him about me.

Barbara being pregnant might provide a good excuse for the visit, but that would be disingenuous. I know at least part of the reason we agree to go is because George has decided that my existence is a reflection of his sexuality. His experiences have been few and his ability to perform will confirm his sex drive is heterosexual and that will set his masculinity free and there will be no reason for me to exist. I will vanish and George will become…A MAN. So George jumps at Charlie's offer and off they go.

The trip is made under the pretense of consulting at a college that requires a late night return and we head out to the little town of La Grange, about sixty miles from Austin. Charlie has been there and knows the location of the little dirt road to the innocent looking, even innocuous, two-story house. And when we arrive, George follows Charlie, politely stepping onto the porch and ringing the bell.

Texas has a whorehouse in it.
Lord have mercy on our souls.

Texas has a whorehouse in it.
    Lord have mercy on our souls.
            [from *The Best Little Whorehouse in Texas*]

Within moments an older black woman in a maid's outfit appears, invites us in, and shows us to the reception room. The walls of the room are a rich dark wooden paneling, but they only reach as high as a chair rail. Above that, they are covered in a dark red wallpaper.

We're shown to a pair of seats alongside one wall as the maid pulls a drawstring hanging in the corner, setting off a series jingling bells.

Neither George nor Charlie say a word as a parade of young women enter the room, each dressed as if auditioning for a different movie genre. There's the 1950's housewife in a prim little polka-dot dress and white apron, the businesswoman in a business suit whose skirt is just a bit too short, the cheerleader (complete with pom-poms), the college co-ed, the airline stewardess, the military girl, the blushing bride, the sophisticate, the slut, the dominatrix, and even a nun. (George tenses up when she enters.) The array covers every possible fantasy that any man might have.

The girls line up in front of the wall on the opposite side of the room and almost immediately Charlie steps forward and starts interrogating them.

"Whatcha got under that skirt?" he asks.

"You like sports?"

"Going to the prom on Saturday?"

"Who's your daddy?"

The questions seem to be more a release for his nervousness than serious inquiries, as most of the girls simply smile, but don't answer.

"Take your pick," he says, waving George over to his side.

We hesitate.

"He's a Yankee," Charlie says to the housewife.

"Go on," Charlie says, waving his arm down the row, then turns to the businesswoman and offers his arm.

She smiles and they walk off together, leaving us standing there, alone, looking up and down the row, debating until, at last, George steps over to the slut and stands directly in front of her.

Without hesitation, she takes his hand and guides him out of the room, towing George and me behind her like a wanton puppy. We walk down the end of the hall and into a sparsely furnished bedroom. There's a sink on one wall, a curtained window on the other, a single bed and night-table with a lamp, and the door where we came in, which she closes and then motions for us to sit on the bed.

The girl seems distant and anxious to have it over with. She stares at us, at George, really, since my mind is racing, considering what it would be like to be her, to do this with strangers every day, without ever knowing anything other than what they look like and their name (if they even use their real name.)

Now the girl steps closer and rattles off a list of sex acts and prices. "Blow Job—thirty minutes, or less if you come sooner, twenty-five dollars; rim job and finger is fifty; missionary fuck is a hundred; Cleveland steamer is one twenty-five; around the world is a hundred-fifty—all those are thirty minutes, or less if you come sooner. For three hundred I can get another girl in here with us. Do you know what you want?"

My god, I think, *it's like the menu at a Chinese restaurant.* George, however, isn't thinking at all. His mind is like a mighty wind blowing down the Grand Canyon and he's feeling a little nauseous. Then suddenly he blurts out "Blow job."

The girl holds out her hand. "Twenty five," she says. "And buy me a soda."

George reaches into his pocket and takes out three tens. She takes them and says "I'll be right back," then turns and steps out of the room.

Almost immediately she's back and carrying a can of soda. She takes a drink, places the can on the table, and says: "Take off your pants."

George obeys and once they're off she points to his crotch. "Those too," she says, and he takes off his jockey shorts. She then guides him to the sink and has him stand close so she can wash his penis. When she's done, she hands him a towel.

We are not aroused and while George is in something of a stupor, I am totally intrigued by the ritual associated with this, a routine that's vaguely like the protocol of a business meeting.

As George dries off, she walks to the bed and begins to undress. He drops the towel in the sink and goes to her. By the time he reaches her she is naked. She pats the space beside her on the bed.

She is young; early-twenties perhaps, and has a perfect figure—slender, curving in at the waist, and shoulder-length blonde hair, though even in her nakedness there's something unkempt in her style.

All she needs is a little bit of fixin' up
To pull herself together
　　She'd be pretty if she'd only try
To pull her self together
And I'll help her,
　　It's as easy as can be
　　Pretty soon she's gonna look a lot like me
　　　　[from *The Best Little Whorehouse in Texas*]

As she begins to go down on us, George reaches out and touches her hair. It's soft and sifts through his hand like sand in an hourglass and then, just as she is about to put his penis in her mouth, she stops, reaches up and moves his hand away. "Kissing is extra," she says, then returns to the matter at hand. But that is short-lived, as George ejaculates before her lips can get there, and he laughs, uncomfortably, as her head jerks back, and she laughs too.

"I'm sorry," he says.

She laughs again. "Nothing to be sorry for," she says, then stands up, retrieves the towel from the sink, and throws it at him.

They get dressed, saying nothing, and she escorts him back to the sitting room where Charlie is waiting.

Years later, we are at a theatre in Houston, watching the touring company of *Best Little Whorehouse*, and we are struck by the accuracy of the set: the dark wood wall paneling as high as the chair rail and the deep red wallpaper. And the array of girls— every fantasy any man ever had, except the girls in the show can sing and dance.

And yes, because I know you are curious. I enjoyed George's orgasms every bit as much as he did. Or maybe even more because, in a way that's hard to describe, I was also that girl.

☜ ❏ ☞

In the summer of 1972, John Zechner Wilkerson is born. Barbara planned to breast feed and for the first few days she tries her best, but the baby wants no part of it. He starts to lose weight.

The problem is a cleft palate—just like his father had, even though the doctor said it's not hereditary and not to worry. But there it is—a gaping hole in the roof of the baby's mouth. He's unable to suck, though his mouth makes the appropriate shape and motions. There's just no suction. So a special feeding bottle must be used and the baby must sit up rather than lie down to take the formula, essentially having it poured down his throat. He is not a happy baby.

THIRTY
An Intern in
Deliverance Land

THE UNIVERSITY PROGRAM REQUIRES AN internship—one semester working at a community or junior college. Bart Herrscher, one of the trainers who worked at the Education Lab, is now President of Mitchell College, a private school in North Carolina and that's where George is assigned. So he and Barbara pack up the kids, rent a house in Statesville, and are all set to move there for a semester. But a week or so before moving, we suffer from a cold so badly that we go to the University infirmary and as part of the examination, the doctor feels our throat, stops for a moment, and lets out a soft "Hmmmm."

"Hmmm?"

He goes to his little table, picks up his prescription pad, and writes down the name of a doctor. "You need to see him," he says. "Get a thyroid scan."

"Thyroid?"

"Just to check. There's a nodule there."

"Nodule?"

The doctor shakes his head. "Just make an appointment."

But we don't. We're leaving town and with the move to North Carolina just a week away there's a lot to get ready. By the time we're on the road, George is over the cold, but when we get to Statesville, George figures he should follow up on the thyroid concern, so he makes an appointment with a local M.D., Dr. Presley. And George asks Dr. Presley about his hunka-hunka thyroid node.

The doc feels our throat and shakes his head. "Nope."

"A nodule?" George asks.

He shakes his head again. "Not that I can feel."

So we are relieved; we needn't worry about it and we put the whole thing behind us. *Nothing to worry about,* I say. *False alarm,* George says. *Second opinions are good,* I think to myself.

Being an intern turns out to be fairly easy. Herrscher is a good man and the college is small, very small. The school started as a women's college, then, during the Great Depression, turned co-ed and opened its doors to men. In 1959 it became an independent community college, but the state supported community colleges were too competitive and the pressure was strong for Mitchell to join the North Carolina Community College System. That eventually would happen in 1973, but for now, it was Herrscher's job to improve enrollment figures and raise donation levels that would keep the college solvent.

One of the tactics aimed at accomplishing that goal is an offer of a money-back guarantee. Students who attend classes, complete assignments, and take all required tests, but still fail can get a full tuition refund. It's a noble experiment, but what we find is that students, knowing they won't flunk, don't pace themselves properly and the tactic doesn't impact the enrollment figures as hoped.

Another tactic is the use of agreements which students sign at the beginning of a semester, contracting for an A, B, or C in a course. That fails as well and Bart decides that the best move for the college is to turn it over to the state.

❧ ❑ ☞

We're getting paid the standard intern salary, which is barely enough to get by, so George works out a deal for a free breakfast in the college cafeteria. While in Austin he began jogging, so now, every morning, he runs around a small lake in a nearby park and then goes to the campus for a plate of sausage and eggs and a cup of coffee. And as Fall slides into full bloom, the brisk runs are less of a workout. The cool, damp air and scent of the trees which are starting to shed their leaves means that our mind is free to roam. And I'm OK with this. I like our time alone, seeing George's thoughts wander and both of us being relaxed. The entire experience in Statesville is actually one of the less stressful for us.

❧ ❑ ☞

In January of 1972 we return to Austin, to the comfort of our married student housing ghetto, and once again we're down with a cold so we go back to the University infirmary and, as luck would have it, the same doctor examines us and is feeling our throat once more when he stops short and pulls his hands away, then looks at us like George is some sort of felon.

"You were here a year ago," he says.

George smiles, sheepishly.

"Did you get it checked?"

He nods. "I had to go to North Carolina, to intern and I saw the doctor there. He didn't find anything."

The doctor is not pleased. "We'll make an appointment for you...<u>now</u>." He motions to the door and we scurry out.

❧ ❑ ☞

The appointment is with an oncologist who schedules George for a thyroid scan. And I wonder—is there a scan that would show me? Maybe an MRI or a Cat Scan. Would I show up? How would that turn out?)

> DOCTOR: *(Holding plastic film against a backlit plate of*
> *glass.)* There it is.
> GEORGE: What?
> DOCTOR: Her. *(Pointing to a shadowy figure)* That woman.
> GEORGE: *(Squinting)* What woman?
> DOCTOR: That woman right there! *(He tilts the film so the light clearly shows the head and arms tapering to the waist and then to the legs.)* How did she get there?
> GEORGE: (Shrugs) Beats me, doc.

The way the thyroid scan works is that they inject us with radioactive iodine and run a Geiger counter across our throat. It's attached to a graphic device that draws a dot-matrix picture of the thyroid. The next day, when we go back to the oncologist, he has the results and explains that there's a 'suspicious node' and schedules surgery for the following day.

A node?

A tumor, the doctor finally says

And the only way of knowing if the 'node' is malignant is to operate. So off we go to have our throat slashed.

Fear is one of those emotions George and I share deeply. We are both frightened. We're scheduled for the surgery early in the morning, so we must check in the night before and, after signing the papers and having 'vitals' checked, we are shuttled off to a room that looks like the set for *General Hospital Meets Dr. Frank-N-Furter…In 3-D*. Everything is white—the walls, the sheets, the furniture. White, white, white. We lie there awake until instinct takes over and we finally doze off, but then…

BLAM! The lights come on and we are blinded by the fluorescence bouncing off the walls. George blinks, we lift our head, and there at the end of the bed are: Tom and Jerry, or Pinky and the Brain, or maybe Wile E. Coyote and the Roadrunner. We blink again. It's none of those. It's Laurel and Hardy in drag, a skinny nurse and a fat nurse. It's some sort of vision, a hallucination, leftover from the dream George was having. If he blinks once more they will go away.

But they don't. They approach from both sides—the skinny one on the left; the fat one on the right. "Give me your arm," the fat one says, and immediately begins wrapping it with the blood pressure cuff. The skinny one, who has been shaking down a thermometer, places it in front of George's mouth. "Open."

He chomps down on the thermometer as the fat one pumps up the cuff, grabs our wrist, squeezes, and looks at her watch. There is a frozen moment, as if a Pause button were pressed, then the thermometer is yanked away and the cuff removed. The fat one smiles. "One-fifteen over sixty. You're nice and relaxed."

George shakes his head vigorously. "I'm a runner," he says, even as she is walking away. "That's high for me. Very High!"

But they're gone, except for the fat hand reaching inside the door and flipping off the lights: *Did one of us imagine the whole thing*, he wonders. *No George*, I say softly, *it was just a scene from a new Mel Brooks movie.*

☜ ▢ ☞

The surgery goes well. While we're on the operating table, a piece of the thyroid is sent to the hospital's lab and very shortly a report that it's negative comes back, so the surgeon decides to remove half of the thyroid, the portion where the tumor was discovered and when we wake up later, in recovery, we're both feeling euphoric. The tumor was benign. We will live a while longer—both of us.

"If you're going to get cancer," the doctor tells us, with a kind of backhanded medical positivity "the thyroid is one of the better places to get it. When a tumor develops there, the thyroid produces an enzyme that encapsulates it, keeps it from spreading." So we were reassured and go home and bask in the pleasures of recovering.

Until a week later.

"We need to see you," the nurse says. "Can you come in this afternoon?"

"I guess so," George says.

And that afternoon, the doctor comes into the examining room and shakes George's hand and explains that they always follow up on the "call" made on the operating table by sending the half –thyroid they removed to a lab for further analysis which involves taking a slice of the thyroid and looking at it under a microscope, while the lab takes hundreds of slices and studies them.

"There were some more tumors," the doctor says. "Smaller ones."

"What does that mean," George asks. "What do we do?"

The doctor shrugs. "There's no agreement. Some say go back and take out the other half. Some say do nothing; just keep an eye on it."

Yes. Well. "What do you say?" George asks.

The doctor pauses, then tilts his head back and smiles. "Hide 'n' watch.

It was a good cancer, but now we have to hide and watch? I ask. That good ol' boy lingo is not reassuring. "Do nothing?" George asks.

The doctor nods. "It's up to you, really."

More surgery? We're thinking. *No way.*

"Hide n' watch." George says. And I concur. I am very good at hiding and watching. I've been doing that for about thirty years now.

The doctor's smile widens. And from that point on, for the next five years, we hide and we watch—thyroid scans every six months and chest x-rays every 12 months. But nothing develops.

About ten years later we're attending a concert of classical music at the University and during the intermission we step out to the foyer of the auditorium and hear a voice calling: "Wilkerson! Hey""

We turn and there's the surgeon, extending his hand. And smiling. "You're still alive!" he exclaims.

GEORGE WILKERSON

THIRTY-ONE
Hey Kids!
Let's Start A College!

I T'S EARLY SUMMER OF 1973. George is finishing his dissertation, completing his Ph.D. and he is contacted by Tom Hatfield who is the newly hired president of a new community college for Austin. "Finish your degree," Hatfield tells George, "before September and you can be my Dean of Instruction."

But the graduate school experience has worn us down. So much of what George does is compounded by <u>my</u> presence and the need for secrecy. It takes a toll. He knows he can't get rid of me and knows that I have to have time to myself, so he has contrived a variety of ways to take care of me without actually setting me loose. He gives me an hour here, a couple hours there, and time to hang out and try on outfits from Barbara's closet. Keeping me at bay means I steal time from his career.

When he goes to defend his dissertation, he discovers within minutes that he knows more about his topic than any of the professors who are there to 'grill him.' In fact, it soon becomes evident that most of them have not read, or at best, only skimmed the dissertation. That means the key to success is to be sure not to embarrass them (no matter how badly he would like to—another trait that's all his; not something I would ever do.)

I may not be a part of all this, but I see what's going on and it's all I can do to keep him from ruining it. Fortunately, John

Roueche, chair of the dissertation committee, has made it clear to the others on the panel that he has thoroughly reviewed the work and that anyone challenging it is, by extension, challenging him, with the end result that the dissertation defense is perfunctory.

So by now, George tells me, he has had enough of the academic bullshit and he tells Barbara what a farce it all is and that he plans to show up at the graduation ceremony, step onto the stage, and reject the degree—throw it on the ground, perhaps, kick it, spit on it. But that doesn't go over well. I'm not the only one who has made sacrifices to get him through school. Barbara has done much more than me and neither of us is about to throw it all away in a remake of *Billy Best and the Riot at Attica*. Of course, Barbara has a lot more clout than me. "So help me," she says, you pull a stunt like that and I'll take the kids and go back to New York." So he takes the degree and within days he is announced as ACC's first Dean of Instruction.

A curious feature of the new Austin Community College is that it opens without a local tax base. The only money for an operating budget comes from the state. The establishment of the college was put to voters twice, each time with a tax base included of about .05 cents on the dollar. And each time it failed. So the third time around, the vote to establish the college district came without a tax base. And it passed. The local school board becomes the board of the college and the college's boundaries are the same as the school district. So, by a clever bit of political maneuvering, the school gets enough money from the state, based on a 'projected' enrollment number which will provide enough funding to get started.

On September 20th, 1973, the college opens in an abandoned high school on the Black and Hispanic side of town. The school building had been shut down ten years earlier during the period of forced integration. It sits on the top of a hill overlooking the east side of Austin.

Surprisingly, the air conditioning system works and the building is in fair condition (although rumor has it that the building is gradually sliding downhill and will one day wind up in the middle of Airport Boulevard.)

☜ ❑ ☞

George and I occupy one of the old administrative offices in a suite along with Tom Hatfield, the President, and Marvin Schwiff, the Dean for Administrative Services. When the school was planned, Schwiff created and supervised the budget. Tom Spencer, a short, overweight bigot who makes no secret of his biases, is his assistant. Spencer openly expresses his disapproval of "niggers?" The prejudice provides an undercurrent of irony in that Schiff, who is Jewish, is in charge of finances. The 'team' moves forward, setting a day in early September for the first day of classes. Without a bit of subtlety, Hatfield describes the road from across the freeway to the new community college as "the route of the virtuous white woman." A 'secure' parking lot is set up, faculty are hired, a catalog is put together, and a string of policy decisions are made.

We have recently read a book about the unnatural separation of Science and the Arts and much of what drives policy decisions is a desire to create a college that brings the two together.

We have artists with no scientific knowledge and scientists with no artistic knowledge and both with no spiritual sense of gravity at all, and the result is not just bad, it is ghastly.

— Robert M. Pirsig, *Zen and the Art of Motorcycle Maintenance*

The catalog is arranged so that courses are not separated into the usual divisions of academic and occupational education or transfer and terminal programs. Instead, they're listed alphabetically, to reflect the equality of the two. A welder's training is regarded as no less valuable than a botanist's. And there are no restrictions on the contents of a student's program. They can design their own collection of courses and receive an *Associate Degree in General Studies*, so long as they complete a total of 60 credit hours,

The policy decisions also include the absence of an 'F' grade. Students who do not successfully complete a course simply receive no credit. "An 'F'" George argues with Tom and Marvin, "just adds insult to injury. We take their money and reward them by labeling them as failures."

The most unique feature of the new school is the accommodation of self-paced learning, which means that courses aren't limited to the standard twelve or sixteen weeks. Students are given additional time (up to a full semester) to complete a course. To help faculty accommodate this, testing centers are set up at locations around the city where a student can take whatever test is appropriate to his or her status in the course. So the teacher doesn't have to use class time to administer tests and students can retake tests (or various forms of the same test) and proceed only when they're ready.

To accommodate the new process, teachers must clearly spell out the requirements for completing their courses. They have to write objectives that specify what the successful student has learned to do and they have to make sure their tests reflect those skills.

It's a variation on the John Tyler CC plan, all very forward thinking and full of promise. But it doesn't last long. It's a hard sell to the faculty. George works nights and weekends to try to make it all happen, but most faculty can't handle the shift from traditional methods of college teaching. From my perch, I can see that they're threatened by this punk from New York who, as they see it, wants them to pass everyone and give up the power of their podium. "The objectives for my course are simple," one instructor says. "Come to all the classes and pass all the tests."

And in what seems like a blind-side, the absence of an 'F' grade is not attacked so much by the instructors as it is by the Veterans Authority, the federal agency that reimburses student veterans for their tuition. If students don't get a grade for a course, the V.A. has no way of being sure they ever attended a class (despite having registered for it), so they won't pay. But ironically, if the student receives an 'F', they happily refund their tuition. The struggle to win this battle for educational equality continues for the next three years.

That struggle and others takes their toll, both physically and mentally. At one point George is buying Pepto-Bismol by the case.

Many hours consist of sitting on a toilet reading the ingredients and warnings:

> *"Pepto-Bismol is indicated for treatment of acute upset stomach symptoms and diarrhea. It is not intended for chronic use. It relieves upset stomach symptoms (i.e., indigestion, heartburn, nausea and fullness caused by over-indulgence in food and drink) without constipating; and controls diarrhea. The active ingredient is believed to work via a topical effect on the stomach mucosa. For diarrhea, it is believed to work by several mechanisms in the gastrointestinal tract, including: 1) normalizing fluid movement via an antisecretory merchanism, 2) binding bacterial toxins and 3) antimicrobial activity."*
>
> *"Pepto-Bismol may cause a temporary and harmless darkening of the tongue or stool. While no lead is intentionally added to Pepto-Bismol, this product contains certain ingredients that are mined from the ground and*

thus contain small amounts of naturally occurring lead. For example, bismuth, contained in the active ingredient of Pepto-Bismol, is mined and therefore contains some naturally occurring lead. The small amounts of naturally occurring lead in Pepto-Bismol are low in comparison to average daily lead exposure; this is for the information of healthcare professionals."

That's some scary shit…figuratively <u>and</u> literally.

THIRTY-TWO
Running On Empty

I N THE MID-1970'S, A jogging/running craze has caught on. We're still living in the University's married student housing in Austin. George has just become Dean at the new community college and his stress level has triggered memories of high school running in cross-country meets. We both enjoyed that, since it gave us time to be together. The endorphins in our system took us to a fantasy world where we could separate ourselves, each having our own identities, George as himself and me as me, brother and sister, floating together.

Some scientific researchers believe that gender identity is formed before birth. They say it's a processes of the Central Nervous System's neurological integration of the fetus during pregnancy. In other words, gender forms in the brain separately from the body, where its formation may or may not be compatible. Hence, female brain-male body, or vice versa. That's a nice theory and George's only comment is: "So what?" And my response is to run away.

So it is that one day, inspired by those high school memories of running free, George puts on tennis shoes and we go across the road from the old army barracks to the city golf course and take off running. And we do it again the next day. And the next. Austin has hike and bike trails, and shortly thereafter George joins the YMCA that's located at the start of one of those trails and each morning we run the five-and-a-half-mile route along Town Lake.

After a while, we're running with a pack of four or five guys who talk as they run and one day the talk goes to the notion of running a marathon. Within a few days, George and his running buddies have picked one out, in Galveston. It's an out-and-back route along the sea wall. We realize we'll have to put in a little more time to get ready for it, so we start working out on a daily schedule, running seven or eight miles in the evenings.

The day of the race arrives and we head for the gulf coast. We've booked a room at the Galvez Hotel, an historic old structure built on a jetty that sticks out into the ocean and as it turns out, only one of the other 'guys, Bill Montgomery, a History professor at A.C.C., stays with the plan and he is there to run as well. But the others never show.

❧ ❑ ☞

The morning of the race the temperature is in the low 40's and it has started to rain. By four or five miles out, George is shivering and I sense he is getting very depressed. He is still only on the 'out' part of the route. Race leaders are passing us going in the other direction, on the 'back' leg. We fall back on a familiar coping mechanism, a daydream. I take him on a journey, to a land where he no longer exists, but is a part of me, and that part is no longer hidden from view. The sound of George's footsteps, clap, clap, on the sea wall, is the monotone that keeps the daydream going. And we manage to finish the race. It takes a little over four hours. Barbara drives us back to the hotel room where we collapse onto the bed.

The next morning, when we awake, we don't feel all that bad. Perhaps there's some leftover euphoria at completing the race. We sit up and look over at Barbara, who is still asleep, smile, and swung our legs over the side of the bed, then stand up and then, without warning, our legs fold underneath us like spaghetti dumped in a colander.

And the rest of the day is spent in bed.

A marathon is 26 miles plus 385 yards. Bill and George compare notes later and learned their results are similar—complete exhaustion. They decide that they probably hadn't trained enough, so when we get back to Austin, George gets into training in earnest. He wakes me every morning for a run of six miles and drags me out to the trail for another run of six or seven miles in the evening. Six days a week we run, chalking up about 75 miles a week. George is feeling a lot better, so when he sees a poster for a marathon in Louisiana he suggests to Bill that they try another and Bill agrees to go.

The Rice Festival Marathon goes from Crowley, Louisiana to Lafayette. It's a flat course, except for a highway overpass near the 18 mile mark. The high for the day of the race is 80 degrees, but we don't mind the heat. The race goes well. It's fun to run past the locals, sitting in their front yards in their lawn chairs waving at us as we go by, some even offering us lemonade or water. And we finish comfortably, learning that our time was around three hours and forty minutes. We had cut 20 minutes off of the Galveston time.

So we continue to run. Maybe because we're addicted to the 'high' running produces, but more likely as an escape. We no longer have to work out to

Mustachioed George
training for marathon

stay in shape, we <u>need</u> to work out, We run a couple of 10 kilometer races and finish third in one of them, boosting George's ego more than I could ever hope to do. We're now running better than men much younger than us and averaging over 120 miles a week.

The only memory of the Austin race: We have to pee so badly that we step to the side of the trail and, with our back to the other runners, pee mightily, not realizing that one of the women runners has detoured to the side as well and is now facing us. "I'm sorry," George says, and she smiles.

"That's OK, she replies. "I wish it was that easy for <u>me</u>."

(And I think, *I wish that <u>was</u> me.*)

We finish the Austin Marathon in a time 20 minutes faster than the Louisiana race. So now George has visions of grandeur and starts talking with Bill about running in the New York City marathon. [I am so left out of these plans, but in an odd way am happy to be forgotten.] It's our home town. We get to run through Brooklyn, past Bishop Loughlin High School (where we had gone for a year and a half before running away). And unlike Galveston and Louisiana, it's well-known; it comes with bragging rights.

☜　❑　☞

George is becoming an expert at running...from home, from me, from his marriage which has become a burden as I struggle to maintain some sort of existence. Eventually he'll learn that he can't run from any of it, especially from me. But now he is running because he can lose himself in the process, outside of his body, just the two of us, because the running somehow causes us to merge more completely, to overlap, and that increases my power somehow. It makes me feel truly equal, like I could head off on my own now, no longer trapped.

George is seriously into distance running now. He subscribes to *Runner's World* and even writes occasional articles for *Texas*

Runner magazine. And he adds 'fartleks' to the workouts (an alternating series of short sprints and short recovery runs). He's got an expensive pair of running shoes and in keeping with the times, he lets his hair grow, maybe envisioning himself as some kind of Greek running god, his long hair flying behind him. But I'm the one who wants the long hair.

He also gets into the "carbohydrate-loading diet." It calls for three and a half days of only protein foods the week before a race. (This, hypothetically, gets the body craving 'carbs.') Then, three and a half days of nothing but 'carbs': pancakes, pizza, spaghetti. George overdoes it and as a result, on the day before we're to leave for New York, he becomes violently ill. Nothing stays down. I argue against going, but George is adamant…he's going to run that marathon.

So the next day we get on a plane and fly to New York. By the time we get there he has stopped throwing up and is able to eat things like Saltine crackers. We spend the night at the Sister's home on Long Island and early the next morning drive into the city and meet up with Bill at his hotel, then go to Fort Wadsworth on Staten Island, the starting point for the race.

☞ ❑ ☜

It's a cool, pleasant morning. We've been told to wear old sweats which we can discard at the start of the race and they would be picked up afterward and donated to Goodwill. Thousands of people are milling around and there's not much order. Signs indicating estimated times to complete the race are staggered along the road and Fred Lebow, the race director, is screaming at people and shoving them this way and that. The friendliness and camaraderie experienced at other races is completely lacking.

Eventually a gun goes off somewhere far ahead of where we are and after a while the crowd we're in begins shuffling forward, a shuffle being the best one can do in such a large crowd. Within a few minutes, though, we're bouncing up the Verrazano Bridge and when we reach the top of its arch all we can see are runners, stretching out ahead of us and down the other side of the bridge leading us into Brooklyn. And a phalanx of men lined up at the bridge railing, pissing into the water below, reminiscent of our time at the army physical. The pissers who have signed up for this draft are fulfilling their promise.

The run is not easy; the city has hills. Where did they come from? The only part of the city where we ever walked was the few blocks in Brooklyn to school and parts of Manhattan and they were all flat. But now, running toward the Queensborough Bridge, we have to lift our head and look up at the long hill leading to the entrance. And once across the bridge and on Second Avenue we see the stream of runners ahead of us, their heads bobbing up and down like cartoon chickens escaping the coop.

At the end of Second Avenue we cross the Harlem River into the Bronx and that's when George 'hits the wall.' This has never happened before. We're fine until, suddenly, I feel him go limp, as if he has been kicked in the stomach. He has no energy, no strength, and I'm sure he is going to collapse and me along with him. I hear George thinking to himself: *OK...so I'll collapse. I've never done that before. It'll be interesting to see what that's like.* But he keeps running, though now the effort is all mental.

We cross the Madison Avenue Bridge out of the Bronx, back down into Manhattan onto Fifth Avenue, alongside Central Park, and all I can hear is George telling himself to keep moving, one foot in front of another, and if he collapses, he thinks, so what. And at last we turn into Central Park and head up to Fifty-Ninth Street, somehow through sheer will, continuing to move, turning onto Central Park South, down to Columbus Circle, and then back into the park to the finish line.

As soon as we cross the line, George collapses. Attendants wrap a foil sheet around us, guide us to a tent, and place us on a cot, at which point every orifice in George's body opens and every bit of fluid drains out of his body.

❧ ❑ ☞

We lay there for at least two hours, having been given an IV to replace fluids and dozing on and off. (Someone occasionally jostles us to make sure we haven't gone into a coma.) When eventually we have enough strength to get up, we check out of the First Aid tent, and go to the hotel. Bill is already there and we share racing experiences. Bill, as it turns out, has fared better—no need for first aid, but George's time is better than his. In fact, once again he has cut off twenty minutes. But the notions of racing glory are gone.

"Why are you doing this to yourself?" I ask. And he doesn't have an answer, but I know it has more to do with matters other than health and fitness.

❧ ❑ ☞

It's weeks before we go for a run again. And gradually we get back into running on a regular basis. We even went back to doing some fartleks, but that move triggers another problem.

When we come home from running one day, we piss blood. And we panic. Memories of the thyroid cancer return and our fear levels spike. We immediately go to a doctor, a friend who is also a runner, and he asks what kind of workouts we're doing. George tells him about the fartleks and he nods knowingly. "You probably bruised your bladder."

Intense running bounces one's bladder against other organs and it can get bruised and produce blood in the urine. "Stop running for a few days," the doctor says. "If it goes away, you're fine."

When we resume running, it's only three or four miles a day, with more days off. The New York City Marathon and the bloody urine have put an end to the serious running. And years later it will become more conclusive when arthritis and meniscus problems arise.

THIRTY-THREE
A Matter of Degrees

WHAT WAS HE THINKING? GEORGE may be something of a creative academic, but when it comes to academic politics, he's more from the Woody Allen school:

> "The Government is unresponsive to the needs of the little man. Under five-seven, it is impossible to get your Congressman on the phone."
> [Woody Allen, from his Speech to the Graduates, originally published in the New York Times, August 10, 1979]

Whether running away from home or running away from life, the race came to a conclusion when George stood up at a college board meeting and spoke against items in the President's budget like carpeting for his office, a car, and a monthly stipend for his personal use. I could have told him how that would go over, but I was so far out of his thinking process that a bullhorn wouldn't have got through. So it wasn't long after that event that the President 'reorganizes the staff, eliminates George's title of Dean and creates what is virtually a position without authority— "Special Assistant to the President for Grant Programs." And he returns to teaching English.

✎ ❑ ☞

George steps down from the job as Assistant for Grant Programs ("strongly encouraged to step down," is a better description) and returns to teaching English full-time. He's still running; the only thing we're halfway good at. He also begins writing articles for area publications like *Texas Runner, Austin Magazine,* and *Third Coast Magazine.* It's a simpler life compared to the madness involved in starting up a college without a tax base or faculty, and having no idea how to do it.

In the meantime, Barbara returns to graduate school, in the same program George had been in and she is now interning at Alvin Community College, a little school outside of Houston. And one night, in a crazy act of desperation, when he is wallowing in his angst, he tells Barbara he wants a divorce.

She is devastated.

And he is unable to reconcile his emotions.

He doesn't really want a divorce. (But I do.) He expects her to fight it, to do something to stop him (though he doesn't know what.) He expects her to get rid of <u>me</u> somehow. *Fat chance,* I whisper. *How many balls can you keep in the air?* I ask, because <u>my</u> life is simple. I have no balls to juggle, no bills to pay, no classes to teach, no races to run. I'm just along for the ride. So I ask. *Three? Four? Five?*

At times like these, when George goes off the deep end, our relationship becomes more difficult. These are the times when the connections between us break, and like mirrors facing mirrors, we each see nothing but ourselves; the demons we each fear see each other's reflection. I am a big part of that pronouncement. The more George has denied me the stronger I have become and so I push back. Nothing matters to me except escape. I don't belong in this show. I need to get out.

George has nothing planned out, nothing thought through or calculated. The way he explains it to himself is like this: *There's a little person inside our heads watching everything we do and if something needs to be done, <u>the</u> little person takes control and the* *rest of our mental activity shifts into auto-pilot. George doesn't really know what's happening. And I am on auto-pilot. Is someone else flying the plane?*

He thinks that the little lady in his head has gotten the better of him, but I refuse to let him use me as an excuse. I am not his pilot. I'm more of a passenger. So then he steals my metaphor. He says that he is trying to juggle too many "balls" at once, that his life is just too complicated, and he has to drop at least one ball, regardless of the consequences. But I can tell that he has no idea of what's driving his behavior.

Barbara rejects all of his theories and labels it an early mid-life crisis. She goes back to New York, to her parents. George goes through the motions of his daily activities. He shuts down everything except essential functions. Routine becomes his escape. He visits Bill Ryan, a fellow Geneseo alumnus who is recently divorced and now lives in San Antonio and asks his advice. Bill's answer: *Don't look back.*

And then Ric Sternberg calls.

A year or so earlier, following a run-in with the law in Vermont involving a little garden with some plants not yet legal even for medical purposes, Ric has moved down to Austin and has worked at the college for a while, but now, he explains, he has hooked up with a local group doing some kind of renegade theater thing and wants to know if George has any of those scripts he produced when they first met at Syracuse University. "We need material," he says.

Yes, we do, but we were sidetracked from creative writing into academia, on a crusade to change the way higher education worked and finding the ivy covered windmills too big and already too tilted, so that work had been all but forgotten. The Esther's group, as Ric describes it, is creating a kind of socialistic theatre;

not the Clifford Odets sort, but something more along the lines of Edward Albee Meets Horatio Alger. So George digs through the detritus of his earlier life, finds the scripts, and joins Ric at Esther's Pool to meet the group.

There are about fifteen people involved: performers Michael Nesline, William Dente, Terry Galloway, Linda Wetherby, Michael Shelton, Shannon Sedgwig, pianists and arranger/composers, Lyova Anderson and Steve Saugey, and lighting director Michael Prokoroff. Shannon Sedwig and her partner, Michael Shelton are the driving forces behind it all and 'ragtag' doesn't even begin to describe the collection of players.

It's a Monday night and everyone has assembled in the bodega Shelton renovated to accommodate bleacher-style seating. The most unique aspect of all is that the stage backs up to a row of floor to ceiling picture windows overlooking Sixth Street with the result that those performing have their backs to those walking along the street outside.

A small group is seated around a table onstage. George passes out copies of one of his scripts. It's called *Solitaire,* a rewrite of the piece written while at Syracuse University and which Sternberg made into a short film when we all lived in New York City. The original version never worked quite right, but the Follies version did because George now realizes that it needs to rhyme and the rhyme generates the timing needed to get laughs.

Of all the games we play or dare
The only game is Solitaire
But no one laughs. Linda blinks and says "I don't get it."

Ric intercedes on George's behalf. "Don't worry…it'll work," he says.

Shannon is shaking her head. "I don't know…"

"It does," we say, "…work…it'll work."

Enough people agree to play the four parts, so it gets put in the line-up. (That's the way it works. A script or an idea is presented to the group and if enough people agree to be in it, it gets in.) And so George becomes a writer for *Esther's Follies* and I am again a muse.

☜ ❑ ☞

The only businesses on Sixth Street in 1977 are the Follies and Wylie's restaurant. Over the next four years, a wave of businesses swoop in and Sixth Street becomes for Austin what Bourbon Street is for New Orleans. But for now, it's considered a dangerous place.

Along with Steve Saugey and Terry Galloway and a few others who occasionally come up with an idea, George becomes one of the main writers. We have something in just about every show. And what makes it even better is the talent of the performers. I might come up with something that's good, and George's script is spot on, but the actors invariably make it better. Often, knowing what they can do, we will write something with one or the other of them in mind. (Once when on a Valentine's Day show, I realize that all we have to do is write a script with William Dente playing the part of Cupid and he would take care of the rest.)

Lyova, one of our musical directors, is responsible for much of the music and she produces a lot of "highbrow" numbers. She does arrangements for pieces like the Blandscrew Sisters train medley (*Chattanooga Choo Choo, Sentimental Journey*, etc.). Steve, on the other hand, writes original musical pieces or adapts music to satirical purposes. One of his cleverest is the *Jalapeno Chorus* (to the music of the *Hallelujah Chorus*) done as a group of customers giving their order to a waiter in a Mexican restaurant. And his masterpiece is *Westward Hose*. The music and lyrics are original and the plot…well, it's years before anyone had the nerve to consider that a cowboy might be gay. It begins with a girl crying in a laundromat because she's just learned that her boyfriend has left her for her brother. In the middle of the song she is interrupted by a drag queen (Stale Evans) who whisks her away to a dude ranch so she can meet her Prince Charming and it concludes with said prince arriving on a white horse and whisking her away. [The prince (a cowboy dressed entirely in white western gear) shows up on the street outside the window on a real white horse. He comes inside the theatre and takes her outside, lifts her onto the horse, and they ride away down the street.]

Apart from teaching and the complications of life at home, which now involves taking care of a son and daughter because Barbara, blindsided by the divorce, has gone home to New York, the *Follies* consumes much of our time It has jump-started <u>my</u> role as writer's muse.

For the next couple of weeks our routine consists of jotting down ideas as George goes to work, picks up the kids, and handles the other required mundane activities. On Sundays, we sit at the typewriter, using the week's notes as reference and carbon paper to produce copies, then go to the little theatre (*Esther's Pool*) on

George and Cass Charboneau
in one of his skits
at Esther's Follies.

Monday night and share our work with everyone else's ideas. After some discussion, we decide what to continue to work on, then rehearse on Tuesday and Wednesday night, perform a dress rehearsal on Thursday night, then do two shows on Friday night and two more on Saturday night. And then, on Sunday, we start all over with new ideas, scripts, and music.

It's like a drug and the highs are only matched by the running highs. It

peaks at those times when we're standing at the back of the little theatre, watching the actors perform our material, and hearing the audience laugh. And like a drug, it shoves aside bad feelings and regrets about the divorce and failed career. We can't get enough of that 'applause.'

GEORGE WILKERSON

THIRTY-FOUR
An Old Companion

"*BEAUTY AND FOLLY*" SAID BENJAMIN Franklin "*are old companions.*" And true to the aphorism, the god of irony steps in and tosses another ball in the air in the form of a girl named Sallie. She's a student in our American Literature class and comes up to us after class one day and invites us outside. "You seem tense," she says.

We follow her to the back of the school gymnasium where she produces a joint, lights it, takes a drag, and hands it to us.

"No..I…er…I…"

She insists and we comply. As it is when he drinks, I'm not affected, although I can feel him drifting away from me. And I can tell he likes the feeling. So I let him go.

They finish the joint and as they return to the classroom building George invites her to the Follies show that Friday. "I'll put your name on the guest list," he says.

☞ ❑ ☞

That Friday she shows up, though we weren't sure she would (I was sure she would; a woman picks up on these things) and after the show they go for breakfast and George vents his spleen for hours, carrying on about the disappointments in his life and everything he's trying to handle and finally culminates with me. Yes. He tells her about me. Or at least he tries to. He puts it in the simplest words possible. "I like to wear womens clothes," he says.

"Nothing wrong with that," she replies.

He hesitates. "Er…underwear…dresses…"

She nods. "OK."

She doesn't know how deep it goes. He's simply presenting himself as a guy who "dresses up," a crossdresser. He's not talking about what's in his soul. He's not talking about me.

But I figure it's a start. Then they move on to another subject because George is uncomfortable with pursuing it further and she doesn't seem all that interested in the topic. They go to her place, a tiny garage apartment with a single bed and the affair begins.

☙ ❑ ☞

Maybe George thought it was macho or maybe it was that Texas makes northerners think they have to own a truck, but George has one now. And after a Follies show one night Ric explains that he has been talking to an old friend (Bennet Spielvogel, professionally known as *The East Side Flash*) who is living in Vermont in the town where he had lived, and that he would be an ideal person to add to the Follies crew. "He's a phenomenal keyboard player and excellent guitarist," Ric explains. "We could drive up and get him over the weekend."

George doesn't know where this conversation is going and I don't want to know.

"It's a straight shot," he says. "Interstate all the way. We could take turns driving."

"George," I say, in my calmest secret voice. "Remember college? The trips to the city that never materialized?"

But he doesn't listen.

Then George (not my George, but Little George, the Follies resident pantomime) chimes in. "You going to Vermont?" he asks.

Ric nods. "Just over the weekend…up and back in one shot."

"Cool," says George. "Could you get my girlfriend? She's in Proctor."

Ric looks at us. I am washing my hands of the whole idea, but George just shrugs. "I suppose…"

"Great!" says Little George.

'My son, too," says Ric. "He's at my parents…in Queens."

In just seconds, the entire thing has got out of hand.

꧁ ❏ ꧂

The following weekend we're on the road to Vermont. The pickup truck has a camper shell with a sliding window behind the front seat and an inflatable seal between the cab and the truck bed, leaving just enough room to crawl back and forth between the cab and the camper/bed. The distance to Vermont is about a thousand miles. Somehow we make it and when we arrive Bennett is ready to go. In addition to his bags, he is bringing his upright piano, which we load into the truck, then stop off to pick up Little George's girlfriend who, it turns out also has a dog she wants to bring along (German Shepherd). We then head down to Queens to get Ric's son Reed. At Ric's parents we have something to eat, load more stuff (including the pieces of Reed's hydroponic marijuana garden), and take off for Texas.

This is not my gig. George is driving, the girlfriend in the middle with the dog's rear end in George's lap and his head in Little George's girlfriend's lap, and Ric is in the 'shotgun position' on the right. In the back, in the truck bed, Bennett and Reed are sprawled out on one side on top of the luggage with their feet propped against the piano, which is on the other side to keep it from falling over on the turns. It's a good thing I don't need any space because there wouldn't be any for me.

Popping pills every four hours or so makes the time fly by and before we know it we're on the Pennsylvania Turnpike and Bennett is now playing the piano. Ric has brought his drumsticks and is beating a rhythm on the dashboard, and we're all singing "Six Days on the Road," but ten years too late to join Ken Kesey's *Merry Pranksters*.

We arrive back in Austin around six p.m.

THIRTY-FIVE
The Heart and Soul of Darkness

THE BEHAVIORIST THEORY OF GENDER identity is based on the belief that when we're born our minds are a blank. Transgender people, they say, simply failed to properly socialize into their correct gender. George and I read this in a college text and considered it for all of a minute. Sure, George doesn't fit the classic male image, but he's not 'feminine.' And I am. And I am very good at hiding.

So there we are. It's 1979 and George is ensconced in the velvet rut of Austin, living with Sallie in a rent house on Lake Austin Boulevard, writing and performing at the Follies, and teaching at ACC. For the most part, it's a comfortable situation, except that the kids spend half their year with us and that entails stepping out of the light and being a responsible parent. It's probably the worst custody arrangement possible. When the son and daughter are with us, I rarely have a chance to get out. And son John is not happy; he "acts out." One day we catch him starting a fire in his bedroom. Another day he jumps down on Sallie's foot and practically cripples her. And Jennifer soothes herself with friends, staying overnight with them or watching *Grease* or *The Shining*; escaping to anywhere else she can.

Then, another life-changing phone call. Stuart Johnson, a mentor from the Education Laboratory in North Carolina, along with his wife Rita, is involved in a training project for a subsidiary of Shell Oil called *Scallop*. He wants to know if George will come to work for him at a salary of $60,000 a year and all living expenses paid.

The job is that of Head Writer for a group of technical writers whose primary job is to develop operations manuals for tasks associated with running oil well flow stations (collection points where a preliminary separation of oil, gas, and water takes place.)

What's the catch?" George asks.

"No catch," says Stuart. "We're doing training in Nigeria and…"

"That's a definite catch," George says and tells him no thanks.

But a week later Stuart calls back and tells us the offer is the same, but we won't have to go to Nigeria. We can work from Houston. So George reluctantly agrees to go to Houston and talk to Stuart about it and a few days later we're in his office and George is reading off a list of caveats associated with taking the job. Among the items on the list: no suit, no tie, and a four day work week every other week so we can spend the three day weekend back in Austin with our round-trip air fare paid by *Scallop*. To our dismay, he agrees to it.

And that's how, in January of 1980, we wind up in Houston, ready to start work. Then Stuart tells us there has been a change in plans. We have to go to Africa after all. (That probably was the real plan all along, but George's naiveté turned a blind eye to it. Now we're here and locked into a contract for 18 months.)

☞ ❏ ☞

Nigeria. Does it stir up romantic images? Or is it just a search for Kurtz in the *Heart of Darkness*? We are very nervous about going there. It takes about six weeks to get visas, since the Nigerian government has all kinds of restrictions on people coming in and going out and on anything having to do with writing and so we can't say exactly what we're going there to do. If we're called writers they think we're journalists, so there are delays while we get visas that call us 'consultants. But we're finally cleared and off we go.

In all, we will travel to Nigeria and back three times, usually with different people. Among them is *Bill Scott*, a friend from the Educational Leadership graduate program at the University of Texas, *Bennet Spielvogel*, who has worked at the Follies with us after we moved him from Vermont, *Charlie Tesar*, a buddy from the Educational Leadership graduate program, *Anne Cramer*, (formerly Ash) from Cortland High School and John Tyler days, *Stuart and Rita Johnson*, the couple who had the Shell contract to design the training program, *Jack*, a friend of the Johnsons, *Betsy*, a woman the Johnsons had worked with before, and *Vladimer Valderama*, a Romanian engineer with the classic vampire-sounding heavy accent, who is working on getting his American citizenship. The *Scallop* people include Jerry, an older Brit, very much the stereotypical blustery gentleman with an accent like that of Simon Cowell.

For the first six weeks we are all housed at the Houston Meridian Hotel. The *Scallop* office is across the street from the hotel, attached by an overpass. *Scallop* pays for everything, but the routine gets boring fast. Breakfast together, then to the office to hang out until coffee break, around 10, then hang out some more, then lunch at the hotel around noon, then back to the office, hang out for the afternoon, then back to the hotel at 4:00 for happy hour, then dinner together, and then off to our rooms.

The hanging out part is occasionally broken up by a meeting where we talk about what we're going to do when we get to Nigeria. Computers arrive so we spend some time learning how they operate. This is 1980 and these are the first desktop computers with word processors built in and printers and plotters attached. George is fascinated by them and spends extra time learning whatever he can. There are no user manuals and no directions, so the learning is all trial and error and occasional sessions with the Hewlett-Packard technology consultant. George thus becomes the computer guy and while the others are busy looking at flow station diagrams and training algorithms, he's writing the directions on how to operate the computer.

~ ❏ ☞

George is no Marlow and there is no Kurtz. We fly out of Houston at two pm and arrive in Amsterdam at seven a.m. There's a short layover, then we fly from Amsterdam to Lagos. We fly First Class. It's all the booze you want, big comfy seats, and special boarding privileges. Drinks are served before the plane even takes off. Slippers are provided and once in the air, a movie, then dinner (and more booze) and after that the shades are drawn and lights lowered, but sleep is spotty at best..

When the lights come up we're about to land in Amsterdam—stretch, yawn, etc. and we're off the plane and hanging out. Eventually we're on the next plane and on our way across the Sahara. Looking out the window there's nothing but desert sand below and we're thinking *If the plane was to go down here no one would ever find us.* So the shades get pulled down and we watch another movie and a couple of hours later the shades are pulled up and we look down and it looks exactly the same as it did before, nothing has changed; it's the same desert. It's as if the plane simply hung in the same air space for that whole time.

~ ❏ ☞

When we arrive at the Lagos airport we're told to watch for a man with a *Shell* sign, but first we must go through customs and Nigerian customs gives new meaning to the word 'chaos.' All we can do is follow the crowd.

Eventually we arrive at a kind of checkpoint, a long counter with half a dozen men in uniform behind it. There are also other uniformed men carrying guns and standing in such a way as to make it clear that we are to line up at one end of the counter and we should not shove or talk or smile. (Shades of the nuns from elementary school, but on a scale only a terrorist could understand.) Slowly, we make our way to the first man. By this time, we have been instructed to have our passport and shot record ready. George holds out his and the man takes the passport, opens it, tucks the shot record between the last page and the back cover, then slides it to the second man. He peruses it, turns a couple of pages, and passes it to the next man who looks at us and asks "What is your business in Nigeria?" George replies (as instructed in Houston) "Educational consultant." He nods and hands the passport to the next man who takes it and immediately slams it with a massive rubber stamp. He then hands it to the next man who closes it and hands it back to us. Five men…five jobs. It's like the scene from the 1949 Lou Bunin Claymation movie of Carol Marsh's "Alice in Wonderland" where the playing-card soldiers sing about communication with the Queen: "The First tells the Second, the Second tells the Third, the Third tells the fourth, the Fourth tells the Fifth, and so on down the line . . ."(All American politicians talk about 'job creation.' These guys have mastered it; however, our politicians would likely look at this process and complain that the government is inefficient and expect the techies to come up with a robot to do it.)

At last we're directed to a doorway, a sliding glass door opens and we're thrust into the total chaos that is Lagos, Nigeria. People everywhere, cars honking their horns, vendors, beggars, and stray animals moving in a blur of dizzying activity. George is about to shit in his pants (our pants, dammit…and I have no control over it. This is one of the drawbacks of being me while being him.) I am busy wondering how in hell I got myself into this, when a hand taps us on the shoulder and there is Bill Scott motioning toward someone with a sign that says *SHELL*. We scurry toward it and the man directs us to a small car parked at the curb. With the help of the driver, we toss our bags into the trunk, climb in and are off and running through the city.

As a child in New York we often heard this: "If you can drive in New York City you can drive anywhere." Clearly, the person who spread that rumor never tried to drive in Lagos. Niceties like stop signs and traffic lights are rare here. If someone could make a video game out of the Lagos driving experience it would be a million-seller. Pedestrians completely disregard the automobiles and drivers generally disregard each other. Gas...brake...horn... gas...brake... horn...it's insane. It makes me wonder why there aren't more Nigerian NASCAR drivers. Rather than avoiding people and other vehicles our driver seems to be aiming at them, but somehow, some way, we make it to the Shell Guest House where, we are told, we'll be staying until our flight to Warri is ready.

The place is comfortable. There are private bedrooms, a common eating area, a living room with a television (though the only thing on TV is the state channel which broadcasts political fare for just a couple of hours each day), and a few easy chairs. So we wait.

George, the "Shell Man" in Nigeria.

The next day we're told we will be leaving for Warri in the

afternoon. We are driven back to the airport, but not to the main terminal. Instead we learn we'll be taking a Shell-owned plane leaving from a private hanger. It's a Fokker twin-engine which we soon discover is barely able to stay above the trees. The only scenery as we fly down the coast is the ocean on one side and forest on the other, with occasional clearings where gas flares from oil wells are burning. Crashing in the desert would have been better. And yet, once again, we make it to Warri, and are taken to the Shell living quarters.

GEORGE WILKERSON

THIRTY-SIX
We Take Care of Him

THE ENTIRE NIGERIA EXPERIENCE IS an eye-opener for both George and me. We live in a rectangular 'compound,' an area that feels more like a prison block, surrounded by high walls of cinder blocks with broken glass cemented into the top. There are a dozen 'flats' (little apartments), six on each side, and a dining hall and kitchen at one end. At the other end there is a single gate and alongside of that there's a huge caterpillar generator which the gatekeeper fires up when the state's power goes out, which is about four times a day.

We eat all of our meals together and travel in and out of the compound to the Shell offices every day. We have the weekends off and some of us use them to travel to various places and take in the local culture. This includes a trip to Benin, an ancient walled-in city where there are a number of craftsmen creating wood carvings and jewelry made of ivory. (We're warned that if the ivory is found when returning to the U.S. it can be confiscated and we could face criminal charges.)

The culture is dramatically different from ours. It's what America might have been like if we had not decimated the Native Americans, but instead superimposed the European cultures on top of them. There are more than 200 tribes in Nigeria, each with its own history and traditions. The Ibo, Housa, and Yoruba are the majority, but many more vie for a place in the government, which over the years has vacillated between that of a democratic republic to that of a dictator or one run by the military.

We do not drive while we're here. Although Shell can get us a temporary license, we are told that it's very risky. If we are involved in an accident, Stuart says, whether we're driving or with a driver, we should not stay at the scene. Leave immediately, is the rule, since the locals often take the law into their own hands and a foreigner is generally considered guilty of whatever happened.

And we have become friends with the Shell pharmacist who often joins us for dinner. Americans, it seems for the most part, are liked by the Nigerians. Not so the English or the Dutch. The impression we get from his stories are that they each have a different attitude toward the 'natives.' The Dutch see them as an ignorant people who must be told what to do. The British have a more paternalistic attitude—the poor beggars, they tell us, need to be guided along.

One evening, in the course of discussing the current Nigerian state, which is modeled after the U.S., with two chambers of elected officials from each of the 19 states and an elected President, the Pharmacist complains that the man elected from his state is corrupt. It is clear to everyone that he is taking tax money for his own purposes and is not representing them as he should

"What do you do with such a man?" he asks.

"Well," George explains. "There are just two options I can think of."

"Yes," the Pharmacist says. "What are they?"

George goes on. "You can have a recall, where if enough people sign a petition there's a special election and they can vote him out."

The Pharmacist nods.

George continues. "Or you can wait until the next election and organize to support an opponent who isn't corrupt."

The Pharmacist again. "Hmmmm."

Then Stuart jumps in. "Or you can file criminal charges, if there's enough evidence that he's breaking the law."

The Pharmacist pauses for a moment, pondering the options. "How quickly can this be done?"

Stuart shrugs. "It depends," he says. "Any of those options could take a year or two."

The Pharmacist shakes his head. "No..no..." he mutters, "no... no...no"

Stuart scratches his head. "Those are the only choices I can think of," he says.

The Pharmacist looks directly at Stuart. "No..." he says, then nods. "We take care of him," he says. "We take care of him." And we know exactly what he means.

❧ ❑ ☞

We have been in Nigeria a couple of weeks when, at the end of one day, we come back to the compound and learn that one member of the team is no longer with us. We have known that Jack, a friend of Stuart and Rita, is gay, but it's never openly discussed. This is still the nineteen-seventies, so if the issue comes up it is skirted or talked about with euphemisms.

What we soon learn is that Jack made a pass at one of the workers in the compound, the young man who operates the gate and the Caterpillar generator. The details aren't clear, but Stuart explains that Jack was hurried out of the country as quickly as possible, having narrowly escaped the wrath of the operator's father and other members of the nearby village where he lived.

The incident is unnerving to me and I can tell it has shaken George. We knew before taking this journey that if I were to come out while here there would be serious repercussions. The only difference between Jack and us is that others on the team knew of Jack's sexual orientation. But gender issues? It's not likely that anyone would understand that. And certainly not the Nigerians. So I was not just in the background during this time; I was in hiding.

❧ ❑ ☞

When there's an opening for a weekend trip to Lagos, we take advantage of it—not to tour the city, but to call home. There are no international phone lines in Warri, so the flight to Lagos and a stay in the guest house, where a working phone line might be established, is the only way to do it.

We get to the guesthouse, drop our bags in the living room, and immediately head to the phone. An operator asks for the number and we tell her it's an international call to Austin, Texas. Then we hang up and wait. And wait. And wait.

There's only one television channel. It's state run and is mostly used to broadcast speeches by the current president—a great way to induce a nap.

It's a lot like planning for a hot night of sex. Sometimes the phone rings and the connection is made. Most times it never happens and we fly back to Warri feeling unsatisfied.

On one occasion, we connect with Sallie. It's not a comfortable conversation. She sounds bothered by it. Her remarks are short and without detail. She's working at *The Omelettry*, going to classes, and not interested in what's happening in Nigeria. There's a sense that something more is going on, but how do we process that 'sense?' As she often does, she takes control of the conversation and soon ends it.

☜ ❏ ☞

When it's time for the team to head back home to Houston, we steel ourselves for the car trip to the little Warri airport. In cartoon-like fashion, the runway crosses the main road. There are gates, like those at a railroad crossing, and a man on each side lowers his gate when a plane is coming in to land. Cars stop behind the gate, but not in lanes. Instead, they line up like runners at the start of a marathon, waiting for the gate to go up—rows of cars facing each other like the Gauls standing across from the Romans, ready to attack. It seems that once the gates go up neither army will survive, but somehow the cars weave in and out and around each other and calmly make their way down the road.

When we arrive in Lagos the seaport is filled with tankers, clearly loaded with oil, but going nowhere. "That's why there's an oil shortage at home," Stuart says.

At the airport, we put our bags down on the scale to check in and the reservations clerk, a large man in a uniform more military than that of the airline clerks we're familiar with, and carrying a swagger stick, slams the stick on one of the suitcases.

"What is in the bag?" the man says sternly.

George smiles. "Souvenirs."

"How many?" he asks.

George shrugs. "Ten…twelve maybe?"

BAM! He slaps the bag again. "Too many!"

George reaches for the bag. "I can leave some here," he says.

BAM! He slaps the bag once more. "NO!"

George is at a loss now. "What should I do?" he asks, in his most polite voice.

"What do you think you should do?" the man asks sweetly, shifting from his autocratic demeanor to an oily purr.

George shrugs again. "I don't know."

The man, exasperated, uses his stick to point to a place across from the counter. "Wait," he says. "There."

George obediently crosses to the designated area, leaving his bags on the platform, and waits. After a few moments, a boy perhaps ten or eleven years old appears at his side and tugs on his jacket. "He send me," the boy says, pointing to the clerk. "He want you to dash him."

'Dash' is Nigerian slang for 'bribe' (or if you want to be more polite, you might say 'tip.')

"Oh," George says, finally catching on. "How much?"

The boy smiles. "How much you got?"

At this, George reaches into his pocket and produces a ten Naira bill (Naira is the standard Nigerian currency.) "That's all I have," he says, lying.

The boy takes the money and nods at the clerk who immediately wraps tags around the two suitcases and places them on the cart to be taken to the plane.

THIRTY-SEVEN
Back to the Heartland

WE TRAVEL BACK AND FORTH from Houston to Nigeria a total of three times and for the last trip, George obtains permission from the head of the project to take along our twelve-year old African-American daughter. Even better, the project head says Shell will foot the bill. So, we tell Jennifer that she's going to see the land of her forefathers and shortly before Christmas, after clearing it with Barbara, Jennifer and George and I head out.

Once on the plane, she takes out a paperback book—*The Diary of Anne Frank*—and explains that she is reading it as a requirement for her English class. So we add a day to the layover in Amsterdam and go to the house where Anne hid. We tour the house and wave at the neo-Nazis who are parked across the street, handing out literature claiming the holocaust never happened. And as an added bonus, we go to the movies to see Mel Brook's *History of the World (Part I)*…in Dutch! What a delight. And in some small way it feels like snubbing our noses at the neo-Nazis.

The next day we're off to Lagos and after a night at the Shell guest house, we're flying down to Warri. We spend a week in the compound there and later learn that one day, while George is at work, the housekeeper comes into our flat and he finds Jennifer asleep in bed, whereupon he crawls in alongside her. She awakes and immediately tells him she needs to use the bathroom, goes there, and locks herself in. After a few moments, the man knocks on the door.

"Are you coming out?" he asks.

"No!" she says. "Go away!"

After some time, he leaves and Jennifer runs to Bill Scott's flat and asks him if she can stay there until George gets back, but doesn't tell Bill what happened, nor does she tell us until we're back in the states. The remainder of her stay is uneventful, but includes time with a pet goat named George (because of his red hair) who one day disappears only to reappear on a platter for dinner.

Jennifer also makes friends with one of the local boys named Christopher Company. He is clearly smitten with her and they will exchange letters for a while after she gets home. But for now, they simply hang out and talk occasionally until it's time for us to return to the U.S.

We fly back to Lagos where we are invited by Henry Omini, the head of Shell Nigeria, to take a tour of the city. We visit a hotel for lunch and get a lecture from Henri on Nigerian history, the colonization by the British and the Dutch and the eventual liberation of the country. He points out that despite the attitudes of the Dutch and the Brits, who both regard the Nigerians as ignorant and backward, when the country's civil war took place (during which some two million Ibo died) Nigerians continued to operate the oil fields.

Following lunch we return to Mr. Omini's limo and continue the tour, which does not include the dead body we spy lying on a street corner. Rigor Mortis has clearly set in. Jennifer's gaze is frozen. She looks at us and George instinctively raises his finger to his lips. She says nothing, and later, back at the guest house, we explain that in Nigeria, as in many parts of the world, there's no infrastructure for dealing with things like that.

The next day we pack up and go to the airport, but once there we discover that flights have been cancelled. There's no plane waiting for us because it never left London. (Foreign airlines don't leave planes at the airport overnight because of the risk of vandalism and theft.) A snow storm has stranded it. So we return to the guest house and begin a series of trips back and forth to the airport until, at last, a plane comes in and we're able to get away.

But not so fast. Once we're airborne the pilot announces that another snowstorm precludes our being able to land in London and that we're going to Scotland instead, but since we don't have enough fuel to get there, we're stopping at Majorca to refuel.

Once on the ground in Majorca, George makes a decision. And I concur. So he calls to the stewardess and tells her we want to get off the plane. She argues with him, but George tells her he is aware of the international rules of flight which say that if a passenger wants to get off he or she must be allowed to do so, even if they have not reached their final destination, and so the stewardess relents and George and Jennifer and I disembark, collect our bags, and catch a cab to a hotel on the beach.

This wouldn't be so bad if it weren't December and a dip in the ocean is out of the question; however, the hotel is nice and at dinner we are treated to a group of tourists from Germany dancing to the music of a little band that plays the chicken dance over and over. The Germans are obviously here to have fun and Jennifer is delighted by them. It helps set us up for a good night's sleep and we're a little saddened in the morning as we watch the sun rise over the ocean and must pack our bags for the trip back to the airport in hopes of catching a flight to Madrid, which we figure is our best chance for connecting to the states.

We manage to book a flight for later that day with a connection in Madrid for New York City and just as we do so we spy the remaining passengers from the flight we came in on coming into the terminal. Scotland, it seems, is snowed out too, so the airline chose to stay and put everyone up at another hotel. Of course, the poor souls didn't get the bonus of a chicken dance with their dinner.

☜ ❑ ☞

We return from Nigeria for the last time and go back to Austin where George has no idea of what he's going to do. The job at ACC is gone, but his connections at the school are still good and he gets a couple of sections of Freshman English to teach as a part-timer.

We move into a rental house with Sallie. She is very concerned with appearances. She says she 'connected' with Katherine Hepburn and carries herself in a rigid posture, her back always straightened and her chin up. And she frets about her hair, which is extremely thin and doesn't style very well. George sees her as the girl from the *Draw Me* ads—the ones in magazines that offered an "home study" art course scholarship. She is the American Beauty who will save him from me. That's all he needs (he thinks) to satisfy the impulse that I am. He doesn't understand <u>our</u> relationship at all. And no effort on my part to warn him about the path he has taken will work.

☜ ❑ ☞

Sallie is now at *Southwest Texas University* working on a degree in Geology (with George footing the bill). Son John and daughter Jennifer live with us from January to June, The Shell/Scallop job has left us with enough money to live on for a short while. Then another ACC connection brings us to work at a little company called Balcones Computer Corporation (BCC). There are about 60 employees and it turns out that George's experience with the Hewlett-Packard desktop computers has some value. There just aren't many technical writers around who know anything about computers.

Lucia McKay, who taught math at ACC and is the head of the BCC Technical Writing group is now George's boss. The floppy disks used by the computers are 7 inches wide and they hold an incredible 400 kilobytes of data. (The one-inch long flash drive you have in your pocket holds 3 gigabytes or more.) We use a word processor called *WordStar* (the same one we used at Scallop) so George knows something about it, but not as much as he fakes in his interview. (George has always been good at faking: *"fake it 'til you make it"* is our motto. He has faked being a male for a long time now.)

The job involves documenting a financial accounting software package called *The Boss*. BCC also makes hardware in the form of a computer they call "the woody" because, like the old station wagons with wood paneling, the computer is actually contained in a wooden box. We also work with a "portable" computer called the Kaypro—portable only in the sense that it has a handle. It is made entirely of metal, with a 9-inch screen, a fold down keyboard and two five-inch floppy disk drives. It runs on an operating system called CP/M and weighs close to 35 pounds.

BCC is owned and run by a trio of friends. In addition to Lucia, there is Bill Gordon, (a black man who these days looks a lot like James Earl Jones), who is a hardware whiz and Maurice Mahlab, who was born in Iran and came to the U.S. when he was 19 to go to Texas A&M University. He eventually got a Ph.D. in Physics and invented a unique style of rotary engine which he patented and then sold to one of the major U.S. automakers. And he created the little trick everyone who has ever used a computer knows for fixing a mistake: <ALT> <Backspace>. It takes you back one set of keystrokes from the one you just entered. But he never bothered to patent it and a while later it showed up as part of Microsoft WORD's features.

Maurice liked to jog in the mornings and he lives close to us and on Saturdays he comes by and we sit outside on our porch and drink coffee and talk. He also comes by frequently on Sunday afternoons to hang out at our pool. (Our house is one of the few in East Austin that has one.)George can always count on Maurice for help if he has a technical question or needs advice. Maurice is smart and sweet and kind-hearted.

One Saturday morning Maurice calls and says he has been depressed and can't shake it off. It makes no sense for him to feel that way. His wife of only about a year is four months pregnant with their first child. He has a good job that he likes. And there is nothing seriously wrong in his life. But something is driving him into a deep depression and he is afraid of what he might do.

George asks if he has seen a professional and he explains that he has, but the doctor did nothing more than write a prescription for an anti-depressant which he has quit taking it because it makes him into a zombie. (That's a description that comes to haunt me a couple years later when a therapist puts George on Prozac as a way to treat the "crossdressing" and we experience the zombie state.)

We had nothing to tell him. Yes, we said, we get depressed, but George won't reveal the cause, though of all his friends, Maurice would likely be the most accepting. Is there something like me that's eating at Maurice's mind? Wouldn't it help if we shared my dilemma with him, I ask George, but he's not listening. As always, the risk of losing a good friend or a loved one is too much.

Ten days later, Maurice hangs himself.

At the funeral we learn that he called others who were as close or closer to him than George. None of them did anything. None thought they could. None even went to see him. But Maurice's suicide has made the specter of depression real. Where there had been light in our lives, there was now darkness and it would be the backdrop for many scenes to come.

THIRTY-EIGHT
Stand Up and Be Counted

O N ARRIVING BACK IN AUSTIN from Africa, George discovers the computer knowledge he has acquired is in demand. But the job he faked his way into at Balcones Computer Corporation (BCC) dissolves when the owners create a portable computer that's operated with a mouse. It's brilliant. There's nothing like it on the market. The Bell brothers, who are the geniuses behind BCC, have been collaborating with Zerox. That's where the mouse idea comes from; however, when Xerox learns of the new BCC machine, they take legal action and everything gets tied up and BCC folds, leaving us high and dry—no job and a sagging economy. George has been saving money to pay taxes, but now he has to dip into it in order to get by without work and when tax times comes, he winds up owing around $10,000 and no way to pay it.

For the next six months, we are harassed by the I.R.S., mostly by phone, asking for a payment of any amount. Sometimes I answer the phone for him:

"Hello."

"Hello. This is Mark Dunner. I'm with the Internal Revenue Service. Is this George Wilkerson?"

I clear my throat. "This is his sister."

"May I speak to Mr. Wilkerson."

"I'm sorry, he's not available."

"Do you know where I can reach him?"

I pause. "Well….you see…he's working as a male escort and…"

"Excuse me?"

"Perhaps your mother would like a date. Is she available?"

"Put Mr. Wilkerson on the phone."

(Slamming the phone on the table). "I'm afraid we have a bad connection. Can you call back?"

Oh yes. Once in a while I get to have some fun.

Despite the harassing calls, we manage to put off the I.R.S. for a while and talk to a friend who is a Vice-President at our bank. He comes up with a solution, though he has George swear that he never heard it from him.

When we get back to Austin, our accountant helps George form a "doing business as" (dba) company called Trainease and we begin doing contract work writing training manuals. Our banker tells us to contact friends and family who might be interested in buying computer equipment. George then gets a small business loan from the bank for $10,000, buys the equipment at a discount, sells it to the friends and family, and uses the resulting cash to pay the I.R.S.

☜ ❑ ☞

As if in response to Maurice's passing, George becomes aware of the increasing popularity of stand-up comedy. It's experiencing a resurgence. Every city has a comedy club now and there are 'touring circuits'. The local comedy club in Austin is *The Comedy Workshop*, an offshoot of the original *Comedy Workshop* in Houston.

I didn't see it coming, but George has decided he might be able to do this. Wasn't he the class clown? Didn't he write for Esther's Follies? So why not?

He begins making notes and working on a routine, writing song parodies and comic poetry. I am not part of this at all. I am not the comedic muse. Comedy has always been a defense for George. So I am nothing more than the girl in the front row, laughing at his dumb jokes and winking at him when he looks at me.

George's mentor at the Workshop is Mark Kishego, someone he met at the Follies. Mark's notoriety came from his imitation of bacon in a frying pan. He is now the manager of the Workshop and has a knack for "funny;" though maybe not for himself, but certainly for others. Each week, much as he had done when writing for the Follies, George jots down notes for jokes and comes to the Workshop on Monday (amateur) night and signs up. There are as many as a dozen people trying out their 'stuff,' so that often means performing at 1:00 in the morning to an audience of half a dozen drunks.

Mark watches the act and gives immediate feedback: "Get rid of the guitar," he says. Then, when George tries performing parodies, Mark says "You're too clever." The stuff is funny, but audiences in comedy clubs have been drinking, they've been working all week, and they don't want to think.

The act winds up being a series of poems. Here's a version of the poem George opens with:

If you look at me what you will see is a refugee from MTV
A devotee of comedy, whose recipe for lunacy is irony and
    joke debris
But never mind, just let that be
I don't need you; you don't need me
On that we'll never disagree
But at least show me some sympathy
This work does not come easily; it's filled with grief and
    misery
You see, there is no easy key, no A B C, no one, two, three
Each joke's a near calamity, reflecting my depravity
It makes me shit, it make me pee, and worst of all, I work
    for free.
So though there is no guarantee of a potpourri of comedy,

If you should absent-mindedly slap your knee and laugh
  at me
Remember, there's just you and me.
I tell the jokes, there is no fee
And only God can make a tree
But jokes are made by fools like me.

This stuff is good enough to get booked as an opening act and after about a year, we get gigs in clubs on the so-called Chitlin' Circuit (Texas, Oklahoma, Louisiana). But it also leaves George wondering why he's doing this. (It leaves George wondering, not me.) A lot of time out of town is spent sharing a motel room with the two comics who are appearing at the local club.

Marquee at The Comedy Workshop in Austin

As an opening act in a club in Houston, George is also the emcee and he asks the headliner how he would like to be introduced.

"Did you see Star Trek II?" He asks.

"Yes."

"You remember the scene where Captain Kirk talks to the aliens?"

We shrug. "Kinda."

"Well," he continues. "I'm the second alien from the left."

And so George must introduce him this way. "Here he is... our headliner for the evening. You saw him in Star Trek II. Give a big hand for...." Which leaves the audience trying to figure out who he was and George tempted to say "Here he is...the second alien from the left! Give a big hand for...."

In addition to their salary, the touring comics are often put up in a motel for their stay, so we end up on some weekends sharing a motel room with two other comedians and sometimes that means living with some very sick people. For just as in 'the real world' comedians come in all forms. One of them spends the entire day watching soap operas and screaming at the television. ("Dump the bitch, you ass hole! She's cheating on you!") Another is teaching himself to play the clarinet and spends half the day practicing. And another (whose name I'll say because he's one of the few sane ones) is Ritch Shydner, who gets up at 8 a.m. every day, makes a pot of coffee, and writes for about four hours.

Others include Emo Philllips, Judy Tenuta, Steven Wright, and my personal favorite, Bill Hicks. Bill is so smart it's intimidating, especially since he's only in his twenties. Watching him, George realizes he doesn't have the insight and comedy bones that are necessary to become a headliner. And watching the others, he realizes, even though he has me to deal with, he's not nearly as 'sick' as many of them. So the stand-up career ends.

The stand-up experience brings us to a realization about life in general. We live on an insignificant planet orbiting a humdrum star, lost in a galaxy in a forgotten corner of the universe. The astronomer Carl Sagan said there are at least 100 billion galaxies, each of which contain something like 100 billion stars and many of those stars have planets and the odds are good that some of them are inhabited. So then, if there is a Creator, don't you suppose he can "tune in" to what's happening on any of those planets, surfing the universe the way we surf cable TV? And if he does, we must be living on the planetoid equivalent of the Comedy Channel.

Despite the disappointing foray into stand-up, George's comedy writing hasn't abated. I'm still in the role of muse and I'm more than happy to provide inspiration, feeding George ideas for all kinds of things.

review

Plays tell tale of 2 marriages with insight

By PATRICK TAGGART
American-Statesman Staff

George Wilkerson's two related one-act plays are to marriage what Woody Allen is to, well — marriage. Both seem to maintain that at their best, relationships are plagued with insurmountable problems, a point of view that sees little difference between relationships at their best and those at their worst.

"On Again/Off Again" is the title given this pair of plays, which will be available for public consumption through Dec. 16 at the Gaslight Theater. The first play traces a marriage as it arrives at its terminus. Both spouses seek comfort and advice from the same friend, Bob (William Dente) — a swishy, wise and wisecracking intermediary who helps articulate what the pair already knows — that the marriage jig is up.

The second play takes place in the real estate office where the former couple is selling their house to a pair of newlyweds. Jerry (Max Evers), the male in the failed partnership, seems to be aware of his mistakes; he just doesn't know at what point they occurred. Daisy (Stella DiFranco) is too hurt and angry to care.

Playwright Wilkerson is deft with his comedic touch and packs his plays with quick quips and humorous insights. The action moves quickly, the performances are relaxed and confident. If Wilkerson is saying anything here, it is that relationships require two persons on roughly the same sense-of-humor wavelength, but that too many punchlines spoil the broth.

As for playwrighting, Wilkerson has the right recipe.

Review of George's Play
(Patrick Taggart, Austin American-Statesman)

One idea is a pair of one-act plays based on his marriages. Max and William, from the *Follies*, are cast as the main character and his friend. The local theater produces it and the local critic likes it. And it set up the occasion for George to connect with Robert aka "Dude" Skiles who heads a popular band called *Beto e los Fairlanes*. They're a salsa group, good musicians, and they always draw a crowd. The city's remaining hippies are big fans. He and George become friends and we hang out at his house and pitch lyrics at him. We write two shows together. The first is called *Mondo Texas* and it's produced at the Gaslight Theatre. It's a collection of Follies-style skits. Some of the pieces we wrote for the Follies ended with musical numbers and that style is reflected in 'Mondo.' The show is well-received and breaks even; good crowds and another good review in the *Austin American Statesman*.

George handles everything for the show—publicity, casting, direction. One of the people cast is Alvin Ventura. (George is in the straitjacket in the photo and Alvin is the guy in the mustache behind him.) Alvin, a friend of The East Side Flash,

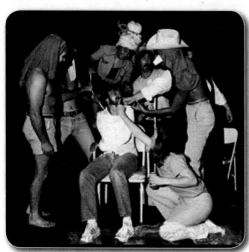

Cast of Mondo Texas

is a wealth of ideas. He has a comic mind and George spends hours hanging out with Alvin and his girlfriend, Jeanette, sometimes making mental notes of his hilarious offhand remarks. And he decides Alvin would be great onstage. Wrong.

Alvin turns out to be difficult in rehearsals and completely chokes in front of a live audience. A lesson is learned—just because someone is entertaining in a small group, among friends, doesn't mean they can translate that to a stage. Alvin has a sense of comedy (as opposed to humor), but Jeanette is the major breadwinner; she's a nurse. Alvin has a job…sort of; he drives a school bus. One of the anecdotes he tells involves his advice to the kids as they board his bus.

"I want you to know that I am not making any judgments, boys and girls. But I know that some of you may be carrying illegal substances and that the school has drug sniffing dogs, so as you leave the bus, please feel free to deposit any items they might be concerned about right here in this little bucket alongside my seat."

He claims this nets him two or three joints a day.

After *Mondo Texas*, George presents Robert with a poem written years earlier with the idea that it might make a nice little children's musical. It's called *The Bogus St. Nick* and I honestly must say it's one of the best things we ever did (as I'm sure I played a part in its creation). It's certainly as good and original as any of the Christmas 'specials' that air on TV every year.

George and Robert put together some songs and work with the community college to launch a 'workshop production.' The children brought in to see it seem to enjoy it, but the show's weaknesses stand out. George is able to revise it, but it languishes until 2014 when it is updated, the title is changed to ROBOCLAUS, and a reading performance is done in Nashville.

GEORGE WILKERSON

THIRTY-NINE
That Geraldo

GEORGE'S SISTER AND I HAVE nothing in common. George and I were born five years after she was. She grew up in the bobby-sox era, swooning over Frank Sinatra and drawing seams up the backs of her legs with an eyebrow pencil because she wasn't allowed to wear stockings. And George had even less. He shivered the first time he heard Ray Charles and the other 'jungle music' (which is how Father referred to the burgeoning sounds of rock and roll). There is one exception though, and it trumps the list of uncommon traits. George and Audrey both divorced after fairly long marriages and then, years later, (spoiler alert!) remarried the same person.

While George was the one to do outlandish things—running away from home at the age of 15, getting arrested at 17—she was the good child, constantly embarrassing us—high school valedictorian, admired by all of her teachers ("Why can't you be more like your sister?"), and always the apple of Father's eye. ("Your sister would never do that.")

That all changed when we became adults. She went to college for one semester, but dropped out to elope with a sailor who had just returned from the Korean conflict. It was a precursor of things to come.

During the years we were married to Second-Wife-Sallie, Sister pulled a stunt that forever washed away the shadow under which we had lived. It was more than George or I could have ever hoped for; the only regret was that our parents weren't alive to see it.

Here's how that went down.

After 20 years, Sister divorces the sailor and George and she develop a weekly habit of talking by phone. Before that time, they never talked seriously, but now they compare experiences, their memories of the parents and of relatives, and engage in long conversations about religion, philosophy, or politics. Such conversations couldn't happen earlier because Sister's marriage had forced her to play 'the dutiful wife;' the kind who needed to be cared for because she was 'just a woman.' Now the Armageddon of divorce has left brother and sister alone in the world. They begin asking questions of one another. Sometimes the talk goes on for hours. Then the phone calls suddenly stop.

After about a month of not hearing from her, we call at a time we're sure she'll be home. And she answers. She's pleasant enough and though George didn't seem to pick up on it, I could tell something wasn't quite right.

"Is everything OK?" George asks.

"I was just writing you a letter...to explain," she says.

"Explain what?"

There's a long pause, then "I'll tell you in the letter," she says, and before we can pursue it any further, she cuts short the conversation and hangs up.

We're completely befuddled, so we check in with our nephew, Danny, who is the second oldest of her four children. We know he often stops by to see how she's doing, sometimes fixing a broken latch or replacing a blown fuse. He recognizes George's voice immediately.

"Uncle George!"

"Hi Dan. I just called 'cause I'm wondering if your mother is OK."

"Aaah....yeah. Well..."

"I just spoke to her and she seemed...awkward."

He tisks. "She didn't tell you?"

"Tell me what?" George asked.

"About Geraldo."

"Geraldo?"

"Yes."

"Geraldo who?"

Danny sighs; his impatience is evident. "How many Geraldos do you know?"

"I live in Texas," George says. "There are a lot of Geraldos here."

There's a snort at the other end, then a deep breath. "Geraldo Rivera," he says.

"Geraldo Rivera?"

"From television…the TV show…"

It takes a moment to sink in. "That Geraldo?"

There's no response

"I don't get it."

"Talk to her," he says. "It's a long story."

But we didn't have to wait. Within a few days the letter comes explaining what she had done.

☜ ❑ ☞

Sister's ex-husband, a truck driver spent a lot of time on the road and though she never said anything about it, we always suspected their breakup was the result of liaisons carried out during the time he was away, but not driving. (We're giving him the benefit of an excuse here, but I suspect he would have been just as unfaithful if the days and nights had been short and he had driven a local beer truck.) The letter explains that Sister is now seeing him on a regular basis. Despite the fact that he has remarried and is living in Florida, he frequently stops by their old house to spend an evening with her. So now, since she is the girl-on-the-road, some of the adventure that had drifted out of their marriage is back.

Sister's letter further explains that they have been considering getting back together. She says that eventually she will explain it all, but doesn't want to get into the details right now.

But I do. So I get George to call her and after some prompting she comes through with the story.

"I didn't know how to tell the kids," she says. "There was this ad in *Newsday*. It said the *Geraldo Rivera Show* was looking for 'childhood sweethearts' who had got back together. So I contacted them."

There is a pause while she searches for the excuse: ""I didn't know how to tell the kids."

"So what <u>did</u> you tell them?"

She sighs. "I told them a friend got me tickets to the *Geraldo Rivera Show* along with a tour of the studio and I asked the kids to come with me."

"But you didn't tell them what it was really all about."

"Right."

"And when did this all happen?"

"Two…no…three weeks ago."

"And then you told them."

She hesitates again. "Not exactly." She sighs. "The people from the show said I should save it…as a surprise…for when we're on the air."

"And you agreed?"

She becomes silent.

"And when does this come on?" We ask.

"I'm not sure," she says at last. "I'll have to let you know."

What she means is that she doesn't want us to know and sure enough, about two weeks later, she calls us at work and says. "It was on this morning."

"This morning?"

"At nine o'clock."

"Oh." We thank her and hang up because she is not aware that although Geraldo's show comes on at nine a.m. in New York, it doesn't air in Texas until three p.m.

We immediately rush home and set the VCR to record the show and that night, as soon as we arrive home, George rewinds the tape and settles back to watch Sister's fifteen minutes of fame.

❦ ❑ ☞

Sister and her ex barely fit into the theme of childhood sweethearts. They met when Sister was in high school. For the Geraldo producers that qualifies as childhood if you're hard up for participants.

The show introduces us to three couples and when Geraldo gets to interview Sister he can't resist tapping into the cliché of the former sailor-now-trucker still having 'a girl in every port.' Then he moves the story along to the point where he can ask them if they have told their children and when they say no, the camera pulls back, a door at the back of the stage opens, and with a sweeping gesture, Geraldo proclaims "Well…here they are now!"

That's where things get dicey. Nephew Dan, steps forward. He stands quietly staring at his parents—the child in the headlights, momentarily paralyzed by a detour on the highway of his life—but not for long. His appearance is the only portion of a longer segment that makes it to the airwaves.

We later learn that his brother's and sister's reactions have been neatly edited out. When the show airs Geraldo's announcement ("Here they are now!") becomes "Here he is now!" And references to the other children are gone.

Three of the four kids, we later learn (the oldest had not come with them) were standing on the other side of that door, having been led there via some ruse by their 'tour guide', and one by one they stepped onstage. The first (the youngest son) caught on immediately. Maybe he figured it out beforehand or maybe he was simply sharp enough to catch on, but no matter. He turned and walked away, finding an exit and leaving the studio, heading for the nearest subway and, ultimately, home.

The second (the youngest girl) on seeing her father (who abandoned her as a child), began to scream at her parents. "They can't do that! He's married to someone else!" (That's something

299

the Geraldo staff had failed to uncover. It was true. He was still married to his third wife who apparently had no idea of the affair with Sister.)

At that point a staff member stepped forward and firmly guided our niece, whose language only George Carlin would appreciate, off the stage, leaving only Nephew Dan. Geraldo then went to Dan and guided him to a place on the platform by his mother and father and asked him what he thought of his mother's plans to remarry his father. And in keeping with his role as the oldest male child, he mumbled "Well…I guess it's OK…if that will make her happy."

Then they cut to a commercial.

☜ ❏ ☞

This is the end of the story so far as Sister is concerned, but what follows may even be better. At the very least, it's more fun, because on the very afternoon that the infamous Geraldo show airs, our African-American daughter, who is away at college (Texas A&M University) is tending to her sick roommate. The two of them have gone to the school infirmary (aka "Quack Shack") and while her roommate is taken to an examining room, Jennifer sits in the waiting room, tending to her schoolwork and occasionally looks up at the TV located in the far corner.

When she had looks up at the television and sees her aunt she exclaims "Oh my god," and points at the TV. "That's my aunt!"

The admitting nurse glances up at the TV set, then over at our daughter. "Where, honey?" she asks.

"There" she says, stepping forward and pointing to the strawberry blonde. "And that's my Uncle!" And she points to the white man beside our sister who is sporting graying hair and a foolish grin."

"I guess it's OK," her Uncle Danny is saying. "If that will make her happy."

"And that's my cousin!"

The nurse squints, searching the screen for dark-skinned people. Geraldo comes the closest.

"Are you sure?"

"Yes," our daughter says, nodding frantically.

"OK," the nurse says sweetly. "How about you lie down for a minute?"

"Lie down?"

"…and take a nice deep breath."

At which point the roommate emerges from the examining room. "What's the matter?"

"It's my Aunt Audrey," the daughter cries, "…and Uncle Ed," pointing to the screen.

The nurse nods benignly and asks "How about some water?" as she moves toward the fountain in the opposite corner.

The roommate turns to the nurse. "That is her aunt," she says. "She's adopted. Her parents are white."

The nurse nods, repeating the sentence in a monotone: "Her parents are white," then turns abruptly away from the water fountain and back to her station.

And that explains the message that is on our answering machine when we get home that evening. "Dad? Did you see…. ah…today? Aunt Audrey? Aunt Audrey was on Geraldo Rivera! What was she doing on Geraldo Rivera?! Call me!"

☞ ❏ ☞

A few weeks later we talk to Sister's oldest daughter, the only one of the children who had enough sense to stay away from it all. "Oh yeah," she says. "I smelled it from the get-go."

George tells her the story of her cousin and the infirmary, the icing on the cake of embarrassment, and they have a good laugh. Then a few weeks later George calls our sister and tells her that part. She laughs too, but it's one of those required laughs rather than one that is heartfelt because she knows that none of her brother's antics will ever top the Geraldo moment. She is the winner; hands down.

Until I come out.

FORTY
Getting With the Program

GEORGE FINALLY MANAGES TO SNAG a couple of short jobs; one is at a little company that produces accounting software for small businesses and that's followed by one at another small company that has a software package for use in medical offices. Then comes another pivotal phone call from one of the people he worked with at Balcones Computer Corp. She asks if he's interested in working where she is, at Dell Computers, and after an interview the next day he is not only hired, but offered about $10,000 a year more than at the medical software company and he gets 700 shares of Dell stock.

These are the salad days for Dell. The company has its own building in the Arboretum, an upscale shopping mall and business center on the northwest side of town. It's a circular building with elevators running up the center. The top floor holds Dell's board room, demonstration center, and visitor meeting room. There are about 1,000 employees. Some of the programmers have cots in their offices and, in keeping with the mythology of the times, they frequently go into trances, writing software code for hours on end and finally crashing on their cots and sleeping for days.

George is part of the technical writing team, producing end-user manuals for the computers. The work load is pretty intense, but the other people are good to work with and his boss, Debbie Rosenquist, is especially competent and supportive. At the end of the first year there he gets a 10% raise.

One day, when we arrive at work a little late and we scurry to catch the elevator we're aware of someone scurrying in behind us. We step aside, turn, and hold the door and see that it's Michael Dell and he's holding a Pee Wee Herman doll the size of a ventriloquist's dummy. Pee Wee is currently at the height of his popularity. His HBO special has become a Saturday morning kids show (drawing more adults than kids) and everyone repeats his catch phrase, "OK! OK!"

Michael, who is not known for being outgoing, steps in, stands to our right, and nods at us. Then, after a moment, he pulls a string at the back of the doll's neck and the doll says "OK! OK!" in that unmistakable high-pitched Pee Wee voice.

We smile, politely.

Michael smiles back. "Cool…huh?" he asks. And all we both can think is that this guy, who is younger than us and clearly more of a nerd, is the CEO of this company that's on its way to being a multi-million dollar business. (*I know he is…but what are you?*)

One of the things we work on at Dell is a new desktop computer system called *Olympus*. We spend over a year working along with the hardware developers to prepare the manuals for the system so they will be ready at the same time as the system is complete. Of course, it would be easier if we simply waited for the hardware and software work to be completed and then wrote the manuals, but that would add too much time to the schedule. Computer system development depends on a 'launch window,' a date the release for sale is planned. The goal is to be first on the market with the latest and greatest. The *Olympus* is our focus. Almost every day we get updates on the development and have to incorporate it into out manuals.

Dell doesn't manufacture the computer's components; we simply put them together and install the software. The few 'original' parts of the system are the box, or case, containing the components and the design for the motherboard, which controls the various components, including the central processing unit (CPU). That's where the *Olympus'* speed comes in. The faster the CPU can run, the faster everything else runs; however, the designers and programmers insist that the maximum speed of a CPU is, and will always be, 33 megahertz. That's the magic number. Beyond that speed, the chip overheats. (They were wrong. Today's systems run a whole lot faster than that.)

In addition to the CPU speed issue, a new 'chip set' was being developed which would be able to diagnose problems. And some other innovations also were in the works. But then, after a year of working on it, the news came that the *Olympus* program was being scrapped. *Olympus* was dead.

On that day one of the other writers comes to us for support. He is clearly distraught. It seems he might even cry. "They killed it," he says.

George shrugs.

"We spent more than a year on it and they just toss it out like it was nothing!"

We nod. "Development is a good tax write-off," George says. "I'm sure they'll salvage some of the work to use on other projects."

"It took a year," the writer says. "And for what? They're not gonna salvage a year of my life!"

"Hey," George says. "Did you get paid?"

He snorts. "Of course I got paid."

"Even some overtime…right?"

He nods. "Of course."

George gets up to leave, shaking his head. "So get over it," he says, and we walk out.

A week later an inflatable ape climbed up the side of the building.

☜ ❏ ☞

The ape was outside of Michael's office, on the top floor of the eight-story building. The day it happens, as we arrive at the Arboretum, we see something unusual hanging on the outside of the building. It's King Kong.

Kong is one of those blow-up dolls and this one is at least two stories tall, so that the feet sit on the ledge of the sixth floor and the head is at the level of the eighth floor, looking into Michael's office.

It's Michael's birthday and the story that's told is that a number of the programmers—buddies of Michael—had sneaked into his office the night before (somehow defeating the security system) and placed the giant inflatable ape outside his window, inflating it once they had it attached. The story goes on to say that Michael is now angry with the 'boys' and takes some kind of action against them, but that it is all dropped when the story makes the newspapers and Michael has to appear to be good-natured.

☜ ❏ ☞

Working at Dell makes George aware of the potential for teaching via the Internet. There's no World Wide Web (WWW) at the time, but there is a text-based internet system and we learn that some schools are offering classes there. Looking further we find that they're using programs known as Bulletin Boards to share information. So we learn how to use one.

George has also started teaching again at Austin Community College, as an adjunct, and so we go to the ACC English Department and propose offering an English course online. Most of the regular faculty scoff at the idea, but George still has some influence with them (he hired most of them when the school first opened) and so he was able to convince them to give it a shot.

To their dismay, the course filled up almost immediately, raising George's nerd score to at least 120%. He runs the course out of our living room using an IBM286 desktop computer, putting together text files that include assignments, a discussion center, and various resources.

Around this time, Sallie has gotten a job at a company called Radian Corporation, an environmental engineering firm, as a Technical Writer and when another position opens George applies.

Radian does 'up front' environmental work. Their engineers go to a site, scope it out, estimate what has to be done, and then pass along the actual clean-up chores to a company that has the equipment needed to dig up buried tanks, scrub the soil, and clean up the water.

In sharp contrast the work Radian does, the Radian switchboard operator, a very sweet, blind man answers incoming calls by singing the company's name: *Ray-Dee-Ann.*

Some people call just to hear him say it.

☜ ❑ ☞

George became the nerd, but not me. When we were kids he was into sci-fi and Popular Science magazine, while I spent my time perusing the *Ladies Fashions* portion of the Sears-Roebuck catalog, totally fascinated by the illustrations of slips and corsets and the like, especially as they contributed to the concept of femininity. There's an engineering component to some of those things, I suppose, but that was never part of my interest.

☜ ❑ ☞

George's first assignment at Radian is with a man named Pat who has developed a software program that monitors dynamos and related equipment at power plants. Sensors on the machines measure vibrations and other factors like oil pressure and flow rates and using that data generates graphs which engineers use to detect potential equipment problems. The program is UNIX –based and runs on a mainframe. Pat had been in the Navy as a submariner and had learned much of what he was doing when developing systems that could measure a submarine's operations and look for potential failures.

Pat writes explanations for the User Manual George is producing and George edits them into more readable prose, then shows his work to Pat to make sure he hasn't changed the meaning. One time, George doesn't understand any of what Pat has given him, so he goes to see him in order to get it clarified.

"Pat," he says, "I don't understand this, and if I don't understand it, it's very likely that our clients won't understand it either."

Pat snorts and shakes his head. "Well," he says "if they don't understand it, they've got no business buying the program."

George, slightly taken aback, considers that for a moment, then says "But…if they don't buy the program, we don't have a job."

Pat shrugs.

Sometimes I admire scenes like that and I wonder how progress is ever made or if it's just an illusion and if the processor ever really got faster than thirty-three megahertz.

FORTY-ONE
Permanently Pressed

ONE DAY WE GET A phone call from Sister telling us that Mother is dying. Mother and Father moved to Florida a few years back and Sister is already there. George books a flight to Tampa, leaving me behind, but of course I went along as an observer.

We get there in time for the funeral service following her cremation. It is strange to see how George reacts. I cannot sense any emotion, no tears, no emptiness. He simply follows protocol, accompanying Father and Sister to the church where it becomes clear that the priest doesn't know either of the parents. He begins his remarks: "I didn't know Pat very well…"

George's mind snaps to attention. Wait a minute! Father's name is Pat. Mother's name is Adele. The damn priest doesn't even know her name!

George looks at Sister and she looks back, raises her eyebrows, and shakes her head. But Father just keeps his head bowed.

Later, as they walk to the car, Father mutters that they had been married for 53 years, and George's mind flashes back to the many times Mother snorted at something Father said or did and said "You see what I have to live with?"

Later, George and Sister sit at the kitchen table back at the little house where their parents lived for the past ten years or so, sighing over coffee and making small talk, Sister tells George of how, when cleaning the house after she got there, she found blood soaked tissues hidden under things and in the trash, the blood most likely having come from Mother's smoke-damaged lungs.

"The doctor told Father he had to quit smoking," Sister says, "so what she used to do was let him smoke half of one, then take it away from him and finish the rest, unaware that the worst part of it was in that second half."

For George, and even more for me, it is all too bizarre. He simply wants to get away from it. And so do I.

☜ ❏ ☞

About a year after Mother dies, we learn that Father is dying. He has sold the house in Florida and moved in with Sister. On hearing from her that he is dying, we go to see him. He and George have a short superficial conversation, but then Father asks George why he has come to New York "all the way from Texas. You have a business meeting here or something?" he asks and George replies "I came to see you."

Father doesn't reply, but later, when George gets up to leave and puts his hand out for a goodbye shake, his father put his arms around him and hugs him. He hugs him for the first time since he was six years old. He holds him tightly for a long time, then steps away. "Take care of your family," is all he says.

☜ ❏ ☞

During his last days with Sister, Father is bedridden and if he needs something, he slams a billy club against the bedpost— Bam! Bam! Bam! It has a leather strap and he uses that to hang it over the bedpost when he doesn't need it. Where he got it, no one can recall and when we come to help Sister sort through everything, George's first impulse is to throw it into the box with the other things he is taking to the Salvation Army, although that was all clothing and in an odd way the billy club seems symbolic of what George and I both recall of him. It reminds us of how he would swat the back of his head because he wasn't holding it over his plate at dinner, or slap his arm because his elbow was resting on the table as he ate. He didn't have the club then, but what if he had? So we keep it. It's hanging in George's office now, as we write this.

We place Father's clothing in a box. All of it is polyester or some blended fabric that doesn't wrinkle—a green jacket that feels like the back of an old easy chair; another jacket with the nap worn down, but retaining the bumps; slacks that can be scrunched up and sat on for a week and still retain their perfect crease.

"He wouldn't let me wash those," Sister says as George closes up the box..

"I'm not surprised," George says. "It's pretty funky in there."

She smiles and sighs. "Need any help?"

George shakes his head. "I'm almost done," he says, and looks back into the closet which now contains only empty hangers. But then, as he turns back toward Sister, he sees a box in the farthest corner, kneels down, and picks it up.

"Oh shoot," she says. "Don't drop that."

"What is it?"

"It's Mom," she says, "Mom's ashes. I didn't know what to do with them."

"Did he know they were in there?"

She nods.

George puts the box on the bed and opens it. There's a ceramic container inside, but he doesn't open it. He recloses the box.

"You want them?" Sister asks.

George snickers. "You crazy?"

"I don't want them," she says. "It's creepy."

They stare at the box, as if waiting for something to happen, a genie to emerge or the ghost of their mother shouting "Eat it over the sink!"

Finally: "You take them," Sister says. "I don't care what you do with them."

George shakes his head. "No way," he says, putting the box on the bed. "Do whatever you want to do with them "

Sister folds her arms and abruptly turns away. "Thanks."

George picks up the box of clothes, carries it through the living room to the kitchen and out the back door, then places it on the ground by the trunk of the rental car.

Sister follows.

"You want a tax receipt for this?" George asks.

"Sure," she says.

We drive to the Goodwill drop-box, pull down the handle, and dump in the clothes.

"Everything OK?" Sister asks, when we return.

"Yeah," George says, except for the alarm.

Her brow furrows. "Alarm?"

"The Goodwill Dropbox Alarm," George says, flashing his hands to illustrate: "POLYESTER OVERLOAD! POLYESTER OVERLOAD!"

She smiles.

He reaches into his pocket and pulls out the billy club. "I think I'll keep this…" he says.

She blinks.

"…for when <u>I'm</u> bedridden and you're the only one left to care for me and I'll bang it on the bedstead when I want you to come."

"Don't you dare," she says.

They chuckle, as I do now, glancing over at the billy club hanging from George's bookshelf.

❧ ❏ ☞

Not long after George comes to work at Radian, Sallie takes a job elsewhere. We're living near the lake now. George and Sallie own a house and a boat and two dogs—all reminiscent of a line from *Zorba, The Greek*. It's "the full catastrophe." George is the yeoman farmer. We grow corn and okra in the back yard and cruise the lake on weekends. It's all so seriously millennial...years before the millennium.

And me? I'm biding my time, enjoying an occasional afternoon out (though not out of the house). George takes me shopping (at Goodwill mostly) and hides my stuff in a suitcase stuffed into a crawlspace under the house. Sallie's clothes don't all fit, but some come close and the trick is to remember where everything is so it's not obvious when it has been 'borrowed.' It's not a pleasant existence for me. On a couple occasions, she comes home early and I rush to the bathroom and lock the door, trying to pretend I'm showering, but she knows what's going on.

Sallie's relationship with the children, whom we have six months out of every year and despite her efforts to have otherwise, is in the mold of the traditional step-mother.

Then, in 1995, Sallie announces that she is having an affair with a guy in the office where she works. She insists it isn't sexual. (*I did not have sex with that man*. A page from the Bill Clinton vocabulary.) She says she wants time to "check it out.". She wants to move out of the house, but not in with him. She'll get an apartment.

George is devastated. But I'm not. I have known all along that Sallie uses people to further her career, or desires (the house, the boat), or whatever it is that drives her and at some point she decided she could do better than George. He has outlived his usefulness. He paid her way through her last two years of college at Southwest Texas State and then trained her in the writing and editing of technical documents. Now it's time to move on to whatever greener pastures the officemate represents. But George's mind is too preoccupied to consider this. Later he'll realize that I nailed it.

So she moves out and we're alone in the house and George is depressed; so much so that one day when we come home from work as he's giving the dog his daily dose of anti-seizure medication (Phenobarbital), he sits down in the yard and stares at the bottle of pills and I know what he's thinking as he starts crying.

I know where he's going, but I am not about to go with him. And so I force myself to the forefront and pry deeper. And what I find is telling, because it is something he has never admitted to himself. I had to bring it into that place where he and I are one.

You left Barbara because of me, I said without speaking. *You were running away from _me_ and when Sallie came along you latched onto her because she was young and attractive and you foolishly thought that having a woman like her would eliminate the need for me. But I'm not a need. I'm you. We are one. And I won't hurt you. Don't leave me.*

For a long time, no thoughts pass between us, but I can feel he is lost, and I wait, and after a while, he gets up, puts the pills away, and goes back into the house.

Divorce is a game no one wins. I'm always suspicious of those who say *but we're still friends.* Sallie told George she wanted to remain friends. In her romance-magazine world that's how it worked. He loves her so much, she thinks, that all he cares about is her happiness. So if she will be happy, then…

Bullshit. George knows it and I know it. It's one of those times where we aren't just on the same page—we're in the same paragraph and in the same sentence. Then the lawyers come into it. George is still living in the house and she's got an apartment, a little ways out of town and the 'discussions' over who gets what are ongoing. Then fate steps in.

Fate is an answering machine. One day, when we get home from work, we find a message. It's a clearly disgruntled Sallie telling us that George is a pervert, that his crossdressing forced her to leave, and if he doesn't acquiesce to her settlement demands she will make sure everyone knows about <u>me</u>—the kids, his friends, his co-workers, and especially Jesus. (OK…not Jesus. I made up that part.)

We are, once again, words in the same sentence, only now the punctuation is bolder. There are lots of exclamation points. When we have calmed down, we take the answering machine's cassette tape with the message to George's lawyer who already knows about me and when she hears the tape she immediately calls Sallie's lawyer, asking if he understands the blackmail laws and how that it could move the dispute from divorce court to a civil to a criminal trial.

And so ends the dispute over the house settlement, who gets the dog, and what becomes of community property. The divorce moves quickly to closure.

☜ ❑ ☞

A curious bit of fallout from the divorce is that I am now free to ask the question George has always avoided. *Do I want to take over?* I know that over the years he has worried that I might do that; that I might insist that he step back and give me <u>my</u> life (and thus give up his.)

Our reading has presented us with that assumption that there are just two motivations for transitioning. One is that we are a homosexual transsexual, i.e. we are attracted to men and since childhood we have been overtly and obviously feminine. On the other hand, we might be a non-homosexual transsexual who wants to transition because we are sexually aroused by the

315

idea that we are really a woman. We 'try them on' but neither of those descriptions fit us. And we reach the conclusion that if we put George away and set me free, I would not be happy. The part-time world that I live in is free of most demands life makes of us. George has a job, meets a variety of family and daily responsibilities and, for the most part, gives me what I want—a new dress, a night on the town, time to live like a 'normal' woman.

So my answer is 'No.' We have come this far together. There's no need to part ways now.

FORTY-TWO
Come Out, Come Out, Whoever You Are

ONE WEEKEND IN 1996 JENNIFER comes home from Texas A&M and tells George that Robert has proposed and she has accepted and the parents will participate and "<u>will</u> talk to each other." She tells Barbara the same thing. So the parents begin to arrange for the wedding.

I really like the whole thing…wedding dresses, bridesmaids, and all the other girly stuff, even though I can't really participate and I have a hard time getting George to get on board. "Your job," Jennifer tells him, "is to keep your mouth shut and your wallet open." So what can I do?

So George and Barbara talk. Finally, George shares things, like how when my need to come out became too intense, he thought there was no way he could survive. So he ran…and took me with him, of course. He had carried around this notion that if he gave in to me, I would take over his life. But what he discovered was that that wasn't going to happen, that what we needed to do was find a life that integrated my life with his…or rather, with the rest of me.

George tells Barbara about me and explains it this way: *The Jeanie (i.e. Bobbi) is out of the bottle and she's not going back.* And Barbara says that the only thing that upset her when she found out about me (which happened long before George ever verbalized it) was that he didn't trust her enough to tell her. And George says that he knows how she must have felt and he apologizes. "Is there anything I can do to make up for it?" he asks.

She smiles and says one word: "Jewelry."

And in the course of these conversations, one day the "click" happens—-like when the little computer mouse in your head seems to glide all by itself over to the LOVE icon and it's… loading 17%....28%....43%.... Done!

And there we are. And now we understand what the Schenectady double rainbow was all about.

☜ ❏ ☞

The irony of the situation is that George's anger at Sallie's attempt to blackmail him gives him the courage, at last, to tell others about me. The motivation also comes in part from the fact that he has grown tired of pretending I don't exist. And I assure him that I don't want to take over his life, that all I want is to have my own life, without denying him his.

He begins with friends and co-workers and to his astonishment no one runs away screaming. No one calls him sick or perverted. No one seems to really care. *That's interesting*, they might say, but it doesn't change the way they act toward him. On some occasions, I'm the one who meets them for lunch or coffee and I introduce myself and yet their reactions are more *So what* than *Oh my god!* Some are actually impressed with how I was kept secret.

"How long have you been doing this?" George's friend Max asks when I come out to him.

I shrug. "I can't remember ever not being part of him," I tell him.

Max shakes his head and takes a deep breath. "You know," he says, hesitating. "I've always wanted to do that."

I point to myself. "This?

He nods. "I just never had the nerve."

And we both laugh.

❧ ❏ ☞

The hardest ones to tell are the kids, so I let George do that.

Daughter Jennifer is OK, but not entirely sure of how she feels.

"Like on Jerry Springer?" she asks.

George laughs and shakes his head. "Oh god no."

"Good."

"But are you OK with it?," George asks.

She nods. "I guess so," she says. "I mean…you've always been weird."

Weird. *That's good enough*, George thinks, and I concur.

He tells our son, John, whose girlfriend has come along to hear the 'news', though neither of them knows what it is.

"You go out?" John asks? "In public, like?"

George nods.

There's a long pause, then a grin comes across our son's face. "Cool," he says.

"Cool?" George asks.

John nods. "Yeah," he says. "This explains a lot. Wait 'til I tell Jerry and…"

"Woah!" (George raises his hand.) "Hold on there. This is <u>my</u> news. I own this, not you. I decide who gets told."

"Oh," John says. "Sorry."

The girlfriend, who has been sitting quietly, is smiling. "Can I ask you something?" she says.

"Sure…anything."

"What size do you wear?"

And the conversation that follows is about sizes and styles and concludes with the girlfriend being shown what's in the closet and trying on some of my things.

About one year later, after being divorced for 17 years, George, and Barbara and I move in together. No more hiding my clothes or struggling to find time to spend away from George. I can get dressed and go out anytime I want.

I am actually more than "out." I have the freedom to come and go as I please, though I don't generally go out during the week and I let George continue to go to work as I'm not ready to dump him. Without him what would I do? He's my only source of income. He's why I don't have to worry about things like rent and shelter. We have become such a team now that I'd hate to lose what we have developed.

And I won't do that to Barbara, although she has never seen me. When I'm going out, she retreats to the living room or to a location where I don't have to cross her path. And that's all right with me. This is not a time for her to be uncomfortable with sharing the house with me.

"Whenever you're ready," George tells her.

So it goes until one Saturday evening, after about a year, when she asks George to have me come and say goodbye before leaving.

I take extra care with my make-up and style that night and when I'm as ready as I'll ever be I walk into the living room. She's sitting on the couch, reading a book. She hears me coming and puts the book down and I walk over to stand in front of her.

"OK?" I ask.

"OK" she says. And I turn and walk away

When I get home that evening she's already in bed and when George wakes up the next morning she's already up. So we crawl out of bed and walk to the kitchen, where we find her, sitting at the kitchen table, reading the newspaper. George pours us a cup of coffee and sits down beside her, whereupon she swats him with the newspaper.

"What was that for?!" he exclaims.

She shakes her head and scowls. "You have nicer legs than me," she says.

And you know what?

She's right.

Me, at the Texas 'T' Party in 1992